Pragmatic Encroachment in Epistemology

Recent work in epistemology has blurred the conceptual line between the epistemic or theoretical, and the practical: knowledge and evidence have become tightly connected in normative ways to one's practical interests and reasons for action. This volume is a welcome collection of new essays which explore this debate and take it in new directions.
—**Matthew A. Benton**, *Seattle Pacific University*

According to philosophical lore, epistemological orthodoxy is a purist epistemology in which epistemic concepts such as belief, evidence, and knowledge are characterized to be pure and free from practical concerns. In recent years, the debate has focused narrowly on the concept of knowledge and a number of challenges have been posed against the orthodox, purist view of knowledge. While the debate about knowledge is still a lively one, the pragmatic exploration in epistemology has just begun.

This collection takes on the task of expanding this exploration into new areas. It discusses how the practical might encroach on all areas of our epistemic lives from the way we think about belief, confidence, probability, and evidence to our ideas about epistemic value and excellence. The contributors also delve into the ramifications of pragmatic views in epistemology for questions about the value of knowledge and its practical role. *Pragmatic Encroachment in Epistemology* will be of interest to a broad range of epistemologists, as well as scholars working on virtue theory and practical reason.

Brian Kim received his PhD from Columbia University and is Assistant Professor of Philosophy at Oklahoma State University. He works on issues at the intersection of epistemology and rational choice theory.

Matthew McGrath received his PhD from Brown and is currently Professor of Philosophy at Rutgers and Professorial Fellow at Arché, the University of St. Andrews. Within epistemology, he has published on topics including pragmatic encroachment as well as perceptual and memorial justification. He is the author, with Jeremy Fantl, of *Knowledge in an Uncertain World*.

Routledge Studies in Epistemology
Edited by Kevin McHale
University of Alabama at Birmingham, USA

Scott Stapleford
St. Thomas University, Canada

Pragmatic Encroachment in Epistemology
Edited by Brian Kim and Matthew McGrath

Pragmatic Encroachment in Epistemology

Edited by Brian Kim and Matthew McGrath

NEW YORK AND LONDON

First published 2019 by Routledge
52 Vanderbilt Avenue, New York, NY 10017
2 Park Square, Milton Park, Abingdon, Oxon OX14 4RN

First issued in paperback 220

Routledge is an imprint of the Taylor & Francis Group, an informa business

© 2019 Taylor & Francis

The right of the editors to be identified as the authors of the editorial material, and of the authors for their individual chapters, has been asserted in accordance with sections 77 and 78 of the Copyright, Designs and Patents Act 1988.

All rights reserved. No part of this book may be reprinted or reproduced or utilised in any form or by any electronic, mechanical, or other means, now known or hereafter invented, including photocopying and recording, or in any information storage or retrieval system, without permission in writing from the publishers.

Trademark notice: Product or corporate names may be trademarks or registered trademarks, and are used only for identification and explanation without intent to infringe.

Library of Congress Cataloging-in-Publication Data
Names: Kim, Brian, 1982– editor.
Title: Pragmatic encroachment in epistemology / edited by Brian Kim
    and Matthew McGrath.
Description: 1 [edition]. | New York : Taylor & Francis, 2018. |
    Series: Routledge studies in epistemology ; 1 | Includes bibliographical
    references and index.
Identifiers: LCCN 2018031826 | ISBN 9781138051829 (hardback)
Subjects: LCSH: Knowledge, Theory of. | Pragmatism.
Classification: LCC BD161 .P7453 2018 | DDC 121—dc23
LC record available at https://lccn.loc.gov/2018031826

ISBN 13: 978-0-367-66513-5 (pbk)
ISBN 13: 978-1-138-05182-9 (hbk)

Typeset in Sabon
by Apex CoVantage, LLC

Contents

List of Figures	vii
List of Tables	viii

1 Introduction   1
MATTHEW McGRATH AND BRIAN KIM

2 Great Expectations: Belief and the Case for Pragmatic Encroachment   10
DORIT GANSON

3 Another Kind of Pragmatic Encroachment   35
KATE NOLFI

4 Pragmatic Encroachment and Practical Reasons   56
ANNE BARIL

5 An Externalist Decision Theory for a Pragmatic Epistemology   69
BRIAN KIM

6 Pragmatic Encroachment and Having Reasons   101
STEWART COHEN

7 Pragmatic Encroachment and Closure   107
CHARITY ANDERSON AND JOHN HAWTHORNE

8 Pragmatic Encroachment on Scientific Knowledge?   116
MIKKEL GERKEN

9 Skepticism and Evolution   141
N. ÁNGEL PINILLOS

vi *Contents*

10 **Deliberation and Pragmatic Belief** 170
BRAD ARMENDT

11 **Doxastic Wronging** 181
RIMA BASU AND MARK SCHROEDER

12 **A Note on Knowledge-First Decision Theory and Practical Adequacy** 206
JUAN COMESAÑA

List of Contributors 212
Index 213

Figures

9.1	Simplified Skeptical Mechanism (SM)	148
9.2	Müller-Lyer illusion	157
11.1	Moral and Epistemic Requirements Without Deontic Conflicts	197
11.2	Morally Forbidden but Epistemically Permissible Beliefs	197
11.3	Coordinated Moral and Epistemic Requirements	199
11.4	Independent Moral and Epistemic Considerations	199
11.5	Moral Requirements Limited by Epistemic Requirements	200
11.6	Epistemic Permissions Limited by Moral Permissions	202

Tables

5.1	Catherine's Decision Problem	74
5.2	Catherine's Decision Problem with [Probabilities] and (Utilities)	76
12.1	Decision Matrix	206

1 Introduction

Matthew McGrath and Brian Kim

Even on orthodox views, knowledge is related to action and to practical reasoning. For, knowledge implies belief, and of course belief influences action. Knowledge also implies truth and justification, and so action on the basis of knowledge will often have good features. It will tend to be successful and reasonable. But if belief is understood, as it often is in the tradition, as merely having high confidence, one won't always be willing to act on one's knowledge. You might have a high degree of confidence that a dish on the menu doesn't contain shellfish, but if you're allergic, a high degree of confidence won't be enough for you to order the dish. Similarly, if justification is understood, as it usually is in the tradition, as merely having good reasons or evidence, one won't always be reasonable to act on one's knowledge in situations in which that knowledge is relevant. You might not be reasonable to order that dish, if you are allergic.

So, on orthodox accounts of knowledge, although there are connections between knowledge and the practical, they hold only for the most part. Perhaps they are part of the "normal" course of events. But they are not strict. When the stakes get high enough or when the odds are long enough, things aren't normal and one will not—and reasonably will not—act on the basis of knowledge. So, all in all, on orthodox accounts, knowledge doesn't require any practical condition. Instead, the relationship between knowledge and action is merely a heuristic and usually holds in normal circumstances.

In its roughest most general meaning, the thesis of "pragmatic encroachment" holds that there are stronger connections between knowledge and the practical than the orthodox account allows. Why think this? We mention two core reasons found in the writings of Fantl and McGrath as well as Hawthorne and Stanley.

It will help to have an example to bear in mind. Consider William Clifford's shipowner, who has good reason to think his ship is seaworthy but some reason to doubt this. He must decide whether to accept payment so that his ship can be used to transport a group of people. For Clifford, even if he has good reason, and even if the belief in shipworthiness is true, this is not enough to make his action on the basis of that belief right. He needs sufficient evidence, and having good reason isn't good enough when lives

2 Matthew McGrath and Brian Kim

are at stake. What goes for action goes for practical reasoning. Clifford's shipowner may have good reasons for his true belief that his ship is seaworthy, and yet he shouldn't use that belief in reasoning about whether to lease his ship for the voyage.

Now for the two core reasons. First, consider criticisms and defenses of action. Consider how, after the fact, we might criticize Clifford's shipowner's action by saying, "The ship turned out to be seaworthy but he didn't know it was". Why would this seem an appropriate criticism if the case is not normal because of the lives at stake? Or consider how the shipowner might try to defend his action and how we would reply to it. He might say, "I knew it was seaworthy, so I knew all would be alright". We would not reply by saying, "yes, you knew it was seaworthy, but you needed to know for sure". We would much more likely say, "no, you didn't know", perhaps adding something like, "you should have taken the ship in for an inspection before sending it out with passengers". But it is hard to see why the shipowner's defense should function to "ward off" the objection that he needed to know for sure, if orthodox theories of knowledge are correct. However, all these phenomena make much better sense if there were a strict connection between knowing something and being appropriate to act on it.

One might object to this argument by insisting that such data show us, in the first instance, only something about how we use "know". Not all features of use reveal features of meaning. Perhaps the orthodox account is perfectly correct and only needs supplementation from Gricean pragmatics to accommodate data about the use of "know" in defenses and criticisms of action. However, if the data about defenses and criticisms did not show us anything about knowledge, then we would expect that it would be difficult to find direct arguments linking knowledge and action which subsume and explain this data. But such direct arguments do not seem difficult to come by, as we point out next.

A second reason to assert a stronger connection between knowledge and reasonable action proceeds from considering general reasoning about knowledge and action. Intuitively, it seems that if Clifford's shipowner knew the ship was seaworthy, then he would be able to conclude and thereby know that it would function well at sea with a normal load of passengers. And if he knew the latter, it seems he would know that the ship's condition would not pose a problem for the proposed voyage. Knowing the latter, together with knowing that the forecast is for calm seas and perhaps some other ancillary propositions, seems sufficient for knowing that all would go well if he hired his ship out in this case. And the shipowner's having *that* knowledge seems enough to make him reasonable in hiring out the ship. Generally, if you know that all would go well if you performed a certain action, then it is reasonable for you to perform it. This makes sense of the phenomena concerning knowledge-citing criticisms and defenses of action, and it is not what we would expect if the orthodox account of knowledge were true.

Introduction 3

Even if these reasons seem initially compelling, we have to ask just what the consequences of pragmatic encroachment are. Most pragmatic encroachment theorists admit and even emphasize that some consequences would be counterintuitive. As Hawthorne puts it, knowledge "would come and go with ease". Fantl and McGrath note that if pragmatic encroachment is true, one could, surprisingly, lose knowledge by writing a big check. But at the same time, it is counterintuitive to think that one could know that a certain action would work out for the best and yet be unreasonable to perform it. Here "working out for the best" can be understood in whatever terms fit one's preferred account—best consequences, best balance of good consequences and satisfaction of certain side constraints, etc. As is familiar in philosophical disputes, it seems there are counterintuitive consequences attending both the orthodox account and accounts embracing pragmatic encroachment. There is a large literature at the moment surveying the consequences of siding with or departing from orthodoxy.

There is a small but growing literature about exactly how to formulate a "pragmatist" theory of knowledge. Here, we will discuss several key issues that arise.

First, which practical conditions on knowledge should the encroachment theorist endorse? Consider three similar conditions: *being rational to act as if* p (Fantl and McGrath 2002), *having* p *a reason for action* (Fantl and McGrath 2009), *being appropriate to use* p *as a premise in practical reasoning* (Hawthorne 2003; Stanley 2005). Which should the pragmatist work with? Does it matter? Are they all equivalent? The answer to the last question seems to be *no*, and therefore it may well matter which the pragmatist selects. To see this, consider what it is to be rational to act as if p, as defined in Fantl and McGrath (2002): to be rational to act as if p is to be rational to do the act(s) that are rational to do *given* p (i.e., conditional on p). This condition is now called the *practical adequacy* condition (Anderson and Hawthorne 2019). Consider a variant of an example given in a lecture by Hawthorne circa 2007. You can choose between two cheese sandwiches, which appear exactly the same. You don't have probability 1 for either of them being cheese sandwiches, but the probability is very high, e.g., .995 (or something of the sort). Hawthorne pointed out that intuitively you know of each sandwich that it is a cheese sandwich, and yet given that sandwich 1 is a cheese sandwich, you should pick sandwich 1, even though you are in fact rational to pick either sandwich as things stand. So, you know sandwich 1 is a cheese sandwich, and yet you are not rational to act as if it is. There may well be ways to block this result by tinkering with the concept of *being rational to act as if* p so as to weaken it. But notice that there is no temptation to think that you don't have, as a reason, the fact that sandwich 1 is a cheese sandwich (and the same for sandwich 2). They both qualify epistemically as reasons. And both count as appropriate to use in practical reasoning. This point suggests grounds for preferring formulating the practical condition in terms of reasons or reasoning rather than practical adequacy.[1]

4 *Matthew McGrath and Brian Kim*

Second, should the pragmatist think that is the practical condition on knowledge a basic condition or can we derive it from something more basic? Consider practical adequacy. If it is a condition on knowledge, it becomes tempting to think that this is only because there is *preferential adequacy* condition on knowledge (Fantl and McGrath 2002). Clifford's shipowner, it seems, is rational to act as if p, only because he is rational to arrange his preferences as if p. Or consider the reasons-based approach. Here it is attractive to think that knowing p is sufficient for having p available as a practical reason only because it is sufficient for having p available as a reason more generally, e.g., as a reason to believe other propositions, but also a reason to have certain emotions. The shipowner intuitively can't reasonably be pleased that his ship will not sink at sea due to structural problems. But if the shipowner had *the ship is seaworthy* available as a reason, it seems he could be reasonably pleased. He could think to himself, reasonably: the ship is seaworthy; so, it won't sink at sea due to structural problems. Or think about the DeRose's high-stakes bank case. Recall that, intuitively, the protagonist (Keith) doesn't know the bank is open Saturday and so can't reasonably plan to skip the long lines today in favor of coming back tomorrow. But consider reasons. Does Keith have *the bank will be open Saturday* available as a reason to rest content that he can successfully deposit his check Saturday? Intuitively, no. Similar observations can be made about the *practical* reasoning condition. It seems it is a condition on knowledge only because there is a general *reasoning* condition on knowledge. Pragmatists therefore might take the practical condition on knowledge to stem from a more fundamental claim on knowledge. In the view of Fantl and McGrath (forthcoming), the more fundamental claim will try to capture the idea that if you know p, then p is something you can *rely* on, *can count on*. The appeal to conditionalizing on p, to reasons, or to reasoning attempt to articulate this core idea.

If the pragmatist sees the practical condition as stemming from a more fundamental and broader condition on knowledge, this might assist her in fending off certain sorts of objections (see Anderson and Hawthorne 2019). For instance, suppose in the high-stakes bank case we offer to pay Keith $50,000 to wait to deposit the check Saturday. Intuitively, this wouldn't affect whether Keith knows the bank is open tomorrow. But it seems to affect *practical* adequacy, because now Keith is rational to do in fact what he would be rational to do given that the bank was open Saturday: wait till Saturday. Now, I think it wouldn't be attractive to think that Keith gained *the bank is open Saturday* as a potential practical reason or as a fact he can appropriately use in practical reasoning. But one might ask why. After all, in this revised case, Keith is reasonable to come back Saturday. Now, just because he is reasonable to do something and some consideration *would* support doing that, it doesn't follow that the consideration is a reason he has (or is something he can appropriately use as a reason). But we can see better why this is so, if we think about what else Keith can't reasonably

Introduction 5

do, which he could reasonably do if he knew. Plausibly, Keith is *not* reasonable to feel assured that he will be able to deposit his check if he waits till Saturday, even if he is reasonable to be assured that he'll be financially fine (because of the $50,000). Similarly, it doesn't seem Keith can now properly employ *the bank will be open Saturday* in his reasoning generally (e.g., reasoning that since the bank will be open Saturday, he will not only have $50,000 but also deposit the $1000 check and so have a total of $51,0000 more money in the bank). Thus, if having p available as a reason, or being appropriate to use p in reasoning, is a necessary condition of knowledge, then the pragmatist can be assured that offering Keith $50,000 didn't magically give him knowledge, which is a good result. And, again, if the core idea of pragmatism is that one can rely on what one knows, this result makes a lot of sense: Keith can't suddenly rely on *the bank is open Saturday* when offered the $50,000 for waiting till Saturday to deposit his check.

Third, the pragmatist also faces the question of the sorts of epistemological theory one might embed a pragmatist theory of knowledge within. A major choice point concerns fallibilism vs. infallibilism about knowledge. Whereas the fallibilist about knowledge takes knowledge to be compatible with the possibility of error, the infallibilist denies this. Thus, Fantl and McGrath's argument that knowledge can vary with practical features depends essentially on the assumption of fallibilism; the arguments from Hawthorne and Stanley do not. Which way a pragmatist goes here might depend importantly on how the pragmatist thinks of the relations between knowledge, probability, and rational credence. If one thinks that knowledge requires probability 1 and rational credence 1, then one will side with the infallibilists. If one thinks that knowledge requires neither of these, one will side with the fallibilists. There is an interesting and relatively unexplored middle ground on which there are two notions of epistemic probability, one connected to knowledge and one not, and two accompanying notions of rational credence, one for each of the notions of epistemic probability. For instance, DeRose (2009, 190–193) distinguishes stable from unstable confidence. If the stakes are high, one might not be willing to rely on p in reasoning, even though one would rely on it in lower stakes situations. We might hope to explain what is going on here, and how it is reasonable, in terms of two notions of rational confidence (or credence), one tied to knowledge and one not.

These are just a few of the many issues a pragmatist must sort out. But what is interesting is that these issues aren't the preserve of pragmatists alone. It seems the disputes about pragmatic encroachment have helped to open up a new area of philosophy, one focused not only on the relatively narrow question of whether the orthodox approach to knowledge is correct or not, but on a range of issues concerning epistemology and its interface with practical philosophy. Previously questions of how the epistemic relates to the practical were mainly restricted to decision theory, with its probabilities and utilities. Now, they are part of normative philosophy generally. The

6 *Matthew McGrath and Brian Kim*

guiding question of this new field is how the epistemic generally bears on the practical and vice versa. Included under the practical is no longer merely prudence or self-interest, but moral statuses, including the rightness and wrongness of actions (and possibly even belief), and moral responsibility. Included, as well, under the practical are not merely actions and plans but states such as *faith, trust,* and *commitment.* In fact, some philosophers argue that we should understand belief as itself a kind of commitment to the truth, a commitment that is not merely a matter of assigning a high credence to a proposition or to feeling a high degree of conviction.

This volume features essays that contribute to this burgeoning field. Moreover, these contributions offer examples of how the recent pragmatic turn in epistemology can inspire new inquiries and explorations into the relationship between the epistemic and the practical. Thus, our aim in this volume is to highlight avenues of research that will broaden and deepen our understanding of the pragmatist perspective, whether from the point of view of the critic or the proponent.

The following essays roughly fit into three camps. The first group of essays present internal explorations into our pragmatist epistemologies. Two of these contributions explore alternative motivations for the pragmatist point of view. Dorit Ganson does so by investigating the relationship between degrees of belief and outright belief. She argues for a *Hybrid Doxastic Pragmatism,* which advocates for a robust connection between outright belief and degrees of belief. Unlike standard reductive threshold views of outright belief, Ganson proposes that the relevant threshold is sensitive to many features of the context, including the subject's practical context, and uses this pragmatic sensitivity to avoid a number of problems with the standard reductive account. Appealing to this new pragmatist view, Ganson proposes that the practical nature of the relation between degrees of belief and outright belief can help explain why there is pragmatic encroachment on knowledge.

Kate Nolfi offers an alternative route to a pragmatist epistemology. While the context-sensitivity of knowledge is often the primary motivation for the pragmatic turn, Nolfi proposes to start with an action-oriented approach to epistemology. This approach focuses on the functional role that belief plays in action production. Nolfi argues that if we consider the role that belief has in subserving action and if the epistemic status of a belief depends upon it fulfilling this role adequately, then we have good reasons to think that the ideal cognitive functioning of belief is sensitive to practical factors. Furthermore, it is argued that the resulting pragmatist account avoids some of the central problems of pragmatic encroachment, particularly the instability of knowledge—a problem highlighted by Cohen's essay.

The next two internal explorations aim to help us understand what a pragmatist epistemology ought to look like. Anne Baril explores how the debate about internalism and externalism about reasons relates to recent discussions of pragmatic encroachment. She argues that adopting one or

Introduction 7

the other account of reasons will result in accounts that make quite different judgments about what we know in various cases. Since these varying judgments can make or break the plausibility of our pragmatist accounts, pragmatists must address the issue.

The topic of externalism continues in Brian Kim's discussion. He argues that Gettier cases bring to light a lacuna with many contemporary pragmatist epistemologies. While such epistemologies have been explicated on the basis of reason-theoretic and decision-theoretic accounts of rational deliberation and choice, these accounts have not been wholly suitable. What is missing is a sufficiently rich externalist account of rational deliberation. Kim proposes that we can enrich expected utility theory by incorporating into the theory an account of how we frame decision problems. By offering the outlines of a novel externalist decision theory and developing a pragmatist epistemology on its basis, Kim argues that we can account for Gettier cases and address some well-known criticisms of pragmatic encroachment, such as the one raised by Anderson and Hawthorne in this volume.

The second group of essays explores criticisms of the pragmatist's approach. Stewart Cohen explores a problematic consequence of pragmatic encroachment on knowledge, arguing that the view leaves us with an implausibly unstable account of knowledge. Cohen reconsiders the arguments that motivated the pragmatist view and identifies a key but problematic inference from knowing that p to possessing p as a reason to act. Cohen acknowledges that it is hard to reject this inference, but he argues that we are already forced to give up this inference in cases of purely epistemic rationality. Given that we must already reject the inference, there is little cost in extending it to cases of practical rationality. Moreover, doing so provides a unified account of both the practical and epistemic cases.

Charity Anderson and John Hawthorne raise a challenge for the pragmatist account of knowledge by exploring its relationship with epistemic closure principles. They consider two versions of the pragmatist theory, one that relies on the notion of practical adequacy and another that appeals to stakes-sensitivity. They show that both versions are incompatible with single-premise closure of knowledge and argue that it is difficult to see how to remedy the problem.

Mikkel Gerken presents a challenge for the pragmatists' account of knowledge by showing that their current framework, with its focus on practical stakes and personal interests, appears unable to account for and explain the trademark features of scientific knowledge. Gerken explores the possibility of combining an anti-realist view of science, such as constructive empiricism, with pragmatic encroachment about scientific knowledge. But he argues that this combination raises new problems about the role of values in science.

The final group of essays expand the scope of our inquiries by identifying under-explored areas where the pragmatist point of view might provide new insight. These essays also expand the scope of the pragmatist's inquiry by considering alternative concepts of the relationship between knowledge and the practical. N. Ángel Pinillos offers a cognitive account of how we make skeptical judgments that one does not know. He proposes that there is a special purpose skeptical module that has been shaped by natural selection and interacts with internalized knowledge-action principles, which are central to the pragmatist account. By understanding the mechanisms behind our skeptical judgments, Pinillos proposes to offer a more satisfactory response to the skeptic's arguments.

Brad Armendt expands on his previous inquiries into how practical factors interact with our beliefs by considering the possibility of stakes-sensitive rational degrees of belief. By appealing to the theory of deliberation dynamics, which explores how self-aware decision makers change their mind over the course of an extended deliberation, Armendt argues that there are cases that can arguably be interpreted as examples of rational stakes-sensitive degrees of belief.

Rima Basu and Mark Schroeder explore the question of whether we can wrong one another by what we believe. Motivating this idea with examples, they focus on addressing two theoretical difficulties that it faces. The first problem is that our beliefs do not seem to be under our voluntary control. The second problem is that there appear to be conflicts between the epistemic and moral norms governing belief. Both problems, they argue, can be resolved given moral encroachment, the view that the epistemic norms governing belief are sensitive to the moral norms governing belief.

Juan Comesaña explores a combination of Bayesian decision theory and the view that knowledge = evidence, which he calls knowledge-first decision theory. He argues that, at first glance, this combined view gives the wrong results in a number of choice problems. However, he suggests that if knowledge-first decision theorists are willing to adopt a practical adequacy condition on knowledge, as pragmatists do, they can address this problem.

Note

1. Alternatively, it may be argued that these competing formulations actually govern different types of reasoning. (e.g. monotonic vs non-monotonic, deductive vs inductive vs abductive). So further exploration of these proposed practical conditions on knowledge may be required.

References

Anderson, Charity and John Hawthorne (2019). "Knowledge, Practical Adequacy, and Stakes." In: *Oxford Studies in Epistemology*, Vol. 6. Oxford: Oxford University Press.

DeRose, K. (2009). *The Case for Contextualism: Knowledge, Skepticism, and Context*, Vol. 1. New York: Oxford University Press.

Fantl, J. and M. McGrath (2002). "Evidence, Pragmatics, and Justification." *The Philosophical Review*, 111.1, pp. 67–94.

Introduction 9

——— (2009). *Knowledge in an Uncertain World*. Oxford: Oxford University Press.
——— (forthcoming). "Clarifying Pragmatic Encroachment: A Reply to Charity.
Hawthorne, J. (2003). *Knowledge and Lotteries*. Oxford: Oxford University Press.
Stanley, J. (2005). *Knowledge and Practical Interests*. New York: Oxford University Press.

2 Great Expectations
Belief and the Case for Pragmatic Encroachment[1]

Dorit Ganson

Then I saw her face, now I'm a believer
Not a trace of doubt in my mind . . .
I'm a believer, I couldn't leave her if I tried.
— The Monkees

According to the thesis of *pragmatic encroachment*, the pragmatic "encroaches" on the epistemic: practical considerations such as the potential costs of acting on p if p is false or benefits of acting on p if p is true can make a difference when it comes to whether or not an agent's belief that p is epistemically rational, epistemically justified, or involves her knowing that p. Two subjects in different practical circumstances can differ with respect to whether they are epistemically justified in believing that p even though they are the same with respect to all truth-relevant, intellectual factors, such as the quantity and quality of their evidence for and against p, the reliability of the methods they rely on in forming their attitudes towards p, etc. Sometimes more evidence is needed to know or to be epistemically justified in believing as the stakes get higher and the odds longer.

Many of the recent criticisms of the case for pragmatic encroachment raise objections to the conclusion itself (how can knowledge come and go with sudden inheritance, new-found indifference, etc.),[2] or take issue with some of the principles connecting knowledge and practical reason that are crucial premises in the central arguments in its favor.[3] Whatever the outcome of such attacks, they leave open the possibility that pragmatic encroachment could still be, surprisingly, true of other significant epistemic relations, as well as the possibility that there are other routes to pragmatic encroachment which don't begin with the principles in question. Perhaps reflection on what it takes for someone's degree of confidence, expectation, or trust to be accompanied by or to give rise to outright belief could help enhance our understanding of the source and scope of pragmatic encroachment.[4]

One convenient way to execute this strategy would be by way of a threshold model of the relationship between *degree of belief* that p and the categorical attitudes of *belief* that p, *suspension* of belief with respect to p, and belief that p is false (*disbelief*). It is rather tempting to think that when expectations become great enough, they somehow tip the scales towards belief; when low enough, towards disbelief. It can certainly appear this way sometimes. One may be inclined at such moments to think that belief is essentially high enough confidence, disbelief low enough, and suspension middling confidence—where the boundaries of these ranges are somewhat vague and variable with circumstance. Say our strength of confidence with respect to p can range anywhere from absolute certainty that p is false (degree of belief or subjective probability = 0) to maximal certainty that it is true (degree of belief or subjective probability = 1). Perhaps there are potentially contextually variant thresholds which set how close to 1 our degree of belief *has to be and is sufficient for it* to serve as belief, or how close to 0 it *has to be and is sufficient for it* to serve as disbelief. We'll call such an account *The Reductive Threshold View of Belief*: degree of belief, or subjective probability, above a potentially contextually variant threshold is necessary and sufficient for belief.

Such an account reduces belief, suspension, and disbelief to degree of belief within certain contextually relevant spectrums of confidence levels. This sort of a view seems to be what's on the table in Hájek (2000).

> I assume here and elsewhere that talk of beliefs and talk of sufficiently high subjective probabilities are intertranslatable.
>
> (Hájek 2000, p. 200)

> Here is a good rule of thumb, I suggest: we should generally associate agnosticism with "middling" probability assignments, belief with "high" probability assignments, and disbelief with "low" probability assignments.
>
> (Hájek 1998, p. 204)

> X is agnostic about A iff x gives a probability assignment to A that is not close to a sharp 0 or 1—the standards for "closeness" being determined by context. That includes all sharp assignments that are not "close" (according to the operative standards) to 0 or 1; and indeed all sets of assignments that include values that are not "close" (according the operative standards) to 0 or 1.
>
> (Hájek 1998, p. 205)

Such a view accords well with the thesis of pragmatic encroachment. Suppose that practical factors are relevant to fixing the placement of the threshold—extreme risk situations with respect to acting on p potentially raising the bar; low risk situations potentially lowering the bar. If we think that it's in the nature of outright belief to be subject to this sort of variance with changes in practical setting, we should expect that the normative epistemic assessment of outright belief will be as well. We can well imagine two individuals who have the same evidence and level of epistemically justified

12 Dorit Ganson

credence for p, but who differ in the peril of their circumstances. For the person in the more demanding setting, say this level of credence falls below the threshold for belief; for the person in the less demanding setting, let's suppose this level of credence is well above the threshold. The second person can, from the standpoint of epistemic evaluation, appropriately believe p; the first cannot and should be agnostic about p. Such a view can nicely be combined with a conception of outright belief as akin to the engagement of heuristics—something that involves fast, energy sparing, and at times inaccurate shortcuts, allowing us to bypass costly calculations with subjective probabilities until the situation demands greater attentiveness to our actual degrees of confidence.

Despite its initial appeal, a simple, Reductive Threshold account of the relationship between categorical belief and degree of belief is not viable, for reasons—some familiar, some unfamiliar—I will present next. Rather than give up on the threshold picture entirely, however, I suggest that we retain part of it, and combine it with a dispositionalist account of belief along the lines of what Ryle envisioned (minus the behaviorism, as Eric Schwitzgebel[5] would say). As Ryle observes in *The Concept of Mind*, belief involves a wide spectrum of proclivities and dispositions—some automatic and some deliberate—involving reasoning, reflecting, asserting, imagining, acting, reacting, and feeling.

> Belief might be said to be like knowledge, and unlike trust in persons, zeal for causes, or addiction to smoking, in that it is "propositional"; but this, though not far wrong, is too narrow. Certainly to believe that the ice is dangerously thin is to be unhesitant in telling oneself and others that it is thin, in acquiescing to other people's assertion to that effect, in objecting to statements to the contrary, in drawing consequences from the original proposition, and so forth. But it is also to be prone to skate warily, to shudder, to dwell in imagination on possible disasters and to warn other skaters. It is also a propensity not only to make certain theoretical moves but also to have certain feelings.
>
> (Ryle 1949, p. 92)

Suspension of belief involves its own spectrum, and the deactivation of these propensities and the engagement of those typical of belief does not *all* come down to a transition from middling to high enough degrees of confidence or expectation. While I won't attempt a full defense of the threshold-dispositionalist hybrid I call *Hybrid Doxastic Pragmatism* here, I at least hope to show that such a hybrid can avert some of the main problems that face the Reductive Threshold View on its own, and yet still provide us with a satisfying sketch of the relationship between belief and degree of belief that can complement and bolster the case for pragmatic encroachment.

1. Interesting and Robust Relations Between Degrees of Confidence/Expectation and the Categorical Attitudes

Even if normative and non-normative facts involving belief, suspension of belief, and disbelief don't supervene on facts involving degrees of belief and degree of belief thresholds, we still have good reason to suppose that there are some kinds of interesting and robust relations between the two realms. Consider our old, reliable belief-desire folk psychology which has served us so well throughout the ages. Countless successful explanations (though not all) work just as well when we substitute "believes that" with "is highly confident that", or "disbelieves" with "has very low confidence that".

(a) Snow White does not give up hope because she believes that someday her prince will come.
(b) Snow White does not give up hope because she is highly confident that someday her prince will come.
(a) Grumpy is crying because he does not believe/disbelieves that Snow White will ever wake from her slumber.
(b) Grumpy is crying because he has very low confidence that Snow White will ever wake from her slumber.

For explanations appealing to belief suspension, the transition is a bit bumpier, but expressions in terms of degrees of confidence seem equally effective and informative (if not more so).

(a) Snow White failed to appreciate the danger of her situation because even after due consideration she remained agnostic/suspended judgment about the existence of witches and evil magic.
(b) Snow White failed to appreciate the danger of her situation because even after due consideration she remained no more confident that witches and evil magic exist than that witches and evil magic do not exist.

Furthermore, some folk-psychological explanations explicitly invoke the notion that opinions are held with varying relative degrees of strength. We are entirely at ease in speaking in comparative terms.

(a) The Queen wasn't absolutely sure, but she strongly believed that one dose of poison would be enough to kill Snow White. Since she believed even more strongly that two doses would be sufficient, and so ardently wished for Snow White's demise, she sprang for the expense of an extra dose.

On occasion we are aware that we are transitioning from disbelief to suspension of belief to belief as evidence steadily accumulates, while at the

14 *Dorit Ganson*

same time we sense a gradual change in our level of confidence. Our expectation is at first very low and grows stronger and stronger still until we finally reach a point where we have reversed our former state of opinion. I had such an experience on the night of the 2016 Presidential Election. I began the evening with little expectation that Hilary Clinton would lose the election, only to see my disbelief that she would lose abandoned and eventually replaced with outright belief that she would lose when all was said and done. Here's another (more fanciful) example, inspired by the case studies in Pinillos (2012).

(a) An unconfident typist, Doc very quickly types out the lyrics to *Heigh-Ho*. At first he disbelieves that the typed document has no typographical errors, i.e. he believes that it is false that it has no typos. He has each dwarf check it over for errors in order from the dwarf least likely to find a mistake (Dopey), and to the one who is the most meticulous (himself), and then carefully checks it two more times. Throughout the process, Doc's confidence that the document contains no typographical errors gradually increases; by the end, his disbelief has been replaced with belief.

When we encounter belief and degree of confidence moving in tandem in this fashion as evidence steadily streams in, it is hard to resist the thought that they relate to one another in a significant way. So what's the problem with the Reductive Threshold picture?

2. Interesting and Robust Relations, but not Reduction

I shall now present a number of objections to the Reductive Threshold View.

(1) Familiar strike: Lotteries

A major and familiar strike against a simple threshold picture is that lottery considerations speak against it. If someone purchases a ticket for a fair lottery with n tickets (where n is very large), that person can have a very high degree of credence *(n-1)/n* for *my ticket is a losing ticket*, yet suspend judgment with respect to, and fail to believe *my ticket is a losing ticket* until the winner is announced and the ticket is tossed into the garbage. It may be reasonable for her to do so, and it is at the very least possible for her to do so. We can image bigger and bigger lotteries, accompanied by ever higher credence levels which fail to ensure belief and exclude suspension. No credence level short of 1 seems to do the job, and that is not a very helpful observation. What's more, before the announcement, the lottery ticket owner can have many other outright beliefs which are accompanied by degrees of confidence much lower than *(n-1)/n*. Outright belief cannot then simply be a matter of a level of credence tipping over a threshold and

Great Expectations   15

falling into a range which is necessary and sufficient for belief: what's good enough for these outright beliefs apparently isn't good enough for *my ticket is a losing ticket.*

(2) Cases where suspension of judgment with respect to conjunctions and disjunctions of propositions one suspends judgments about is possible and rationally permissible

Another consideration strongly telling against the simple threshold picture concerns the alleged boundaries of the credence range for suspension of belief or agnosticism with respect to p. (What I raise here is a simplification of a central idea developed and defended with greater sophistication by Jane Friedman (2013)). Such boundaries would, if they exist, hover somewhere around the middling section of the 0 to 1 credence spectrum. On the Reductive Threshold View, to suspend belief with respect to p is *essentially* a matter of having a degree of belief which falls into this middling range: too far from 0 to count as disbelief, and too far from 1 to count as belief. Imagine someone is confronted with a series of n independent claims which she understands but is powerless to adjudicate given her lack of relevant background knowledge. (In Friedman's example, a woman is given a series of different images of snowflakes, and is asked to consider of each image whether or not she thinks it will exactly match a given concealed image of a snowflake.) She suspends belief with respect to each claim. She also suspends belief with respect to both the disjunction, and the conjunction of the n claims. Such a set of attitudes seems possible, as well as reasonable. A person who suspends judgment with respect to each of a set of claims should also be entitled to suspend judgment about their conjunction or disjunction. But the simple threshold view cannot sanction this set of attitudes. For any genuinely middling span (short of 0 to 1), there's an n such that the agent's credence for the disjunction must (on pain of incoherence) fall into the belief span, and for the conjunction, fall into the disbelief span.

(3) An epistemically appropriate transition to outright belief even though epistemic probability goes down

Sometimes a factor that from the standpoint of epistemic rationality appropriately tips an agent into genuine, robust outright belief with respect to a claim is a factor that lowers the epistemic probability of the claim. In such a case, the transition to outright belief on the part of this rational agent cannot be a matter of her degree of belief finally becoming high enough to cross a belief-demarcating threshold. (We'll take it for granted here that being able to and inclined to rely on p in relevant practical and theoretical reasoning is a significant aspect of outright believing it; for the rational believer, in turn, such reliance will be entirely appropriate.) Imagine Sherlock—an excellent detective who is, as Spock would say, very *logical.* Suppose Sherlock has

16 Dorit Ganson

already determined that a single individual committed a murder, and has narrowed down the suspect list to 10,000 individuals in the ballroom on the cruise ship. All but two, a chef and Joe the plumber, are lawyers. The evidence Sherlock has so far is indifferent between all these suspects: his degree of credence that any given suspect committed the crime is 1/10,000, and hence for *Either Joe or some Lawyer did it* ($J_p \vee L_1 \vee L_2 \ldots L_{9,998}$) it is 9,999/10,000. Later, he uncovers evidence E that strongly implicates the plumber when he comes across a box of plumbing tools stained with the victim's blood, hidden in a sewage chamber only plumbers (in all but the rarest of cases) have access to. His evidence justifies him in believing J_p (say to degree 999/1000). Let's suppose as well that Sherlock recognizes that the chef has very difficult, but still far better access to the chamber than any of the lawyers. While Sherlock regards it as exceedingly unlikely that the chef is the guilty party, he figures that given his evidence E concerning the location of the murder weapon, strictly speaking it is nine times as likely that the chef did it than that some lawyer or other did it. In light of E, say Sherlock's credence for

> Jp goes up from .0001 to .999
> *The chef did it* goes up from .0001 to .0009
> *Some Lawyer did it* goes down from .9998 to .0001
> *Either Joe or some Lawyer did it* goes down from .9999 to .9991 (= .999 + .0001).

Now that Sherlock is justified in believing *Jp*, he is entitled to believe other things he competently deduces from it, such as $J_p \vee L_1 \vee L_2 \ldots L_{9,998}$, which in turn he can now rely on to conclude the chef is innocent and should be allowed to go home. The evidence which provides him with epistemic reason to believe that J_p is also a newly gained epistemic reason he has to believe that $J_p \vee L_1 \vee L_2 \ldots L_{9,998}$, even though the evidence ultimately has a downward impact on his rational degree of credence in this case. Before the evidence in question came along, and despite his very high level of credence, Sherlock couldn't outright believe *Either Joe or some lawyer did it* and legitimately rely on it in reasoning—to conclude, say, that the chef is innocent and should be allowed to go home. After all, a similar line of reasoning could then be used to conclude, of each and every suspect, that the suspect is innocent and should be allowed to go home (i.e. infer S_1 *is innocent* from S_2 or S_3 or . . . $S_{10,000}$ *did it*, etc.). But after the bloody plumbing tools are found, then it is acceptable for Sherlock to rely on *Either Joe or some Lawyer did it* to conclude that the chef should be allowed to go home.

Indeed, there is a telling, more direct route to the belief that the chef is innocent and should be allowed to go home. In light of E, Sherlock's credence for

> *The chef did it* goes up from .0001 to .0009 (a slightly higher, but still negligible chance of guilt)
> *The chef didn't do it* goes down from .9999 to .9991.

Great Expectations 17

E gives Sherlock strong reason to believe *Joe did it*, which in turn he can rely on to conclude that *The chef didn't do it*. This more direct path also illustrates how acquiring an epistemic reason to believe a claim can end up lowering the epistemic probability of the claim. At the end of the day, Sherlock appropriately outright believes that the chef is innocent and lets him go home. Whatever the transition to this state of outright belief amounts to, it cannot be simply a matter of Sherlock's credence now becoming high enough to finally cross the lower bound of a *close-to-1* belief-demarcating threshold.

(4) The beliefs that constitute the acceptance of the terms of decision matrices are not reducible to credences

Another case against a simple, reductive threshold view is derived from what seem to be basic presuppositions of the Decision-Theoretic framework for practical rationality itself. Degrees of belief are indispensable to such a framework. But it turns out some kind of category of outright belief— irreducible to credences—is as well. Robert Nozick stresses this point in *The Nature of Rationality* as he explains why a radical Bayesianism which simply makes do with credences will not do.

> Despite these apparent strengths, it is unclear that this position of radical Bayesianism can be formulated coherently. Probabilities of statements (rather than simply beliefs in them) are to be applied in choice situations, but a choice situation is one a person believes he is facing, that is one where he believes that he can perform various alternative actions A1, . . . An, believes that A1 can have various possible outcomes Oi (perhaps depending on which state of the world Sj obtains), and so on. To be sure, the person then acts upon probabilities, prob(Oi/A1) or prob(Sj/A1), but these occur *within* a structure of beliefs about the situation of choice . . . The very setup of theories of personal probability and utility, or the background commentary they require, involves the existence or attributions of beliefs to the person whose choices are taken to indicate preference or probabilistic judgments. Without those beliefs about the situation he was in, his choices would not indicate these particular preferences or probabilistic judgments. The theoretical definition of these latter notions presupposes attributing certain beliefs to the person.
>
> (Nozick 1993, p. 95)

Any decision matrix which is taken as realistically representing or approximating how an agent is or should be reasoning through a practical decision problem cannot take too many epistemically possible but highly unlikely states of the world into account. An agent who thinks through the potential effects of a choice of action given too many remote possible

18 *Dorit Ganson*

happenings in the world, or takes into account too many remote possible outcomes for a given action and state of the world will get bogged down in pointless, costly calculation. A choice of action might be indefinitely postponed as a seemingly endless array of possible states and outcomes enter into consideration. At some point, the terms or partitions of a decision matrix have to be accepted. The agent has to be seen as having beliefs about what choice situation she is in. To identify such beliefs with credences (short of 1) is to invite the pursuit of ever more finely divided decision matrices. To identify such beliefs with maximal degree of confidence is equally problematic. You are not certain that the possibilities you are not taking into account are false, nor should you be. The beliefs that constitute the acceptance of the terms of the decision matrices are not reducible to credences.

(5) Psychological attitudes are most plausibly taken as attitudes towards p itself, rather than p *is likely*

Some of the emotional states that can accompany/are caused by coming to believe that p (crossing the Rubicon to now outright believing that p) are in certain circumstances more plausibly regarded psychologically as attitudes towards p itself, rather than p *is likely* (especially when preceded by belief that—p): surprised that, dismayed that, disappointed that, relieved that, dejected that, overjoyed that, ecstatic that, outraged that, indignant that, frustrated that, shocked that p . . . . The Munchkins in *The Wizard of Oz*, for example, are overjoyed that the wicked witch is dead, not that it is likely that the wicked witch is dead. My daughter was thrilled that she was accepted at Hamilton College, not that it is likely that she was accepted at Hamilton College. My husband Todd was disappointed that the Browns lost the football game, not that it is likely that the Browns lost the football game. These states of mind are simply best explained by appeal to B*p*, *not* B(p *is likely*). If outright belief were just a matter of a high enough credence (often short of 1), the difference in explanatory value between B*p* and B(p *is likely*) in these cases would be puzzling.

One has come to have these feelings in these sorts of cases because one has now come to outright believe that p. It would be absurd to suggest that since outright believing p really amounts to a high degree of credence that p (accompanied by a small degree of credence that—p), strictly speaking one is relieved, surprised etc. to a large degree that p, and devastated, not surprised etc. to a small degree that—p. Sometimes one can be ecstatic or profoundly relieved that p *is likely* (e.g. when finding out after a scan that it is likely that the cancer has not yet spread to other organs), but such circumstances seem to be the exception rather than the norm. If we take the propensity to have these feelings as among the dispositions relevant to or typical of categorical belief, that is another reason to resist the idea that categorical belief is simply high enough credence.

3. Distinctive Epistemic Norms for the Categorical Attitudes

There is a further, significant reason why the Reductive Threshold View fails. Norms involving Bp, Sp, and Dp (the doxastic attitudes of belief, suspension, and disbelief with respect to p) are not readily reducible to those involving degrees of confidence in the way that would be expected if the simple threshold view were correct.[6] I shall argue that, from the standpoint of epistemic rationality, we are sometimes required to Bp (vs. Sp or Dp), permitted to Bp, permitted to Sp, and these requirements are not simply reducible to requirements governing degrees of confidence.

Here are a few potential requirements from the standpoint of epistemic rationality concerning a proposition under consideration. The requirements and permissions at issue concern the tripartite attitude choice of belief, suspension of belief, and disbelief with respect to p, not the choice to believe that p vs. available alternatives incompatible with p.

(a) If you have considerably more reason to Bp than to Sp or to Dp, then Ought(Bp) (you ought to believe that p) and OughtNot(Sp) (you ought not to suspend belief with respect to p).
(b) If you have considerably more reason to Sp than to Bp or to Dp, then Ought(Sp) and OughtNot(Bp).
(c) If you have at least as much reason to Bp as to Sp or to Dp, then Perm(Bp) (it's permissible for you to believe that p); if you have at least as much reason to Sp as to Bp or to Dp, then Perm(Sp).

Constraint (c) does not entail that belief is permitted when you have at least as much or slightly more evidence for p than counterevidence against p. When you have no evidence either way, or the evidence for and against p is equally or very nearly balanced, that can itself be an overriding reason to favor Sp. Under what conditions could both Bp and Sp be permitted but not required options? Perhaps some situation where Bp is allowed, but so is B(p *is likely*) combined with Sp. *My lottery ticket is a losing ticket* may sometimes fall into this category. Another example that comes to mind is when my radiologist said to me "this looks like cancer" before biopsy results confirmed the diagnosis. You are not permitted to Bp when you have more evidence for some alternative which is incompatible with p than you do for p.

(d) If Kp (you know that p), then Ought(Bp) and OughtNot(Sp).[7]
(e) If Jp (you are justified in believing that p), then Perm(Bp).

We can also acknowledge an obligating vs. permitting notion of *being justified in believing*, in which case

(f) If Jp, then Ought(Bp) and OughtNot(Sp).

20   *Dorit Ganson*

If the Reductive Threshold View of belief were correct, epistemic obligations and permissions involving Bp, Sp, and Dp would boil down to what spectrum (high, middling, low) in the 0 to 1 range our confidence for p ought to or is permitted to fall. Ought(Bp) would be a matter of (from the standpoint of epistemic rationality) being obligated to have a credence sufficiently high to constitute belief, and of having more reason to have a degree of confidence in the belief-spectrum than either the suspension-spectrum or the disbelief-spectrum. Perm(Bp) would be a matter of being permitted to have a credence sufficiently high to constitute belief, and of having at least as much reason to have a degree of confidence in the belief-spectrum as in the suspension-spectrum or in the disbelief-spectrum. But when would that happen? This last condition is especially hard to picture.

I take it this condition sounds forced and strange because the only kinds of reasons to which our degree of credence states are appropriately responsive (epistemically speaking) are evidential. The only kind of considerations which, from the standpoint of epistemic rationality, ought to move what part of the spectrum your degree of confidence for p falls into over a period of time is the strength, quality, and quantity of the evidence for and counter-evidence against p that you acquire. The reasons to which our BSD doxastic attitudes are appropriately responsive include, but are not limited to, evidential considerations. Among such reasons are: that conclusive test results are expected very soon, that opportunities for low cost double-checking await, that there is little to gain and much to lose by a rush to judgment, that only action animated by decisive conviction will allow for continued inquiry, that continued inquiry would be very costly and unlikely to yield relevant new information, that treating p as true and acting on p if p is false would be devastating, that not treating as p as true and not acting on p if p is true would involve missing out on some major goods . . . . As William James famously observes in "The Will to Believe":

> Whenever the option between losing truth and gaining it is not momentous, we can throw the chance of *gaining truth* away, and at any rate save ourselves from any chance of *believing falsehood*, by not making up our minds at all till objective evidence has come. In scientific questions, this is almost always the case; and even in human affairs in general, the need of acting is seldom so urgent that a false belief to act on is better than no belief at all.
>
> (James 1948, p. 101)

All of these candidates are potential reasons which have a bearing on which of the doxastic attitudes (Bp, Sp, or Dp) we ought to or are permitted to adopt—even when we take pains to stress that we are making our evaluations from the standpoint of epistemic rationality.

Consider these different kinds of cases which all concern *very high credence*, but involve different permissions and obligations with respect to Bp, Sp, and Dp:

Great Expectations 21

(1) For a wide range of cases involving very high levels of credence for p, Sp can be successfully and permissibly combined with the high credence and an attitude of B(p *is likely*). In such cases an agent might say "while I believe p *is likely*, I'm still going to keep the matter open and continue investigating; I'm still going to suspend judgment with respect to p", or "while I believe p *is likely*, conclusive evidence is coming soon to settle the matter, so I won't fully make up my mind about p until then". Lottery cases seem to show that there's no threshold short of 1 which in principle excludes or disallows combining that high a credence for p with Sp and B(p *is likely*).

(2) Sometimes a very high credence for p can appropriately be accompanied by Bp or by Sp and B(p *is likely*) as a reasonable alternative (as in my cancer diagnosis example, before the biopsy results come in). If having the attitude of Bp is essentially just a matter of having a credence for p which falls within the (contextually determined) B part of the spectrum, and having the attitude of Sp is essentially just a matter of having a credence for p which falls within the (contextually determined) S part of the spectrum, it is hard to see how an agent with a given degree of confidence in a given circumstance could genuinely have these two options, Bp or Sp and B(p *is likely*).

(3) If we assume fallibilism, sometimes a very high credence for p can only appropriately be accompanied by Bp, and not by Sp and B(p *is likely*)—namely when Kp. [Recall: If Kp, then Ought(Bp), and OughtNot(Sp).] The reasons which are playing a role in settling which of Bp, Sp, or Dp is permitted or required go beyond the reasons relevant to settling in which part of the 0 to 1 spectrum a credence is permitted or required to fall.

Two factors over and above a justified level of confidence which could potentially have a bearing on which categorical attitude a subject will or ought to adopt with respect to a proposition include the kind of proposition in question, as well as the kind of evidence that comes along. For example, for an anti-realist such as Bas van Fraassen, if a well confirmed scientific claim concerns unobservable theoretical entities, he thinks we ought to be agnostic about it, and accept it only as empirically adequate. That the claim is of that type is (for him, given various philosophical arguments he finds compelling) a general reason to be agnostic about it. He will also deny that we have knowledge of the existence of unobservables.[8] According to van Fraassen, when it comes to such claims, we Ought(Sp) and—Kp.

When something of great importance to a person's well-being is at issue (such as whether or not the person has a particular form of cancer), more confidence might be required for outright belief than for something of lesser significance. Furthermore, certain kinds of evidence and counterevidence might be particularly impactful (such as hearing your radiologist say that all the biopsies are positive for cancer) when it comes to adopting or changing a categorical attitude.

22   *Dorit Ganson*

Sometimes you find yourself in a situation where now in light of particularly decisive evidence you should/ought to believe p itself, and not simply p *is likely*. At times like these when now you know, you get the kind of evidence that seems to make you now know p, not just p *is likely* (which you already knew before).

So it looks like there is no answer to the question *how much confidence is enough to constitute or serve as belief?* Whether or not your degree of confidence that p involves or is accompanied by Bp is not fully a matter of your confidence crossing the lower bound of a fixed or contextually variable sufficiency threshold for belief.

4. Pragmatic Credal Constraints on Outright Belief

Perhaps these further, non-evidential reasons, which apply to the Bp, Sp, or Dp attitude choice, could potentially be regarded as relevant at least to fixing the location of credence *requirements*—how high or how low a level of confidence for p is required (but not sufficient) for Bp or Dp. Some settings might involve more or less demanding requirements concerning how close to 1 a degree of belief *has to be* in order to be accompanied by belief. (Now we are talking simply about necessary constraints: how confident we have to be to have belief. When there's much to gain or lose with a choice of action depending on whether p is true or false, it makes sense to suppose that a higher degree of confidence in p is required for p to serve as a principle of action—motivating and justifying our choice.) There are potentially some constitutive or normative links between our degree of confidence and our BSD doxastic attitudes. Here is one plausible candidate.

(A) Bp requires that you are more confident in p than any alternatives you know to be incompatible with p.

Let's also consider what necessary requirements or links to credences are plausible if we adopt a broad, dispositionalist understanding of belief of the sort Ryle (1949) and Schwitzgebel (2002) propose. (If you prefer to privilege a particular class of dispositions involving assertion or practical and theoretical reasoning, feel free to make the appropriate substitutions in what follows.) We'll call the position *Hybrid Doxastic Pragmatism*, because it is a form of doxastic pragmatism that combines dispositionalism about belief with aspects of a threshold view. According to this view, to believe *the ice is dangerously thin* is to be to prone (under the right circumstances) to act, react, reason, and feel in certain sorts of ways, to engage in various sorts of activities and reflections—some automatic, instinctive, and habitual, others more reflective and deliberate . . . but all on the basis of *the ice is dangerously thin*, with *the ice is dangerously thin* as one's motivating reason. Furthermore, this hybrid view involves the claim that without *some* measure of trust, confidence, and expectation that *the ice is dangerously thin* on our

Great Expectations 23

part, *the ice is dangerously thin* cannot serve this psychological role as motivating reason for us—enabling us to have the relevant sets of dispositions typical of *the ice is dangerously thin* categorical belief. Equipped with this hybrid form of doxastic pragmatism, we can still draw some kind of essential link between credences and categorical belief, even if a simple reductive threshold account isn't viable.

So suppose you are in a situation where you are faced with the issue of which doxastic attitude to adopt: Bp, Sp, or Dp. You are at the pond with your ice skates, and you will ultimately come to believe, suspend judgment with respect to, or disbelieve that *the ice is dangerously thin.*

> *Hybrid Doxastic Pragmatism*: Bp requires that you are confident enough that p
>
> - for you to be able to have the spectrum of dispositions typical for outright belief that p under these conditions
> - for p to be able to serve as a motivating reason for you to have or engage in the relevant sorts of activities, actions, reactions, feelings, habits typical for belief that p here.[9]

Whatever minimum confidence that p is required for you to able and willing to act, etc. on the basis of p (in the current situation, and perhaps also for at least a wide range of typical or ordinary circumstances when p is relevant),[10] Bp presupposes that you have that level.

Maybe we can go for something somewhat stronger:

> *Hybrid Doxastic Pragmatism**: Bp requires that you are confident enough that p
>
> - for you to be able to have the spectrum of dispositions typical for outright belief that p under these conditions
> - for p itself (rather than something more hedged like p *is likely*) to be able to serve as a motivating reason for you to have or engage in the relevant sorts of activities, actions, reactions, feelings, habits typical for belief that p here.

If you don't meet this condition, you may be more accurately described as B(p *is likely*), and not really as Bp.

While Hybrid Doxastic Pragmatism supposes that there is an essential link between categorical belief and degree of belief, it does not equate Bp, Sp, and Dp with having a degree of belief for p within a (contextually variant) spectrum. Unlike the Reductive Threshold View of belief, it does not reduce outright belief to degree of belief above a lower-bound threshold, or identify a change from Sp to Bp with a change from a middling to a high enough degree of belief that p. As a result, Hybrid Doxastic Pragmatism is able to avoid the main problems that we examined for the Reductive

24   *Dorit Ganson*

Threshold View. With Hybrid Doxastic Pragmatism, we can well allow that our *acquiring certain kinds of compelling evidence*, or *no longer needing to rely solely on considerations of indifference* could mark the point where we transition to outright belief (in a way that is epistemically appropriate). We can also acknowledge the crucial role that the acquisition of various sorts of dispositions in reasoning, acting, and feeling can play in marking the transition to belief.

To showcase this advantage, let's return to the lottery. The following interpretation of the transition to outright belief is available to Hybrid Doxastic Pragmatism, but not to the Reductive Threshold View. When we're newly confronted with a wide range of exhaustive, mutually exclusive possibilities, and we have no evidence yet which could potentially weigh them differently, we're often not inclined to *outright believe* rather than *suspend/withhold* with respect to the claim that a particular possibility does not obtain—even though our credence for such a claim is very high. If all we have to go on are considerations of indifference, *withholding belief* about the possibility not obtaining will often strike us as just as appealing or reasonable an option as *believing* that the possibility doesn't obtain—all the more so when we expect some evidence to come along to end our state of complete ignorance. When we have nothing but considerations of indifference to go on, the chance of falsehood can remain relevant and active for our reasoning, even when it's small. We won't yet have the relevant reasoning dispositions to count as outright *believing* that the possibility does not obtain. Given a lottery of 10,000 tickets for a million dollar prize, for instance, it seems perfectly fine for the ticket holder to outright believe, and to be disposed to rely on *my ticket is* most likely *a loser* in practical and theoretical reasoning. The same cannot be said for *my ticket is a loser*. (Would you have her sell it for a penny then? Or dispose of it before the winner is announced? Can't she quite reasonably say "Most likely the ticket is a loser, but I won't take the matter to be fully settled until the winner is announced"?) Once the winner—ticket X—is announced, there's some evidence to discriminate between all those possibilities. Now our ticket holder should and will take it as true that ticket X is the winner, and reason that, since her ticket is not ticket X, her ticket is not the winner. Now she has reason to outright believe *my ticket is a loser*, and to throw it in the trash. To continue withholding on *my ticket is a loser* at this point is no longer reasonable.

A similar story could be told for Sherlock and Joe the plumber. At the outset, despite his very high level of credence, Sherlock doesn't have the right reasoning dispositions to count as outright believing that *Either Joe or some lawyer did it*. He *isn't* inclined to rely on the claim in reasoning to conclude that the chef is innocent and should be allowed to go home. After all, a similar line of reasoning could then be used to conclude, of each and every suspect, that the suspect is innocent and should be allowed to go home (i.e. infer S_1 *is innocent* from S_2 *or* S_3 *or* . . . $S_{10,000}$ *did it*, etc.). But after the bloody plumbing tools are found, Sherlock *is* inclined to rely on *Either Joe or some lawyer did it* to conclude that the chef should be allowed to go home. Now he counts as a believer.

5. Hybrid Doxastic Pragmatism and the Case for Pragmatic Encroachment

We shall now explore some potential ways the Hybrid Doxastic Pragmatist framework can enhance the case for pragmatic encroachment. Recall:

    (d) If Kp, then Ought(Bp) and OughtNot(Sp).

According to Hybrid Doxastic Pragmatism*, if Bp is true of you, then you have sufficient confidence in p for p to be able to serve as a motivating reason for you for the relevant sorts of actions, reactions, feelings, etc.[11] Since Kp entails Ought(Bp) and OughtNot(Sp), your knowing that p entails that you ought to have sufficient confidence that p for p itself (and not just p *is likely*) to be able to serve (in the current situation) as a motivating reason for you for the relevant sorts of actions, reactions, feelings, etc. If you tend to require atypically low confidence to have sufficient confidence for p to serve as a motivating reason for you (because you are somewhat foolhardy and devil-may-care) it will be easier to fulfill this condition. If you tend to require atypically high confidence to have sufficient confidence for p to serve as a motivating reason (because you are very cautious and a bit of a worry wart) it will be harder to fulfill this condition.

We generally are aware that many of the things we outright believe in principle could be false, so once we're given reason to move to Sp, it's pretty easy to fall back to B(p *is likely*) and take the possibility that p is false into account in our activities, reactions, and deliberations about what to do. If a subject who outright believes that p encounters a situation where she recognizes that there is now, surprisingly, an extremely high cost for acting on the basis of p/treating p as true in your choice of what to do if it is false—that *could* sometimes be a newly introduced reason for her to Sp and go with B(p *is likely*). In such a case, unless she is foolhardy, she no longer satisfies the necessary constraint on Bp articulated by Hybrid Doxastic Pragmatism. Because Sp is permitted in this case, and hence—Ought(Bp), here we conclude that—Kp is true of the subject. If we suppose that she could have previously been in generally low-risk-with-respect-to-acting-on-p environments where she did satisfy the credal pragmatist constraint on Bp, as well as the further conditions for Kp, we have an example of pragmatic encroachment. If it's in the nature of outright belief to be subject to variance with changes in practical setting, we should expect that the normative epistemic assessment of outright belief will be as well. Hybrid Doxastic Pragmatism accords well with the thesis of pragmatic encroachment.

26 *Dorit Ganson*

In their signature work in defense of pragmatic encroachment, Fantl and McGrath (2009) argue in favor of a pragmatic necessary condition on knowledge:

(KJ) If you know that p, then p is warranted enough to justify you in both belief and action.

If you know that p, then no insufficiency of warrant stands in the way of p justifying you in further beliefs and actions suggested by p in your circumstances. You can put what you know to work as a reason for belief and action.

Quite a few weighty objections to KJ have been raised in the literature.[12] Fantl and McGrath (2009) introduce various possible responses, and Hybrid Doxastic Pragmatism may be able to add to these resources. We shall explore this possibility by considering one particularly well-known objection to KJ.

Brown (2008) argues that, contrary to KJ in light of fallibilism, knowing that p does not always ensure that a subject has sufficient warrant to rely on p in practical reasoning. In an extremely risky situation, knowledge may not be good enough; only something closer to absolute certainty will do. She illustrates this point with the example of a surgeon who knows a patient's left kidney is diseased, but nonetheless takes the trouble to double-check the patient's records just before surgery.

I take it that Brown's (2008) surgeon example is supposed to be one where Kp, and hence Ought(Bp) and Bp is true of the subject. The surgeon knows and hence does and ought to outright believe p (*the left kidney is the one to be operated on*), but double-checks the patient's chart anyway in order to be even more sure since so much is on the line.

The Hybrid Doxastic Pragmatist can argue that in these circumstances the surgeon *lacks* sufficient confidence (the minimum required) to be able to have the full spectrum of dispositions associated with belief here, and lacks sufficient confidence to be able to be motivated/willing to act on the basis of p, to have p itself as a motivating reason in her choice of what to do. But having such a minimum is required for outright belief that p. In these circumstances, the surgeon is more accurately described as outright believing p *is likely* and suspending with respect to p until she completes the check. Furthermore, it doesn't seem right say that, from the standpoint of epistemic evaluation, Ought(Bp) is true of her. Perm(Sp) and B(p *is likely*) is true of her. So a Hybrid Doxastic Pragmatist will be inclined to say that—K(p) is true of the surgeon, an outcome favorable to the defenders of pragmatic encroachment.

Note that some cases of acting as if you don't know/acting as if the matter isn't closed when the matter really should be considered closed can bear non-trivial costs. Obsessively checking and re-checking and then checking again (when you're *sure* the paper has no typos) can take valuable time and energy that would be better spent on other pursuits. Being in a position to know that a build-a-bear is not dangerous and does not contain explosives because you saw it being put together, but nonetheless tearing it apart to make extra sure it is safe, is a serious problem. Here it seems that you may have enough confidence that p to be able to have some of the propensities and dispositions typically associated with categorical belief that p under the circumstances, but crucially in some respects you exhibit behaviors and reactions more characteristic of someone who does not yet fully believe, someone who has not yet fully resolved the matter to their satisfaction and made up their mind that p. These cases perhaps constitute instances of what Schwitzgebel (2001) calls "in-between believing". If you are an in-between believer with respect to p, you are not a knower and are not categorical believer of p. The double-checking doctor could potentially be handled in the same way too.

6. Don't Leave Great Expectations out of a Dispositionalist Account of Outright Belief

The credence-level constraint (necessary condition) on outright belief of Hybrid Doxastic Pragmatism is similar to a constraint on outright belief I suggest in Ganson (2008).

> C: believing that p to a degree which is high enough to ensure that one is willing to act as if p is true, where one's being willing to act as if p means that what one is in fact willing to do is the same as what one would be willing to do, given p.
>
> (Ganson 2008, p. 451)

> C as a necessary constraint on outright believing: In order to count as outright believing that p in the circumstances, an agent must believe that p to a high enough degree such that she is willing to act as if p in the circumstances.
>
> (Ganson 2008, p. 453)

It accords well with the kind of modest pragmatism about belief that Fantl and McGrath (2009) take to be required by the pragmatic epistemic principles they defend.

These kinds of pragmatic credal constraints on belief have been (I think perhaps uncharitably) construed as a form of credal reductivism about belief (e.g. Ross and Schroeder 2014), so it's important to keep in mind that some members of this family of views can be seen as predominantly concerned with necessary constraints on belief (or, to be more specific, credence-related necessary conditions on pragmatic necessary conditions for belief), not necessary and sufficient credal conditions for outright belief. A bi-conditional version of credal pragmatism is potentially a variant of the Reductive Threshold View, and is subject to a similar set of objections. At

28   Dorit Ganson

times Fantl and McGrath (2009) do discuss a bi-conditional version,[13] but in other passages it's clear that a conditional reading (presenting a necessary, but not sufficient pragmatic condition on belief) is what's at issue.[14]

> The truth of JJ, we have seen, does not require that belief be strong pragmatic belief. But does it require that belief be at least weakly pragmatic, where by this we will mean that the believing requires that there be some ϕ such that one's credence in p is high enough for p to move one to ϕ?
>
> (Fantl and McGrath 2009, p. 140)

> Consider the view that belief doesn't require credal sufficiency to move you to any ϕ, especially wildly unrelated ϕs, but does require credal sufficiency to move you to any relevant or connected or perhaps salient ϕ.
>
> (Fantl and McGrath 2009, p. 143)

> Bayesians will naturally want some motivation for thinking that there are important doxastic states other than credences . . . Roughly the importance might be as follows: if belief doesn't amount to credence 1, then belief marks a movable yet important confidence threshold in relation to relevant sets of actions, intentions, feelings, etc.: if you believe that p, your credence is high enough so that it doesn't stand in the way of the proposition being your basis for the actions, intentions, feelings, etc. relevant in your situation.
>
> (Fantl and McGrath 2009, p. 155)

Here's the *Knowledge-Action Principle* to be potentially accommodated by an account of belief, according to Ross and Schroeder (2014):

> *Knowledge Action Principle* For any agent S and proposition p, if S is in a choice situation in which S could not rationally act as if p, then S does not know that p (where to act as if p is to act in the manner that would be rationally optimal on the supposition that p is true).
>
> (Ross and Schroeder 2014, p. 262)

Ross and Schroeder (2014) provide the following gloss on the relevant family of views they call "pragmatic credal reductivism":

> To a first approximation, they all maintain that what it is to believe that p is to have sufficiently high credence in p to rationalize acting as if p when choosing among relevant actions under relevant circumstances— where the relevant circumstances and actions include, but may not be limited to, the agent's actual circumstances and the actions available therein.
>
> (Ross and Schroeder 2014, p. 263)

> [T]o believe that p is to have sufficiently high credence in p to rational-
> ize acting as if p in the relevant choice situations (i.e. when choosing
> among the relevant actions under the relevant circumstances).
>
> (Ross and Schroeder 2014, p. 264)

There are a couple uncharitable things about this gloss (at least as a gloss on the sort of pragmatist view of belief at issue in Ganson (2008), and Fantl and McGrath (2009)). First is the emphasis placed on *credence high enough to rationalize acting as if* p—a normative quality, not a strictly psychological feature. Consider hesitant Worry Wart. She has sufficiently high justified credence to make what's best/rationally optimal for her to do the same as what's best for her to do, conditional on p in the relevant choice situations. None-theless, she fails to be inclined, willing, or motivated to reason and to act on the basis of p and do what's best. Why? Because she psychologically requires a super, abnormally high confidence in p before she is moved to or willing to act, etc. on the basis of p itself. Consider foolhardy Devil-May-Care. He does not have sufficiently high justified credence to make what's best for him to do the same as what's best for him to do, conditional p. But he is inclined, willing, or motivated to reason, act, and react on the basis of p itself anyway. He psychologically requires only an abnormally low confidence in p in order to be moved to or willing to act etc. on the basis of p itself. We don't want a view linking outright beliefs and confidence that forces us to say that Worry Wart counts as believing that p and Devil-May-Care does not. If anything, Devil-May-Care is the believer, and Worry Wart is not. What seems most relevant to whether or not they outright believe that p is whether or not they indeed are motivated, inclined or willing to reason, act, and react on the basis of p, not whether they would be reasonable/rational to do so. It's plausible that Kp requires that the subject have sufficiently high credence (i.e. high enough to be able) to be rational to act as if p, but not Bp.

The bi-conditional form of the gloss is the second uncharitable thing. When you have to settle on Bp, Sp, or Dp, then Bp involves your having sufficiently high confidence in p (i.e. high enough to meet the minimal level required by you . . .) for you to be able to be motivated by p itself, to be able to base your activities, reasoning, emotions, and reactions on p itself. But having that sufficiently high credence is not itself sufficient for you to be indeed motivated by p itself, to base your activities and emotions and reactions on p itself. It's not all a matter of your confidence level reaching a point where it is big enough to hit some sort of trigger/release a valve to all the belief-relevant propensities of the sort Ryle mentions. Still, you aren't able to have these propensities unless you have at least a certain amount of confidence that p.

Now we shall look at why *high confidence in* p,[15] while not the whole story about outright belief, shouldn't be left out of the picture either.

Ross and Schroeder (2014) favor an account of outright belief that emphasizes *the defeasible, automatic disposition to treat a proposition as*

30   *Dorit Ganson*

true in reasoning. To *treat* p *as true* in practical reasoning is to evaluate your options and determine what choice is best in the same way that you would if you were evaluating your options conditional on p. When you are *treating a proposition as true* in this sense, you are ignoring the possibility that it is false. You are not taking p's possible falsity into account as you engage in practical and theoretical reasoning that pertains to or involves p. To avoid regress problems (whereby any proposition we are using in reasoning would first have to be subject to our reasoning about whether we ought to treat that proposition as true in reasoning), Ross and Schroeder stress that the disposition in question is automatic. To capture the stability of belief, Ross and Schroeder stress that the disposition *to treat* p *as true in reasoning* involved in outright belief that p is defeasible. It may be overridden, for instance, when the costs of mistakenly acting as if p is true (so acting when p is false) are particularly salient and great.

> But if we concede that we have such defeasible dispositions to treat particular propositions as true in our reasoning, then a hypothesis naturally arises, namely that beliefs consist in or involve such dispositions. More precisely, at least part of the functional role of belief is that believing that p defeasibly disposes the believer to treat p as true in her reasoning. Let us call this hypothesis the *reasoning disposition account* of belief.
>
> (Ross and Schroeder 2014, p. 267)

(I will not address the argument they provide in order to show how the Reasoning Disposition Account of belief accounts for KAP, and hence, for pragmatic encroachment.)

In their view, belief is a kind of heuristic device which serves two primary ends: to enable the believer to arrive at good conclusions (the end of reasoning), and to prevent cognitive overload (e.g. the cognitive overload that would result from always taking degrees of credence into account). This aspect of their account may very well be on the right track. When construed as a potentially reductive account of belief, however, the Reasoning Disposition Account is not so appealing. Consider attitudes of acceptance that fall short of belief, such as acceptance as empirically adequate, acceptance as useful for certain purposes, etc. Acceptance can involve our *treating* certain propositions we know to be false *as true in reasoning* (e.g. when idealizing assumptions are made to simplify calculations in physics), and also potentially in a way which is automatic, given the proper background and training. So just as there's more to belief than the confidence required to engage the variety of dispositions typically associated with belief, there's more to belief than one (granted, highly significant) subclass of these dispositions. First, there are other sorts of dispositions important to belief—such as those involving emotions, and other activities besides reasoning. Second, we need the confidence required to set all these dispositions into motion. What makes *belief that* p fundamentally different from *acceptance that* p? At least

Great Expectations   31

part of the answer seems to be that belief requires us to have a fairly high level of confidence, trust, and expectation that the p is true. The advocates of the Reasoning Disposition Account might retort that they never intended their view to be taken in a reductive way, as spelling out both necessary *and* sufficient conditions for belief. (Other doxastic pragmatists like me could reply in kind.)

A further potential worry is raised by Tang (2015), who takes issue with the Reasoning Disposition Account's ability to successfully accommodate the fact we often do have *beliefs* that reflect our lack of epistemic certainty about things we believe: we believe that p, and also believe that there's some small/non-zero chance that—p. The Reasoning Disposition Account saddles us, then, with two competing automatic, defeasible dispositions: the automatic disposition to treat p as true in reasoning, and the automatic disposition to treat *there's a small chance that*—p as true in reasoning. Being disposed to treat p as true in reasoning involves being inclined to ignore or set aside the possibility that—p in reasoning; being disposed to treat *there's a small chance that*—p as true in reasoning involves being inclined not to ignore such a possibility in reasoning. The decision matrices apt for modeling the exercise of the first (which look the same as the decision matrices for reasoning about what's best conditional on p) will be very different from the ones apt for the second (which do not). It's difficult to make sense of the idea that we are automatically inclined both to ignore and to not ignore something when engaged in a particular sort of activity. So it looks like being automatically, defeasibly disposed to treat a proposition as true in reasoning is not necessary for believing it.[16]

Hybrid Doxastic Pragmatism is not subject to this objection. If you B(*there is a small chance that*—p), then you have enough confidence that *there is a small chance that*—p for you to be able to have *there is a small chance that*—p as a motivating reason for your activities, actions, emotional states, reactions, etc. in the relevant circumstances. Such circumstances could include: when the small chance of falsehood becomes salient or relevant, such as a lottery situation (for *my ticket is a losing ticket*), or when you become aware that now acting on p if p is false has suddenly become very costly. Or suppose someone asks: "Do you think there's a small chance that—p?" You can have this level of confidence that *there is a small chance that*—p (implicitly) while at the same time, when faced with a Bp, Sp or Dp situation, you have enough confidence in p (the minimum required) to be able to have p itself as a motivating reason for your activities, actions, emotional states, reactions, etc.

Maybe there are some easy modifications or refinements to the Reasoning Disposition Account which help it to avert Tang's objection. I'll remain agnostic about the matter for now. Also, don't get me wrong. I do think that the disposition to engage in practical and theoretical reasoning on the basis of p itself (when p is relevant) is one among a wide array of dispositions that we typically associate with the attitude of Bp, and it does contribute

32 Dorit Ganson

to making Bp a different sort of attitude than Sp. But when construed as a potentially reductive account of belief, the Reasoning Disposition Account ultimately fares no better than the Reductive Threshold View. Furthermore, when it comes to our beliefs, we may not wish to focus so exclusively on what we are inclined to base our *reasoning* on. Our beliefs bestow us with motivating reasons for many kinds of activities and emotional states. My cats and daughters when they were babies seemed to have something akin to belief, or at least something on its way to belief—something like a level of trust, confidence, expectation that can lead to hesitation, surprise, delight . . ., confidence informed by the past, and subject to upward and downward revision as expectations are thwarted or met.[17]

We are far from understanding exactly how levels of confidence and categorical doxastic attitudes relate to one another, but it seems likely from our current vantage point that progress in our understanding will help to make, rather than break, the case for pragmatic encroachment. We can well allow that non-evidential, practical factors do not legitimately enter into the normative assessment of degree of belief. But how close to 1 our degree of belief *has* to be in order to be accompanied by belief, or how close to 0 it *has* to be to accompany disbelief, is potentially subject to change as our practical circumstances change. Whether we have enough confidence in p for us to be able to have the propensities of the sort Ryle takes to be constitutive of belief and whether we have enough confidence in p for p (and not simply p *is likely*) to be able to be a motivating reason for us—such things are sensitive to practical circumstances. We have reason, then, to think we will find such sensitivity to practical circumstances reflected in the epistemic norms governing outright belief itself.

Notes

1. I presented earlier versions of this chapter at the 2017 Arizona State University Pragmatic Encroachment Philosophy Conference, Sedona organized by N. Ángel Pinillos, and the 2017 Annual Meeting of the Society of Exact Philosophy, University of Calgary. I thank the audience members and gracious hosts for these events. Being able to present my work to two groups of such smart, exacting philosophers was a great privilege. I also wish to thank Jeremy Fantl and Matthew McGrath for their inspiring, ground-breaking work; Brian Kim and an anonymous reviewer for their extremely helpful comments on an earlier draft; and my philosopher husband, Todd Ganson, for his supportive feedback and unwavering confidence in me through the most challenging of circumstances.
2. Russell and Doris (2008), and Gerken (2017) pursue this sort of criticism.
3. See Brown (2008) and Anderson (2015), for example.
4. Accounts of the relationship between degree of belief and outright belief are sometimes used to frame a critique of the thesis of pragmatic encroachment, as in Weatherson (2005). My project is not of this sort.
5. Schwitzgebel (2001 and 2002).
6. We'll go a bit beyond the usual points that are made to highlight the *prima facie* case for thinking that the norms that apply to categorical beliefs are different from those that apply to credences: logical coherence norm for belief vs. probabilistic coherence norm for credences; norm of *correct if true, incorrect if false* for belief, not for credences.

Great Expectations   33

7. For a nice discussion of why knowing is in normative conflict with suspending judgment and inquiring attitudes (IAs) quite generally, see Friedman (2017). Here are some telling quotes from that work.

> So, I think we should say that there is a sort of incompatibility between knowing Q and having an IA towards Q but that incompatibility is not incompossibility but normative incompatibility. There is something epistemically inappropriate about having that sort of combinations of attitudes . . . If one knows the answer to some question at some time then one ought not be investigating the question, or inquiring into it further or wondering about it, or curious about it, and so on, at that time.
>
> (Friedman 2017, p. 310)

> Knowing Q and suspension about Q are conflicting sorts of attitudes or orientations towards Q. And so the reason that one ought not to inquire into Q, or have any IA towards Q, when one knows Q is that inquiring into Q always involves suspension of judgment about Q.
>
> (Friedman 2017, p. 311)

By a startling coincidence, around the time I first read this piece by Friedman, my youngest daughter was watching an old re-run of the TV show *Drake and Josh* in which the brothers are at work on some concoction and have the following exchange.

> Josh: I wonder why it's bubbling?
> Drake: Do you know why it's bubbling?
> Josh: If I knew why it was bubbling, would I be wondering why it's bubbling?

8. Van Fraassen (1989).
9. I use the awkward locutions "to be able to have" and "to be able to serve" in order to try to stress that passing a confidence threshold is necessary but not on its own sufficient to bring it about that you have the relevant dispositions and motivating reason.
10. I leave aside the tricky issue of just how broad a scope is appropriate here. At the very least, a constraint concerning credences is imposed in the current situation where you are faced with the issue of which categorical attitude to adopt.
11. You have sufficient confidence in the current situation and perhaps also in a wide range of typical or ordinary circumstances when p is relevant.
12. See, for example, Neta (2007), Brown (2008), and Anderson (2015).
13. Fantl and McGrath (2009, p. 137, p. 139, p. 143, p. 143, p. 158, and p. 160).
14. Fantl and McGrath (2009, p. 137, p. 140, p. 143, and p. 155).
15. By "high confidence in p" I mean confidence enough for you to be able to have the relevant dispositions, and confidence enough for p to be able to serve as a motivating reason for you to have or engage in the relevant sorts of activities, actions, reactions, feelings, habits, etc.
16. Tang offers an alternative account of the heuristic relevant to reducing our risk of credence-related cognitive overload:

> More precisely, the proposal says that when our credence is close enough to 1 (or 0), we're disposed to reason as if it equals 1 (or 0); furthermore, if its content has the form "The chance of p is x", where x is sufficiently high (or sufficiently low), we're disposed to round up x to 1 (or round it down to 0).
>
> (Tang 2015, p. 257)

I don't think anything I've committed myself to here is at odds with the notion that we do employ this heuristic, which Tang calls "the Cournotian Heuristic".

17. Railton (2014) develops an account of the origin of belief along these lines.

References

Anderson, Charity. (2015). "On the Intimate Relationship of Knowledge and Action." *Episteme* 12(3): 335–342.

Brown, Jessica. (2008). "Subject-Sensitive Invariantism and the Knowledge Norm for Practical Reasoning." *Noûs* 42(2): 167–189.

Fantl, Jeremy and McGrath, Matthew. (2009). *Knowledge in an Uncertain World.* Oxford: Oxford University Press.

Friedman, Jane. (2013). "Rational Agnosticism and Degrees of Belief." *Oxford Studies in Epistemology* 4: 57–81.

Friedman, Jane. (2017). "Why Suspend Judging?" *Noûs* 51(2): 302–326.

Ganson, Dorit. (2008). "Evidentialism and Pragmatic Constraints on Outright Belief." *Philosophical Studies* 139: 441–458.

Gerken, Mikkel. (2017). *On Folk Epistemology: How We Think and Talk About Knowledge.* Oxford: Oxford University Press.

Hájek, Alan. (1998). "Agnosticism Meets Bayesianism." *Analysis* 58(3): 199–206.

James, William. (1948). "The Will to Believe." In *Essays in Pragmatism.* New York: MacMillan Publishing.

Neta, Ram. (2007). "Anti-Intellectualism and the Knowledge-Action Principle." *Philosophy and Phenomenological Research* 75(1): 180–187.

Nozick, Robert. (1993). *The Nature of Rationality.* Princeton: Princeton University Press.

Pinillos, N. Ángel. (2012). "Knowledge, Experiments and Practical Interests." In *Knowledge Ascriptions* (Eds. Jessica Brown and MIkkel Gerken). Oxford: Oxford University Press: 192–219.

Railton, Peter. (2014). "Reliance, Trust, and Belief." *Inquiry* 57(1): 122–150.

Ross, Jacob and Schroeder, Mark. (2014). "Belief, Credence, and Pragmatic Encroachment." *Philosophy and Phenomenological Research* 88(2): 259–288.

Russell, Gillian and Doris, John (2008). "Knowledge By Indifference." *Australasian Journal of Philosophy* 86(3): 429–437.

Ryle, Gilbert. (1949). *The Concept of Mind.* New York: Harper & Row, Publishers.

Schwitzgebel, Eric. (2001). "In-Between Believing." *The Philosophical Quarterly* 51(202): 76–82.

Schwitzgebel, Eric. (2002). "A Phenomenal, Dispositional Account of Belief." *Noûs* 36: 249–275.

Tang, Weng Hong. (2015). "Belief and Cognitive Limitations." *Philosophical Studies* 172(1): 249–260.

Van Fraassen, Bas. (1989). *Laws and Symmetry.* Oxford: Clarendon Press.

Weatherson, Brian. (2005). "Can We Do Without Pragmatic Encroachment?" *Philosophical Perspectives* 19(Epistemology): 417–443.

3 Another Kind of Pragmatic Encroachment

Kate Nolfi

1. Introduction

What sorts of considerations help to determine whether S's belief that p has the epistemic status that it has? If S's belief that p is, e.g., epistemically justified, what sorts of considerations make it so? Common sense and philosophical orthodoxy agree that, at least in paradigmatic cases, evidential considerations—i.e. considerations that are truth-relevant; considerations that affect the (subjective or objective) likelihood of p—play a crucial role in determining the epistemic status of S's belief that p. If S believes that p on the basis of considerations $c_1, \ldots, c_n$, and if $c_1, \ldots, c_n$ provide especially good evidential support for p, then it certainly seems that these facts are part of what makes it the case that S's belief that p enjoys the positive epistemic status that it seems to have. But do non-evidential considerations ever help to determine the epistemic status of our beliefs? That is, do considerations ever help make it the case that S's belief that p has the epistemic status that it does *without* affecting the likelihood that p is true? And if they do, when and how do such non-evidential considerations help to determine the epistemic status of our beliefs?

Any epistemological account according to which non-evidential considerations help make it the case that a belief has the epistemic status it does will endorse

> **Pragmatic Encroachment (PE)**: some of the considerations that help to determine the epistemic status of S's belief that p do so without being truth-relevant (i.e. without affecting the subjective or objective likelihood of p).

But different accounts that embrace PE will develop PE in different ways, by offering alternative characterizations of when and how non-evidential considerations help to determine the epistemic status of our beliefs.

This chapter introduces a new way of developing PE, one that is both motivated by and grounded in an independently attractive action-oriented

36 *Kate Nolfi*

framework for epistemological theorizing. On the resulting epistemological account, non-evidential considerations help to explain the epistemic status of our beliefs by explaining when and why believing that p on basis b makes it the case that one's belief that p is epistemically justified.[1] An action-oriented approach to epistemological theorizing suggests that non-evidential factors bear on the epistemic status of S's belief that p not by raising or lowering the evidential standard that must be met for S's belief to be justified and knowledgeable, but rather by helping to determine the degree of epistemic-status-conferring support, strength, power, or force that the considerations which serve as S's basis for belief have.

2. A Familiar Version of PE

It will be useful to be able to contrast this new kind of pragmatic encroachment to which I call our attention in the following with a more familiar alternative. This familiar alternative is

> **Standard-Shifting Pragmatic Encroachment (SSPE):** some considerations that influence the epistemic status of S's belief that p do so without being truth-relevant (i.e. without affecting the likelihood that p), but rather by determining the level of evidential support (where evidential support is understood in straightforwardly probabilistic terms) required for S's belief that p to achieve a certain epistemic status.[2]

According to SSPE, the bar or threshold for evidential support that a belief must surpass in order to achieve a positive epistemic status (e.g. to be epistemically justified, or to constitute knowledge) is determined (at least in part) by features of the believer's circumstances that have no effect on the likelihood of p. Proponents of SSPE generally construe the evidential support relation in straightforwardly probabilistic terms. Accordingly, SSPE says that non-evidential considerations help to determine the epistemic status of S's belief that p by determining whether the probability that p, conditional on whatever evidence serves as S's basis for belief, is sufficiently high so as to make S's belief epistemically justified or knowledgeable.

SSPE is most often motivated by our common-sense reactions to certain sorts of now-familiar cases involving high- and low-stakes situations. Consider Jeremy:

> Jeremy is at Back Bay Station in Boston preparing to take the commuter rail to Providence for a vacation. He asks a man, "Does this train make all those little stops in Foxboro, Attleboro, etc.?" It does not matter much to Jeremy whether the train is express or not. The man answers, "Yeah, this one makes all those little stops. That's what I was told when I bought the ticket". Jeremy believes what the man says.

Another Kind of Pragmatic Encroachment 37

And contrast Jeremy with Matt:

> It is of dire importance that Matt gets to Foxboro, and the sooner the better. While he has a ticket that gets to Foxboro in two hours, which is just in the nick of time, a train rolls into the station and he overhears the conversation above. Matt thinks to himself, "That guy may have misheard. After all, he doesn't care so he probably didn't pay careful attention. I better go check it out myself".[3]

It seems that Jeremy makes no mistake in believing—indeed, we are even inclined to say that he knows—that the train will stop at Foxboro. After all, Jeremy has no reason to think the man who tells him as much is being deceitful. And the man claims that the information he passes along comes from a reliable source: the ticket counter agent. Jeremy's case seems to be a paradigmatic case of justified—indeed, knowledgeable—belief based on testimony. And certainly we think it would be quite strange for Jeremy to withhold belief until he uncovers additional evidence that the train makes the Foxboro stop. But, given how important it is that Matt get things right in this particular situation (remember, Matt desperately needs to get himself to Foxboro as soon as possible—it would be disastrous if he got on a train that didn't make the Foxboro stop!), Matt's inclination to withhold belief, even after hearing the man's testimony, strikes us as understandable, reasonable, and perhaps even mandatory. And this suggests that Matt is not justified in believing, and that he does not know, that the train stops at Foxboro. Jeremy and Matt have precisely the same evidence that the train makes the Foxboro stop; their cases are identical in this respect. The only difference between Jeremy's and Matt's cases is that whether the train stops at Foxboro is of great practical importance to Matt, but not to Jeremy. And so, the proponent of SSPE reasons, since Jeremy's belief appears to be justified and, indeed, Jeremy appears to know, whereas were Matt to hold same belief on the same basis, his belief would not be justified and would fail to constitute knowledge, it must be the practical importance of getting it right in Matt's case and the practical insignificance of getting it right in Jeremy's case that explains why.

More carefully, the proponent of SSPE can offer the following vindicating explanation of our common-sense reactions to these two cases. The level of evidential support required for Matt to be epistemically justified in believing (and so, to know) that the train stops at Foxboro is relatively high. And the reason is that it matters a great deal, practically speaking, that he board the first available train which stops at Foxboro. Because of this straightforwardly non-truth-relevant feature of Matt's idiosyncratic situation, Matt needs more or better evidence in order to be epistemically justified in believing that the train will make the Foxboro stop than the man's testimony can supply. But nothing of practical significance is at stake in Jeremy's case. It just doesn't matter, practically speaking, whether Jeremy boards a train that makes the Foxboro stop. And, for precisely this reason, the level of evidential

38   Kate Nolfi

support required for Jeremy to be epistemically justified in believing (and so, to know) that the train stops at Foxboro is relatively low. At least it is low enough such that the testimony Jeremy hears provides sufficient evidential support for the proposition that the train will stop at Foxboro to reach or exceed this level.

My aim here is not to refute SSPE. Instead, I want to contrast SSPE with another version of PE, one that offers an alternative characterization of when and why non-evidential considerations help to determine the epistemic status of our beliefs. My hope is that developing the contrast with SSPE will help clarify the contours of this less-familiar alternative. Nevertheless, it is worth noting that, although SSPE accounts for our common sense reactions to Jeremy's and Matt's cases with relative ease, it has proved difficult to reconcile with our common sense reactions to a slew of other sorts of cases.[4] One reason that SSPE runs into trouble is that SSPE makes the epistemic status of S's belief that p fragile or unstable in specific ways.[5] In particular, a subject's practical situation certainly can, and often does, change over time. And, as a result, S's belief that p may be practically advantageous or beneficial at one time and practically disastrous at another. So, if SSPE is right, then the right sort of change in S's practical circumstances can change the epistemic status of S's belief that p without altering S's evidential position with respect to p in any way (e.g. without giving S new evidence, without defeating some of S's evidence, without changing the strength, weight, or force of S's evidence). S's belief can be epistemically justified, even knowledgeable, at one time, and epistemically unjustified, failing to constitute knowledge, at another time, even as S's evidential position with respect to p remains fixed. Of course, that SSPE entails this counterintuitive result doesn't show that SSPE is untenable. But, if another version of PE can lessen or avoid this kind of tension with common sense, then I suggest that, *ceteris paribus*, we have reason to prefer it over SSPE.

3. First Steps: Introducing Action-Oriented Epistemology

I turn now to the task of developing an alternative to SSPE, one which offers a different sort of answer to the question of when and how non-evidential considerations help to determine the epistemic status of our beliefs. Let me begin by describing an independently attractive approach to epistemological theorizing—what I'll call an *action-oriented approach*—that both inspires and motivates this alternative.

An action-oriented epistemologist takes a familiar idea about what our beliefs are *for* as her starting point for epistemological theorizing. The idea is this: our beliefs are meant to fulfill a map-like function in the service of action production.[6] And she precisifies the idea in two steps.

First, belief, simply by virtue of being the distinctive kind of mental state that it is, has a certain proper function. That is, there is a distinctive job or role that beliefs paradigmatically perform or play within the believer's

Another Kind of Pragmatic Encroachment   39

mental economy, and the fact that beliefs paradigmatically perform this job or play this role is part of what makes beliefs the kind of mental states that they are. Accordingly, beliefs constitutively "aim" at being well-suited to perform their distinctive proper function. And the constitutive norms of ideal cognitive functioning with respect to belief-regulation are just those norms conformity with which most effectively results in believers like us having beliefs that achieve this constitutive "aim".[7]

Second, belief's proper function is characterized by the distinctive way in which our beliefs paradigmatically subserve action production. More precisely, beliefs function to facilitate successful action by equipping us with flexible-use predictive tools (a kind of "map" of the facts) which enable environmentally sensitive action selection. Our beliefs put us in a position to predict which courses of action will best further our various ends across a wide range of different scenarios, and so to act accordingly. In this sense, then, the proper function of belief (and so, we might say, belief's constitutive aim) is fundamentally action-oriented. Crucially, since our ends, as well as our circumstances, are varied and evolve over time, beliefs that are most well-suited to successfully fulfill their particular action-oriented function will, much like useful maps, be quite versatile: they will be well-suited to facilitate successful action across the wide range of circumstances that we might face, and in the service of the wide variety of potential end(s) that we might adopt.

On this picture, ideal cognitive functioning with respect to belief-regulation is just functioning that most effectively equips believers who have the kind of cognitive equipment that we have and operate in the kind of environment in which we operate with beliefs that are well-suited to fulfill belief's particular action-oriented proper function. So, patterns of ideal cognitive functioning are those patterns of cognitive processing which most reliably yield beliefs (as output) that are well-suited to serve as flexible-use predictive tools to facilitate environmentally sensitive action selection across a variety of different circumstances and in the service of a variety of different potential ends.

An action-oriented epistemologist takes the fact that beliefs constitutively "aim" at being well-suited to subserve action by operating as flexible-use predictive tools as her point of departure for specifying the content of epistemic norms. And, accordingly, for the action-oriented epistemologist, evaluation qualifies as *epistemic* by virtue of being evaluation with respect to the constitutive norms of belief and belief-regulation that derive from belief's having its distinctive action-oriented proper function.[8]

Most fundamentally, on the action-oriented approach, a belief enjoys one kind of positive epistemic status—i.e. a belief is appropriately subject to a species of epistemic praise—when it is well-suited to fulfill this action-oriented proper function. Any belief that is not well-suited to fulfill belief's proper function is faulty or defective *qua* belief, and is thereby criticizable along at least one fundamental dimension of epistemic evaluation. The action-oriented epistemologist might put the point like this: belief, simply by

40 Kate Nolfi

virtue of being the kind of cognitive state that it is, is governed by a certain explanatorily fundamental norm: a norm of correctness. This norm dictates that a belief is correct to the extent that it is well-suited to fulfill belief's action-oriented proper function.

Crucially, however, belief's constitutive action-oriented proper function gives rise to additional norms that govern the way in which cognition regulates belief. These are norms of ideal cognitive functioning with respect to belief-regulation for believers equipped with our cognitive equipment and our cognitive limitations, operating in an environment like our own, and whose mental economies are wired up in the service of action production in the way that ours are. They characterize the particular ways in which cognition ought to regulate our beliefs—the ideal way(s) in which our cognitive processing will translate a particular set of inputs (e.g. perceptual experience as of p) to doxastic output (e.g. belief that p)—so as to equip us with beliefs that are well-suited to serve as flexible-use predictive tools in the course of action production. And evaluation with respect to these additional norms constitutes another species of epistemic praise and criticism. So, these further epistemic norms characterize how belief-regulation will ideally proceed in creatures who have the kind of cognitive equipment that we have, and who operate in the environment in which we operate, so as to generate and sustain a corpus of beliefs that are well-suited to fulfill belief's action-oriented proper function.[9] And evaluation with respect to these norms is genuinely *epistemic* in character *because* these norms govern belief-regulation simply by virtue of belief having the constitutive action-oriented proper function that it has.

4. How an Alternative to SSPE Comes Into View

At least at first pass, it can appear obvious that our beliefs must be true in order to be well-suited to play the role of map-like flexible-use predictive tool in action selection.[10],[11] After all, a subway map that misrepresents the order of the stops on the subway lines will be fairly useless when it comes to navigating the city. But there are compelling reasons to doubt that a belief's being well-suited to fulfill its action-oriented proper function always and inevitably requires accuracy. Without pretending to settle the empirical question at issue here, let me briefly canvas two of these sources doubt.[12]

First, empirical research on what psychologists have called "positive illusions" suggests that we are, as a general rule, more successful in achieving our various ends when our beliefs about ourselves and about our relationship to the world around us are systematically distorted in particular ways.[13] If my belief corpus includes slightly overly optimistic or inflated representations of the degree to which I am, as well as the degree to which others think of me as, intelligent, hard-working, resilient in the face of adversity, kind, caring, etc.—if, that is, my beliefs about myself and about the way in which others view me generally code a mild, but systematic distortion of

Another Kind of Pragmatic Encroachment 41

the relevant facts—then it seems that, e.g., I will have an easier time making friends, I will perform better in job interviews, and I will be more successful in my efforts to convince others to invest in my business venture. And if my belief corpus slightly overestimates the degree to which I am responsible for the good in my life and slightly underestimates the degree to which I am responsible for my misfortunes, then it seems that I will be more resilient in the face of tragedy and hardship. My distorted view of the relevant self-regarding facts leads me to, e.g., slightly underestimate my own chances of failure in any given endeavor, and so to embrace an ultimately advantageous course of action where my success is uncertain, one that my aversion to risk might otherwise lead me to reject. In systematic and predictable ways, I will be more successful in selecting courses of action so as to achieve various of my ends across a wide range of different circumstances if my beliefs in certain domain(s) systematically distort the facts, than I would be were my beliefs in these domain(s) to accurately represent the facts as they are.

Second, certain of our interpersonal relationships, or, indeed, our relationship to ourselves as the authors of our own lives, seem to demand a kind of distortion or bias in our beliefs or belief-regulation. Theorists have suggested that friendship, faith in others, as well as in ourselves, and the kind of agential perspective on our own future actions that makes it possible to promise or resolve in the face of temptation without succumbing to bad faith, all require some form of what has come to be known as epistemic partiality.[14] Friendship, for example, may constitutively involve a disposition to give one's friend the benefit of the doubt, so to speak, interpreting evidence so as to put the friend's behavior in a favorable light.

If these theorists are right, then it may well be that the beliefs that best equip us to participate in friendship, to have faith in ourselves and others, and to understand ourselves as the authors of our actions are beliefs that represent reality in a way that our evidence does not, strictly speaking, support. So, if friendship, faith, and understanding ourselves as the true authors of our actions are (or are prerequisites for achieving) paradigmatic human ends, then some paradigmatic human ends will be straightforwardly unachievable for us if we always and invariably regulate our beliefs by responding to our evidence in a strictly probabilistic way. And, accordingly, it seems that ideal belief-regulation, at least when it comes to beliefs about our friends, ourselves, and our control over our future actions, is not plausibly a matter of straightforward probabilistic calculation on the basis of available evidence and belief in accord with these conditional probabilities.

All this suggests that, at least for creatures who are psychologically constituted in the way that human beings are, certain beliefs which are moderately (but not wildly) skewed or distorted may well make for *better* flexible-use predictive tools not by virtue of supporting more accurate predictions, but rather by virtue of supporting predictions that, although strictly speaking inaccurate, are nevertheless better-suited, given our human psychological constitution, to facilitate action selection across a wide range of potential

42 Kate Nolfi

circumstances we may expect to face and in the service of a wide range of paradigmatic human ends (i.e. potential ends for us). Because of our peculiar psychological constitution (e.g. our aversion to particular sorts of risk), we are, at least as a general rule, better able to select courses of action that will, in fact, lead us to achieve our various ends when our predictions about the likely outcomes of various courses of action are grounded in a slightly, but systematically distorted view of certain facts.[15]

Moreover, ideal human cognition will involve the operation of certain domain-specific belief-regulating mechanisms which generate and sustain systematically inaccurate beliefs. These belief-regulating mechanisms are ideal in part because they are straightforwardly unreliable: they operate by *introducing* and *maintaining* a kind of advantageous systematic distortion into the way in which our belief corpus represents the facts; they are designed, as it were, to engender and sustain a certain kind of misrepresentation.

If the beliefs that are well-suited to fulfill belief's action-oriented proper function sometimes code a kind of systematic distortion of the facts, then the action-oriented epistemologist should concede that epistemically correct beliefs are not always accurate. And if belief-regulating mechanisms which distort the facts really do better subserve action than their accurate counterparts could, then pursuing an action-oriented epistemological approach will involve embracing the result that the (domain-specific) belief-regulating mechanisms which routinely introduce and sustain this kind of kind of systematic distortion in our belief corpus are epistemically ideal. For the action-oriented epistemologist, belief-regulation that is the product of these mechanisms is belief-regulation that conforms with epistemic norms, and so the beliefs that these mechanisms generate and sustain are epistemically justified or warranted.[16]

5. Weight-Shifting Pragmatic Encroachment

If all this is right, then any attempt to explain why regulating one's beliefs in any particular way constitutes (or fails to constitute) *ideal* belief-regulation will have to appeal to non-evidential, non-truth-relevant considerations. So, an action-oriented approach to epistemological theorizing suggests that non-evidential, non-truth-relevant considerations help to determine whether and why any particular pattern of belief-regulation manifests (or fails to manifest) conformity with epistemic norms. Accordingly, for the action-oriented epistemologist, non-evidential considerations can and do help to make it the case that our beliefs have the epistemic status that they have. And they do so by helping to fix what conformity with epistemic norms looks like for believers like us.

More precisely, an action-oriented approach maintains that facts about what sorts of beliefs are most well-suited to play a map-like role in facilitating successful action for creatures like us determine which doxastic output epistemic norms pair with any specified set of inputs in ideal cases of

Another Kind of Pragmatic Encroachment 43

cognitive processing. And these facts go beyond simple facts about the likelihood that various propositions are true conditional on our evidence. In particular, whether and to what extent S conforms with epistemic norms in believing that p is partly determined by facts about, e.g., the systematic, species-level advantages of having certain empirically identifiably "biases" built into our cognitive architecture, the nature and value of friendship and faith as paradigmatic human ends, and/or the importance, for creatures like us, of understanding ourselves as the authors of our actions. Although these sorts of facts are not straightforwardly prudential, they are, broadly speaking, practical. And, in any case, they are paradigmatically non-truth-relevant. So, an action-oriented epistemological approach leads to the conclusion that non-truth-relevant factors can help to determine the epistemic status of our beliefs by determining which sorts of cognitive transitions are sanctioned by epistemic norms. Or, put differently, non-truth-relevant factors can help make it the case that S's belief that p has the epistemic status that it has by determining whether and to what extent the particular set of considerations on the basis of which S believes that p lend epistemic support to S's belief.

We can distinguish two different ways in which a consideration might help to determine the epistemic status of S's belief that p. On the one hand, a consideration can help make it the case that S's belief that p has the epistemic status that it has by constituting (or potentially constituting) S's basis for believing that p.[17] A consideration which operates in this way helps determine the epistemic status of S's belief by serving as one of the *reasons for which* S believes. Imagine I believe that we're out of milk on the basis of my partner's reliable and trustworthy testimony to this effect. Then my partner's testimony that we're out of milk helps to make it the case that my belief is epistemically justified by serving as the reason for which I believe. On the other hand, however, a consideration can help make it the case that S's belief that p has the epistemic status that it has by determining whether S's believing that p on some particular basis, b, constitutes an instance of conformity with epistemic norms. A consideration which operates in this way does not help to determine the epistemic status of S's belief by serving as a *reason for which* S believes. Instead, it helps determine the epistemic status of S's belief by determining whether, and to what extent, the reasons for which S believes are capable of rendering S's belief epistemically justified. So, considerations that operate in this latter way explain why I'm epistemically justified in believing we're out of milk on the basis of my partner's testimony (and why I would not be epistemically justified in so believing were my belief to be based instead on, e.g., the particular pattern of tea leaves left in the bottom of my tea cup).

It is the considerations which operate in the latter way that are of particular interest here: an action-oriented epistemologist ought to embrace the conclusion that considerations which operate in this latter way are sometimes non-evidential in character.[18] Accordingly, non-truth-relevant considerations sometimes help to determine whether, and to what extent, the

44   Kate Nolfi

particular reasons for which S happens to believe that p render S's belief epistemically justified. So, an action-oriented epistemological approach suggests that non-truth-relevant considerations help to determine the degree to which any particular consideration has epistemic-status-conferring strength, force, or power when it serves as (part of) S's basis for believing that p. More succinctly, we might say that non-truth-relevant considerations determine the *epistemic weight* of those other considerations that serve (or might potentially serve) as S's basis for believing that p. Thus, the action-oriented epistemologist must embrace:

> **Weight-Shifting Pragmatic Encroachment (WSPE):** some considerations that help to determine the epistemic status of S's belief that p do so without being truth-relevant (i.e. without affecting the likelihood that p), but rather by determining the epistemic weight of the considerations which serve as S's basis for believing that p.

In effect, WSPE says that non-truth-relevant factors sometimes determine the epistemic status of S's belief that p by determining the amount of epistemic support that those considerations on the basis of which S believes that p lend to her belief. As such, WSPE entails that the epistemic support relation is not the evidential support relation, at least insofar as the evidential support relation is understood in straightforwardly probabilistic terms.[19]

Notice that, strictly speaking, WSPE is compatible with its more familiar cousin, SSPE. In principle, non-truth-relevant considerations might help to determine the epistemic status of our beliefs in both the ways that WSPE and SSPE describe. But I have motivated WSPE here by appealing to an action-oriented account of epistemic norms. And, at least at first pass, SSPE seems to fit rather less naturally within an action-oriented framework for epistemological theorizing. Thus, it is hard to see why the epistemologist who embraces WSPE as a consequence of her commitment to the action-oriented approach should be inclined to embrace SSPE as well.[20]

In light of this result, it is worth noting that the action-oriented epistemologist's way of endorsing WSPE leaves the epistemic status of our beliefs more stable than SSPE can. Thus, an action-oriented approach that embraces WSPE is well-positioned to provide a largely vindicating explanation: the commonsensical idea that the epistemic status of S's belief that p is stable so long as S's particular evidential position remains unchanged. In particular, an action-oriented account entails that certain sorts of common and predictable changes in stakes will neither elevate nor diminish the epistemic status of her beliefs. If S's evidential position remains constant (and if S's friendships remain stable), then the epistemic status of S's belief that p will remain constant as well, even if it is practically advantageous for S to believe that p at t_1, but practically disastrous for S to believe that p at t_2.[21] And this is because the role that non-truth-relevant considerations play in determining the epistemic status of S's belief that p involves a kind of abstraction away from the particular believer's idiosyncratic situation. Just as norms of ideal functioning for the human circulatory system are specified as the level of the species, rather than at the level of the individual, so too, according to the action-oriented epistemologist, are norms of ideal cognitive functioning with respect to belief-regulation. So, if the action-oriented epistemologist who embraces WSPE is right, then non-truth-relevant considerations do not influence the epistemic status of our beliefs by helping to specify what constitutes belief-regulation that most efficiently and effectively equips *a particular believer* with beliefs that facilitate successful action *in her particular circumstances and in the service of her particular ends*. Rather, they influence the epistemic status of our beliefs by helping to specify what constitutes belief-regulation that most efficiently and effectively equips believers who are psychologically constituted in the way that we are with beliefs that are well-suited play a map-like role in action selection across a wide range of potential circumstances and in the service of a wide range of potential ends. And the idiosyncratic features of any particular believer's situation at a particular moment in time simply have no bearing on whether a particular pattern of belief-regulation most efficiently and effectively equips believers who are psychologically constituted in the way that we are with beliefs that are well-suited play a map-like role in action selection across a wide range of circumstances and in the service of a wide range of ends that, on the action-oriented approach, constitutes conformity with epistemic norms.

6. Situating PE Between Strict Evidentialism and Straightforward Pragmatism

The pragmatic encroachment thesis is usefully situated between two more extreme theses, both of which deny that non-evidential considerations ever help to explain the epistemic status of our beliefs. On the one hand, epistemic purism maintains that the epistemic status of S's belief that p is exclusively a function of truth-relevant considerations (e.g. S's evidence for and against p). Thus, the epistemic purist rejects PE by embracing the thesis that considerations only ever help to determine the epistemic status of a belief by virtue of their truth-relevant character (i.e. by virtue of affecting the likelihood that the proposition believed is true).[22] On the other hand, the straightforward pragmatist maintains that the only normative standards by which we might evaluate S's belief that p are practical standards. So, straightforward pragmatism entails that all and only considerations that bear on whether S believing that p is practically advantageous or beneficial help to determine the normative status of S's belief that p. In effect, then, the straightforward pragmatist rejects PE by simply denying that there is any distinctively epistemic way of evaluating belief.[23]

For the epistemic purist, the epistemic domain is thoroughly encapsulated, isolated, and autonomous. Epistemic evaluation is entirely *sui generis*. And for the straightforward pragmatist, the epistemic domain simply collapses or dissolves. The only normative evaluation of belief is straightforwardly practical evaluation, and the only normative standards governing belief are straightforwardly practical standards. There is no *distinctively epistemic* species of normative evaluation, and there are no *distinctively epistemic* normative standards governing belief. In contrast, the defender of PE aims to offer an intermediary position, according to which the epistemic domain remains distinctive, but is not *sui generis*. If she is right, then the epistemic domain is not a fully autonomous normative domain. Epistemic evaluation is unique in character, and epistemic standards are certainly distinguishable from standardly practical standards, but epistemic evaluation is not thoroughly independent of or encapsulated from practical evaluation.

Since my primary aim is simply to introduce a novel way of developing and defending PE, I do not offer decisive arguments against PE's competitors here. But by way of illuminating what I take to be an attractive result of the action-oriented version of the pragmatic encroachment thesis that I develop in the preceding text, it is worth pointing out that epistemic purism and straightforward pragmatism both stand in tension with certain facets of our common-sense reactions to certain cases. Consider:

> Bella knows that she can secure a great sum of money merely by believing that there are an even number of stars in our galaxy. An eccentric billionaire has promised the payout as a prize for anyone who manages to believe this particular evidentially-unsupported proposition.

Or, a somewhat less contrived case:

> Denise is the public defender in a criminal case. Denise's evidence (e.g. the information included in the case file, her gut feeling after meeting and chatting with her client) suggests it is overwhelming likely that the accused, her client, is guilty. Nevertheless, Denise believes that it is reasonably likely that her client is innocent. Intuitively, at least, Denise's belief is both epistemically irrational and unjustified. Let us stipulate that Denise believes in a way that violates epistemic norms.[24] Yet, as a result of believing that her client is likely innocent, let us stipulate that Denise is able to present a much more compelling defense in the courtroom than she otherwise could. In effect, having an epistemically unwarranted belief about her client's innocence guarantees that Denise more successfully discharges her legal and moral obligations to her client and furthers her own professional ambitions than she otherwise could.

In such cases, the subject's idiosyncratic circumstances guarantee that she stands to gain a substantial practical benefit if she adopts a belief that is not supported by her evidence. And, crucially, that there is some significant practical advantage to believing that p for the subject is entirely independent of whether p is, in fact, the case.

Another Kind of Pragmatic Encroachment 47

Common sense tells us that if Bella does manage to believe that there are an even number of stars in our galaxy, it seems clear that her belief will be regrettably faulty, imperfect, or flawed, at least along one important dimension of evaluation. And if Denise believes her client is innocent, it seems similarly clear that she will be appropriately subject to a kind of criticism. That Bella's and Denise's beliefs manifest a lack of regard for their evidence bothers us. And we think this ought to bother them. Nevertheless, common sense also tells us that there is some very important, perhaps overriding sense of "should" in which these subjects' practically advantageous, but evidentially unsupported, beliefs are precisely the beliefs they should have. We can easily imagine encouraging Bella and Denise to do whatever it takes to adopt and sustain these practically advantageous beliefs. Indeed, we can even imagine being moved to help Bella or Denise discount or ignore evidence that makes it difficult for them to form or sustain their practically advantageous beliefs.

The epistemic purist is poorly positioned to vindicate our common-sense reactions to Bella's and Denise's cases.

To see why, imagine both Bella and Denise somehow manage to form and sustain the relevant evidentially unsupported, but practically advantageous beliefs. If the epistemic purist is right, then Bella and Denise do make a kind of mistake here. Both subjects fail to believe in accordance with their evidence, and so, according to the epistemic purist, both subjects' beliefs are epistemically faulty, defective, or flawed. Moreover, epistemic purism is certainly compatible with the position that epistemic evaluation is one species of evaluation among many. And so the epistemic purist can acknowledge that from some non-epistemic (plausibly practical or prudential) perspective, Bella and Denise make no mistake: they believe precisely as they should, given their circumstances.

But once the epistemic purist concedes that epistemic evaluation is one species of evaluation among many, and that, at least in these cases, different species of evaluation pull in different directions, then she faces a dilemma. On one horn, the epistemic purist might deny that epistemic evaluation is genuinely and inescapably normative in its own right. That is, she might endorse a kind of error-theoretic account of the fact that we think that Bella or Denise (or a third party, for that matter) ought to be troubled by the fact that their beliefs are so flagrantly lacking evidential support. On such an account, this sort of reaction is just mistaken or confused. So, adopting this horn of the dilemma amounts to suggesting that, contra common sense, we should not regard the epistemic shortcomings of Bella's and Denise's beliefs as genuine shortcomings at all.

On the other horn, the epistemic purist can embrace the idea that epistemic evaluation and, e.g., practical (or prudential) evaluation are both genuinely, but entirely independently, normative. Epistemic shortcomings and practical shortcomings are both genuinely regrettable, and independently so. But if the epistemic domain and the practical domain are wholly independent and both genuinely normative in their own right, then we should

48   *Kate Nolfi*

feel no pressure to navigate conflicts between epistemic and practical evaluation when they arise. However, we do feel such pressure, especially when we focus on cases like Bella's and Denise's. Moreover, we have no trouble navigating the conflict between epistemic and practical demands that these cases generate: practical demands trump epistemic demands. Although we think Bella and Denise should regard the fact that their beliefs are flagrantly lacking evidential support as genuinely regrettable, we also think it is obvious that the practical virtues of their beliefs outweigh or overpower this flaw. And the emerging purist picture is poorly positioned to supply a vindicating explanation of why this is. Rather, it seems the epistemic purist must offer an error-theoretic account of why our reactions to Bella and Denise give a kind of priority to practical standards for evaluation.

So, whichever horn of this dilemma the purist adopts, it seems she is forced to concede that epistemic purism won't vindicate (all of) common sense.

At least at first pass, it seems that the straightforward pragmatist fares no better. The straightforward pragmatist maintains that the only normative standards that govern belief are practical standards. Common sense suggests that our subjects' evidentially unsupported beliefs are the beliefs that they should have precisely because these beliefs are uniquely practically advantageous or beneficial in the circumstances these subjects face. From a strictly practical point of view, we think Bella and Denise believe precisely as they ought to believe. But if this is right, it seems the straightforward pragmatist must concede that Bella's and Denise's beliefs are flawless. And, in turn, she must concede that Bella and Denise are thoroughly uncriticizable for believing as they do. So, straightforward pragmatism seems poorly positioned to provide a vindicating explanation of the fact that our commonsense reactions to Bella and Denise involve thinking that both these subjects make a genuine and regrettable, if understandable and forgivable, mistake by holding beliefs that lack sufficient evidential support.[25]

7. Applying WSPE to Cases

The action-oriented epistemologist who embraces WSPE is particularly well-positioned to vindicate our common-sense reactions to cases. Grant that Bella's and Denise's evidentially unsupported beliefs are uniquely well-suited, given each subject's peculiar circumstances and ends, to facilitate their own successful actions. Still, an action-oriented epistemologist might argue that the belief in question wouldn't have similarly facilitated successful action across the wide variety of different circumstances that human beings normally face, and in the service of the wide range of paradigmatic human ends. Thus, Bella's and Denise's beliefs are not, in fact, well-suited (in the relevant sense) to fulfill belief's particular action-oriented function as *flexible-use* predictive tools. Metaphorically speaking, they are overly specialized: perfectly suited for use in a very narrowly circumscribed situation, but rather poorly suited for use across the wider range of situations

Another Kind of Pragmatic Encroachment 49

that our subjects might reasonably be expected to face. Alternatively, the action-oriented epistemologist might argue that Bella's and Denise's beliefs are generated and sustained by belief-regulating processes that do not reliably give rise to beliefs that are well-suited to fulfill belief's action-oriented function, and cite this result as grounds for a kind of negative epistemic evaluation. Here, the particular species of epistemic criticism in question is, in the first instance, criticism leveled at the pattern of belief-regulation that underwrites Bella's and Denise's beliefs, and then (derivatively) at the belief itself. In effect, the diagnosis here is that Bella and Denise get lucky: their cases are cases of serendipitous malfunction or malfunctioning with respect to belief or belief-regulation.

Interestingly, however, the action-oriented epistemologist might contrast Bella and Denise with Frida or Jayla.

> Frida overhears an acquaintance mentioning that she heard Frida's close friend made a truly cruel and tasteless remark at a recent social gathering. Frida, herself, was not present at the gathering, and she has no independent evidence that the acquaintance is lying or otherwise untrustworthy. Moreover, Frida knows that although her friend is generally sensitive and respectful, her offhand remarks can, on rare occasion, be cruel and tasteless. Frida's evidence makes the proposition that her friend made a cruel and tasteless remark more likely than not. And let us stipulate that a third party with all the same evidence would reasonably believe as much. Still, Frida remains skeptical. She believes that it's more likely that her acquaintance has misperceived real cruelty and tastelessness in what was, in fact, a harmless and inoffensive remark (perhaps, she might speculate, the acquaintance has failed to fully appreciate the contextualized meaning of her friend's use of a certain word, or has failed to detect the sarcastic, even satirical tone of her friend's remark).
>
> Jayla is a job candidate. She has no evidence that she is especially well-qualified for the position to which she has applied as compared to her competitors, and she has no evidence that either her credentials or her personality are more likely than her competitors' to impress the hiring committee. Given the evidence that Jayla has, a third party might reasonably believe that Jayla is an average candidate, somewhere in the middle of the pack, and not particularly likely to stand out from her competitors. But Jayla remains optimistic about how she measures up. She believes that, although the competition is stiff, she is a good candidate for the position, and that the hiring committee will recognize as much. Jayla is not delusional—she recognizes that there is a good chance she will not get the job. But her beliefs about her chances of getting the job manifest slightly more optimism than they would were they to perfectly match the probability that she will get the job, conditional on her evidence.

50 *Kate Nolfi*

Like Bella and Denise, Frida and Jayla have beliefs that are not supported by their evidence (at least insofar as evidential support is understood in straightforwardly probabilistic terms). And, as the earlier discussion of positive illusions and of epistemic partiality in friendship suggests, both Frida's and Jayla's beliefs seem to be practically beneficial or advantageous. But, that earlier discussion also suggests that it is no happy accident—no merely lucky result—that Frida's and Jayla's beliefs are well-suited to facilitate action. It is easy to imagine how, in general, giving one's friends the benefit of the doubt as Frida does here will lead one to act in ways that build and sustain friendships. Indeed, this is part of what makes it plausible that a disposition to give one's friends the benefit of the doubt just as Frida does here is partially constitutive of true friendship. And, quite plausibly, it is precisely because the kind of optimistic bias that Jayla manifests engenders more successful action that this kind of bias is wired into our psychology.

So, it seems that general facts about human psychology and the nature of friendship guarantee that a systematically distorted way of responding to one's evidence in situations like Frida's and Jayla's reliably best equips believers like us with beliefs that are well-suited to fulfill their proper function in facilitating successful action in the service of paradigmatic human ends. If the belief-regulating mechanisms that govern Frida and Jayla's beliefs are sufficiently encapsulated, restricted to a circumscribed domain, then the action-oriented epistemologist who endorses WSPE will say that Frida and Jayla are models of ideal belief-regulation, and, indeed, that this fact explains why their beliefs turn out to be well-suited to guide their actions. More precisely, the action-oriented epistemologist who embraces WSPE will explain that, from the epistemic perspective, the testimony that Frida's acquaintance gives carries less epistemic weight for Frida than it would for a third party. And it is the fact that it is Frida's friend whose behavior is at issue that explains why this is. Jayla's evidence that she is well-qualified for the position, and that she is likely to make a good impression in her interview, carries more epistemic weight for her than it would for a third party. And this result is explained by the fact that, when it comes to our beliefs about our own talents, abilities, chances of success, etc., ideal cognitive functioning for believers who are psychologically constituted as we are involves belief-regulation that manifests an optimism bias. Accordingly, the action-oriented epistemologist will say that, unlike Bella and Denise, Frida and Jayla are not epistemically criticizable for believing as they do; their beliefs are epistemically flawless. Still, the same will not hold for a third party to either case who believes as Frida and Jayla do. And, crucially, explaining why involves an appeal to paradigmatically non-truth-relevant factors.[26]

Notes

1. And so, if justification is a prerequisite for knowledge, then non-evidential considerations help to explain the epistemic status of our beliefs by helping to

determine when and why believing that p on basis b helps to make one's belief knowledgeable.

2. Prominent defenders of SSPE include Fantl and McGrath (2002), Hawthorne (2004), and Stanley (2005). Kim (2017) provides a contemporary survey of the relevant literature.
3. Both these cases are lifted directly from Fantl and McGrath (2002).
4. See, e.g., DeRose (2009), Reed (2010), or Neta (2012).
5. For further discussion, see Anderson and Hawthorne (2019) and Eaton and Pickavance (forthcoming).
6. This action-oriented approach is at least foreshadowed in the work of the American pragmatists (see, e.g., Peirce 1877), and also in one of the theoretical commitments that stands behind embodied/enactive research programs in psychology and cognitive science (see, e.g., Clark 1997 or Engel et al. 2013). I've argued that we ought to favor an action-oriented approach to epistemological theorizing over an alethic or truth-oriented alternative in Nolfi (2015).
7. This way of thinking about the nature of belief is not new (see, e.g. Burge 2010; Kornblith 2002; Lycan 1988; Millikan 1993). I remain neutral here among competing (e.g., etiological vs. dispositional) accounts of function.
8. Notice that, at least insofar as the action-oriented epistemologist is committed to the thesis that epistemic evaluation is genuinely normative, she owes an account of *how and why* the constitutive norms for belief and belief-regulation that derive from belief's action-oriented proper function come to have genuinely normative authority and force. I have tried to show that the action-oriented epistemologist can discharge this explanatory burden in other work. So, without pretending that there isn't significant philosophical work for the action-oriented epistemologist to do to secure this result, I will simply assume in what follows that the action-oriented epistemologist has a story to tell that explains how and why norms that derive from belief's constitutive action-oriented proper function come to enjoy genuine normative authority and force.
9. On the action-oriented approach, then, the project of spelling out these norms of ideal cognitive functioning with respect to belief-regulation is very much like the project of spelling out the norms of ideal operation of any particular part of the human circulatory system. As will emerge in what follows, just as an attempt to characterize the norms of ideal functioning that govern the operation of the human heart must be informed by empirical inquiry, and will be hostage to empirical results, so too must an attempt to characterize the norms of ideal cognitive functioning with respect to belief-regulation. And just as norms of ideal functioning that govern the operation of the human heart will be specified with respect to the paradigm of the human circulatory system, so too will the norms of ideal cognitive functioning with respect to belief-regulation be specified with respect to proto-typical or paradigmatic human psychological constitution.
10. After all, as Quine (1969) puts it, "creatures inveterately wrong in their inductions have a pathetic but praiseworthy tendency to die before reproducing their kind".
11. Papineau (1987), Lycan (1988), Kornblith (1993 and 2002), Millikan (1993), and Burge (2003) develop the action-oriented approach along precisely these lines. I suspect that a (sometimes suppressed—see Millikan (1993), sometimes explicit—see Kornblith (2002)) assumption that accurate representation *is just what it takes* for beliefs to be well-suited to serve as predictive tools in guiding action often underwrites the popular thought that beliefs constitutively aim to accurately represent the facts. But, as the arguments that follow show, this assumption ought to be rejected.
12. See Hazlett (2013) for a more extensive discussion.
13. For an overview of the relevant psychological results, see, e.g., Taylor and Brown (1988) and (1994) or Johnson and Fowler (2011), Sharot (2011). See Hazlett

52 Kate Nolfi

(2013) or McKay and Dennett (2009) for a philosophical discussion of some of the relevant psychological research.

14. On friendship, see Keller (2004) and Stroud (2006). On faith, see Preston-Roedder (forthcoming). On promising and resolving in the face of temptation without succumbing to bad faith, see Marušić (2015).

15. Of course, a particular believer might encounter circumstances in which this kind of typically advantageous systematic distortion in her belief corpus happens to frustrate her efforts to achieve some particular end. The point here is more general: in abstraction from the actual ends any particular believer might happen to have and from the idiosyncratic circumstances in which any particular believer finds herself, believers who are psychologically constituted in the way that we are and who operate in the kind of environment in which we operate are best-equipped to act in the pursuit of ends (as yet unspecified) if we have a belief corpus that encodes the relevant sort of systematic distortion.

16. Insofar as the action-oriented epistemologist embraces something like the idea that, at least in normal circumstances, epistemic justification/warrant converts correct belief into knowledge, then these considerations should persuade the action-oriented epistemologist to reject the thesis that knowledge is factive.

17. This is the way in which my having a visual experience of my coffee cup's being empty typically helps make it the case that I am justified in believing that my coffee cup is empty: my belief is based on my visual experience and, at least in the usual sort of case, my belief is epistemically justified as a result.

18. I have argued elsewhere (see Nolfi 2018) that considerations which operate in the former way to confer positive epistemic status on our beliefs are always truth-relevant. But those arguments are independent of the arguments on offer here (which concern considerations that play a different sort of role in determining the epistemic status of our beliefs).

19. Indeed, one might take the philosophical import of WSPE simply to *be* that we ought to embrace an alternative account of evidential support, one that is not straightforwardly probabilistic, but instead practically infused.

20. Perhaps it is possible to motivate WSPE in a way that proves to be more friendly to SSPE, without relying on an action-oriented epistemological framework. Or perhaps it is possible to develop an action-oriented epistemological account in a way that is ultimately congenial to SSPE, as well as WSPE. Although I am somewhat skeptical on both fronts, I simply cannot give either the attention each deserves in this piece.

21. Of course, if S's belief that p is a belief about F, who is S's close friend at t_1, but with whom S has fallen out by t_2, then, assuming true friendship really does require having a positively skewed view of your friend's actions and character, the epistemic status of S's belief that p may well change from t_1 to t_2 even as her evidential position remains constant. In this sort of case, an action-oriented approach suggests that the changing status of S's relationship with F may change the epistemic weight of the evidential considerations on the basis of which S forms beliefs about F's actions and character. Thus, WSPE does not remove all potential instability in epistemic status of S's belief, even while S's evidential position remains constant. It does, however, avoid the particularly pervasive and predictable species of instability that seems to plague stakes-motivated versions of SSPE.

22. Actually, matters are slightly more complicated here since the epistemic purist might embrace both a truth condition and an anti-Gettier condition on knowledge, and so might accept that whether S's belief that p constitutes knowledge depends on more than just whether S's belief that p is based on evidence conditional on which p is sufficiently likely to be true.

23. Stich (1993), Papineau (2013), McCormick (2014), and Rinard (2015) express some sympathy for straightforward pragmatism.

Another Kind of Pragmatic Encroachment   53

24. It is worth making explicit that this stipulation is compatible with a very wide range of views about what, precisely, conformity with epistemic norms in any particular instance requires.

25. Perhaps the straightforward pragmatist can do better here. Indeed, I am indebted to Susanna Rinard for helping me appreciate ways in which the straightforward pragmatist might endeavor to account for our intuition that Bella and Denise make some sort of genuine and regrettable mistake. For example, the straightforward pragmatist might point out that believing in the absence of evidence is often practically disastrous. And so, the way in which Bella and Denise ignore or disregard their (lack of) evidence in regulating their beliefs is risky. Accordingly, then, the straightforward pragmatist might suggest that Bella and Denise are criticizable for subjecting themselves to an objectionable (or, perhaps, simply regrettable) level of risk in believing as they do. And perhaps this is enough to account for our intuition that both Bella and Denise make some sort of genuine and regrettable mistake. Bella's and Denise's circumstances might well be such that the risk they incur here is ultimately justified or reasonable. Sometimes one's situation is such that taking on what would generally be an unacceptable level of risk is precisely the thing to do. But incurring this risk might still be regrettable. It might be unfortunate the Bella and Denise find themselves in situations where engaging in a risky form of belief-regulation turns out to be the thing to do. And, all things considered, it would be better if these subjects' circumstances simply did not require them to engage in this kind of risky belief-regulation in order to secure the relevant practical benefits. Notice that the straightforward pragmatist's strategy here involves distinguishing at least two different species of evaluation: one that yields a positive result (i.e. Bella and Denise believe in precisely the way that they ought to believe), and another that yields a negative result (i.e. Bella and Denise accept a regrettable level of risk by believing as they do). But once we have distinguished these two different species of evaluation, then the distance between the straightforward pragmatist's view and the action-oriented epistemologist's view shrinks considerably, perhaps to the point of being merely terminological. As we will see, the action-oriented epistemologist might propose that Bella and Denise make a kind of regrettable mistake because they engage in a risky kind of belief-regulation: this kind of belief-regulation is unacceptably likely to yield beliefs that are not well-suited to facilitate successful action. In effect, then, the action-oriented epistemologist can vindicate our intuitive reactions to Bella's and Denise's cases by distinguishing a straightforwardly practical species of evaluation from a species of evaluation according to which Bella's and Denise's beliefs fall short by virtue of being the product of belief-regulating processes that fail to reliably produce beliefs that are well-suited to facilitate successful action. And so the real disagreement between the action-oriented epistemologist and the straightforward pragmatist seems to be a disagreement about whether this second species of evaluation is properly classified as *epistemic* evaluation. But given the principled way in which the action-oriented epistemologist circumscribes the epistemic domain (recall that, epistemic evaluation is evaluation with respect to standards or norms that derive from the constitutive proper function of belief), it seems that the straightforward pragmatist simply begs the question against the action-oriented epistemologist in resisting the action-oriented epistemologist's suggestion that the relevant sort of criticism of Bella's and Denise's beliefs is paradigmatically *epistemic* criticism.

26. I am grateful to participants at the 2017 Northern New England Ethics and Epistemology Workshop for invaluable feedback on this material, and I am especially indebted to Tyler Doggett, Brian Kim and Susanna Rinard for their extensive written comments on earlier versions of this piece.

54 *Kate Nolfi*

References

Anderson, C., and Hawthorne, J. (2019). Knowledge, Practical Adequacy, and Stakes. In *Oxford Studies in Epistemology*, Vol. 6. Oxford: Oxford University Press.

Burge, T. (2010). *Origins of Objectivity*. Oxford: Oxford University Press.

———— (2003). Perceptual Entitlement. *Philosophy and Phenomenological Research* 67(3): 503–548.

Clark, A. (1997). *Being There: Putting Brain, Body, and World Together Again*. Boston: MIT Press.

DeRose, K. (2009). *The Case for Contextualism*. Oxford: Oxford University Press.

Eaton, D., and Pickavance, T. (forthcoming). Evidence Against Pragmatic Encroachment. *Philosophical Studies*: 1–9.

Engel, Andreas et al. (2013). Where's the Action? The Pragmatic Turn in Cognitive Science. *Trends in Cognitive Science* 17(5): 202–209.

Fantl, J., and McGrath, M. (2002). Evidence, Pragmatics, and Justification. *The Philosophical Review* 111(1): 67–94.

Hawthorne, J. (2004). *Knowledge and Lotteries*. Oxford: Oxford University Press.

Hazlett, A. (2013). *A Luxury of the Understanding: On the Value of True Belief*. Oxford: Oxford University Press.

Johnson, D. D., and Fowler, J. H. (2011). The Evolution of Overconfidence. *Nature* 477(7364): 317–320.

Keller, S. (2004). Friendship and Belief. *Philosophical Papers* 33: 329–351.

Kim, B. (2017). Pragmatic Encroachment in Epistemology. *Philosophy Compass* 17(12): e12415. doi:10.1111/phc3.12415

Kornblith, H. (1993). Epistemic Normativity. *Synthese* 94(3): 357–376.

———— (2002). *Knowledge and Its Place in Nature*. Oxford: Oxford University Press.

Lycan, W. G. (1988). *Judgement and Justification*. Cambridge: Cambridge University Press.

Marušić, B. (2015). *Evidence and Agency Norms of Belief for Promising and Resolving*. Oxford: Oxford University Press.

McCormick, M. S. (2014). *Believing Against the Evidence: Agency and the Ethics of Belief*. New York: Routledge.

McKay, R., and Dennett, D. (2009). The Evolution of Misbelief. *Behavioral and Brain Sciences* 32: 493–561.

Millikan, R. G. (1993). Naturalist Reflections on Knowledge. In *White Queen Psychology and Other Essays for Alice*. Cambridge, MA: MIT Press, pp. 241–264.

Neta, R. (2012). The Case Against Purity. *Philosophy and Phenomenological Research* 85(2): 456–464.

Nolfi, K. (2015). How to Be a Normativist About the Nature of Belief. *Pacific Philosophical Quarterly* 96: 181–204.

———— (2018). Why Only Evidential Considerations Can Justify Belief. In C. McHugh, J. Way, and D. Whiting, eds., *Normativity: Epistemic and Practical*. Oxford: Oxford University Press.

Papineau, D. (1987). *Reality and Representation*. New York: Blackwell

———— (2013). There Are No Norms of Belief. In T. Chan, ed., *The Aim of Belief*. Oxford: Oxford University Press.

Peirce, C. S. (1877) The Fixation of Belief. *Popular Science Monthly* 12: 1–15.

Preston-Roedder, R. (forthcoming). Three Kinds of Faith. *Philosophical Topics*.

Quine, W. V. (1969). Natural Kinds. In Jaegwon Kim and Ernest Sosa, eds., *Ontological Relativity and Other Essays*. New York: Columbia University Press, pp. 114–138.

Reed, B. (2010). Self-Knowledge and Rationality. *Philosophy and Phenomenological Research* 80(1): 164–181.

Rinard, S. (2015). No Exception for Belief. *Philosophy and Phenomenological Research* 91.

Sharot, T. (2011). *The Optimism Bias: A Tour of the Irrationally Positive Brain*. New York: Vintage.

Stanley, J. (2005). *Knowledge and Practical Interests*. Oxford: Oxford University Press.

Stich, S. (1993) *The Fragmentation of Reason: A Preface to a Pragmatic Theory of Cognitive Evaluation*. Boston: MIT Press.

Stroud, S. (2006). Epistemic Partiality in Friendship. *Ethics* 116(3): 498–524.

Taylor, S. E., and Brown, J. D. (1994). Positive Illusions and Well-being Revisited: Separating Fact From Fiction. *Psychological Bulletin* 116(1): 21–27.

——— (1988). Illusion and Well-being: A Social Psychological Perspective on Mental Health. *Psychological Bulletin* 103(2): 193–210.

4 Pragmatic Encroachment and Practical Reasons[1]

Anne Baril

Defenders of pragmatic encroachment in epistemology hold that practical factors have implications for a belief's epistemic status. Paradigm defenders of pragmatic encroachment have held—to state their positions roughly— that whether someone's belief that p constitutes knowledge depends on the practical reasons that she has (Stanley 2005), that knowing p is necessary and sufficient for treating p as a reason for action (Hawthorne and Stanley 2008), or that knowing p is sufficient for reasonably acting as if p (Fantl and McGrath 2009: 66). Although their defenders may not always pose their theses in the language of practical reasons, the idea of a practical reason is central to each of these views. Yet there remain issues concerning the nature and basis of practical reasons on which defenders of pragmatic encroachment have not taken a position, including—as I will explain—the issue of whether internalism or externalism about reasons is true. It may be thought that the position the defender of pragmatic encroachment takes on this does not make a difference to the truth or falsity of her main thesis. In this chapter, I will show that it does matter, in the sense that her view will generate different verdicts about cases depending on whether she endorses internalism or externalism about reasons. Given the role of cases in providing intuitive support for or against the theory, this, in turn, makes a difference to the plausibility of pragmatic encroachment.

1. Pragmatic Encroachment

Traditionally, epistemologists have assumed that whether or not a belief is justified, warranted, or (in the case of true beliefs) an instance of knowledge, "depends exclusively on truth-related factors: for example, on whether the true belief was formed in a reliable way, or was supported by good evidence, and so on" (Grimm 2011: 705; see further Stanley 2005: 2; Fantl and McGrath 2007: 558; Kim 2017: 1). Pragmatic encroachment theorists deny this. They argue that there are non-truth-related factors—specifically, practical factors—that have implications for a belief's epistemic status.[2]

To see why defenders of pragmatic encroachment think this, we may consider some of the cases that many take to provide *prima facie* motivation

Pragmatic Encroachment and Practical Reasons 57

for pragmatic encroachment. One pair of cases was introduced by Keith DeRose (1992) and stated by Jason Stanley (2005) as follows:

Bank Case 1

Hannah and her wife Sarah are driving home on a Friday afternoon. They plan to stop at the bank on the way home to deposit their paychecks. It is not important that they do so, as they have no impending bills. But as they drive past the bank, they notice that the lines inside are very long, as they often are on Friday afternoons. Realizing that it isn't very important that their paychecks are deposited right away, Hannah says, "I know the bank will be open tomorrow, since I was just there two weeks ago on Saturday morning. So we can deposit our paychecks tomorrow morning".

(Stanley 2005: 3–4)

Bank Case 2

Hannah and her wife Sarah are driving home on a Friday afternoon. They plan to stop at the bank on the way home to deposit their paychecks. Since they have an impending bill coming due, and very little in their account, it is very important that they deposit their paychecks by Saturday. Hannah notes that she was at the bank two weeks before on a Saturday morning, and it was open. But, as Sarah points out, banks do change their hours. Hannah says, "I guess you're right. I don't know that the bank will be open tomorrow".

(Stanley 2005: 4)

Even if we suppose that the bank will be open the following day, it seems to many that Hannah's remarks are true in *both* these cases: that she knows in the first case and doesn't know in the second case. Yet there is no difference between the two cases when it comes to purely truth-related factors: no difference, for example, in how reliably formed Hannah's belief is, how well-supported by the evidence, and so on. The difference, rather, is a practical one: Hannah has more at stake in the second case than the first.

A second set of cases comes from Jeremy Fantl and Matthew McGrath (2002):

Train Case 1

Matt is at Back Bay Station in Boston preparing to take the commuter rail to Providence. He's going to see friends. It will be a relaxing vacation. He's been in a rather boring conversation with a guy standing beside him, who is also going to visit friends in Providence. As the train rolls into the station, Matt continues the conversation by asking the guy, "Does this train make all those little stops, in Foxboro, Attleboro, etc.?"

58 Anne Baril

It doesn't matter much to Matt whether the train is the "Express" or not, though he'd mildly prefer it was. The guy answers, "Yeah, this one makes all those little stops. They told me when I bought the ticket". Nothing about him seems particularly untrustworthy. Matt believes what he says.

(Fantl and McGrath 2002: 67, edited to give the person a name)

Train Case 2

Matt absolutely needs to be in Foxboro, the sooner the better. His career depends on it. He's got tickets for a southbound train that leaves in two hours and gets into Foxboro in the nick of time. He overhears a conversation like that in Train Case 1 concerning the train that just rolled into the station and leaves in 15 minutes. He thinks, "That guy's information might be wrong. What's it to him whether the train stops in Foxboro? Maybe the ticket-seller misunderstood his question. Maybe he misunderstood the answer. Who knows when he bought the ticket? I don't want to be wrong about this. I'd better go check it out myself".

(Fantl and McGrath 2002: 67–68, edited to give the person a name)

It seems to many that Matt is warranted in believing, or has "good enough evidence to know",[3] in the first case, but not in the second case. Yet, again, the difference is not a matter of truth-related facts, but a matter of practical factors: Matt has more at stake in the second case than the first.

We can accommodate our intuitions about these cases, and others like them, if we hold that practical factors have implications for a belief's epistemic status (e.g. whether it is warranted, justified, or counts as knowledge). To account for this, defenders of pragmatic encroachment hold that there is a connection between knowledge and practical reasons. They may hold, for example:

> **KRN:** If it is appropriate for S to treat the proposition that p as a reason for action, then S knows that p.[4]
>
> **KRS:** If S knows that p, then is it appropriate for S to treat the proposition that p as a reason for action.[5]
>
> **KR:** S knows that p iff is it appropriate for S to treat the proposition that p as a reason for action.[6]

These principles explain the truth of our intuitions about the Bank and Train Cases. First, consider KRS. In the second of each pair of cases, the high-stakes case, it wouldn't be appropriate for S to treat the proposition that p as a reason for action, because the stakes have gone up, in contrast with the first case of the pair. KRS implies that, because of this, the subject does not know—which, indeed, is in line with our intuitions about those cases.

Pragmatic Encroachment and Practical Reasons   59

KRS thus explains the truth of our intuitions about the second, high-stakes cases. Second, consider KRN. KRN explains the truth of the intuitions we have about the first of each pair of cases, the low-stakes case. In these cases, it's appropriate for the subject to treat the proposition that p as a reason for action. KRN implies that, because of this, the subject knows that p—which, again, is in line with our intuitions about the cases. KRN thus explains the truth of our intuitions about the first, low-stakes cases.[7] Finally, KR, being the conjunction of KRS and KRN, explains the truth of the intuitions we have about both sets of cases.

2. The Practical Implications of the Appropriateness of Treating a Proposition as a Reason

My thesis in this chapter concerns the practical reasons that play a role in pragmatic encroachment. Notice that whether or not it is appropriate for a subject to treat p as a reason has implications for the subject's practical reasons. We can see this by reflecting on the Bank and Train Cases. In Bank Case 2, it is *not* appropriate for Hannah to treat the proposition that p— that the bank will be open the following day—as a reason for action (in this case, a reason for leaving the bank and returning the following morning). The implication is that Hannah has certain practical reasons: reason to double-check the bank's hours, or to change her plan and wait in line. In Bank Case 1, by contrast, it *is* appropriate for Hannah to treat p as a reason for action; here the implication is that—other things being equal—she does *not* have reason to double-check the bank hours, or to change her plan. Likewise, in Train Case 2, it is not appropriate for Matt to treat the proposition that p—that the train isn't an express—as a reason for action, and, correspondingly, he has reason to double-check the train schedule, or to take a different train that is more obviously not an express; in Train Case 1, by contrast, it *is* appropriate for Matt to treat p as a reason, and, correspondingly, he does *not* have reason to double-check or to take a different train.

In light of this, we should accept the following principle:

> **TPR:** It is appropriate for S to treat the proposition that p as a reason for action iff S does not have reason to double-check whether p.[8]

(To simplify, I have made the principle concern double-checking in particular, but it should be clear how the same general point may be made, *mutatis mutandis*, to other actions on the subject's radar, such as, in Hannah's case, waiting in line on Friday to make sure her check is deposited, or, in Matt's case, taking a different train.)

What TPR makes explicit is that, although the KR principles concern the appropriateness of the subject's treating a proposition as a reason for action, these principles have implications concerning the practical reasons the subject has, or lacks—for example, reasons to double-check whether p. This is

60   *Anne Baril*

important because, as I will argue in the remainder of the chapter, there are issues concerning the nature and basis of practical reasons that will make a difference to the practical reasons subjects have in variants of the previous cases, and, thus, to the plausibility of KRN, KRS, and KR. Hereafter, I will focus exclusively on KR, assuming it will be obvious how the points I make here bear on KRN and KRS as well.

3. Pragmatic Encroachment and Practical Reasons

Bringing practical reasons to the fore in pragmatic encroachment reminds us of the rich philosophical literature exploring the nature and basis of practical reasons. The practical reasons of central concern here are normative reasons, where, on one popular definition, a normative reason to φ is a consideration that counts in favor of φ-ing (Scanlon 1998). Questions raised in this literature, about which there is no consensus, include the following: Can we have practical reasons that are not ultimately rooted in our desires or preferences? Are claims about what we have reason to do capable of being literally true or false? Are some kinds of reasons, such as moral reasons, overriding, such that "even the weakest moral reason trumps the strongest nonmoral reason" (Portmore 2008: 370)? Even the very definition of a practical reason I mentioned previously—that a reason is a consideration that counts in favor of an action or attitude—is disputed (Hieronymi 2005, 2011).

It may be thought that issues concerning the nature and basis of practical reasons are of limited importance in a discussion of pragmatic encroachment. After all, although the position a defender of pragmatic encroachment takes on these issues may help us understand her view in its entirety, the way she answers these questions will—it may be argued—make no difference to our evaluation of the principle she defends. By way of analogy: people hold a wide range of views about the nature of justification, but this does not prevent us from evaluating the analysis of knowledge as justified true belief. Just as we can evaluate this analysis of knowledge independently of how the individuals who accept this analysis understand justification, so too—it may seem—can we evaluate principles like KR independently of how their defenders understand practical reasons.

Whatever we wish to say about the evaluation of this analysis of knowledge, we cannot, I propose, evaluate KR independently of questions about the nature and basis of practical reasons. This is because practical reasons play a central role in KR, and the way that they are understood can make a difference for what it implies about cases, and thus for how plausible it is.

We can see this by considering an example. Consider these two possible, alternative, views of what agents have reason to do:

Subjective Desire Theory of Reasons (SDR): "what agents have reason, or ought, to do or intend is just what, given what they believe their

Pragmatic Encroachment and Practical Reasons 61

circumstances to be, would best satisfy their strongest, present intrinsic desires taken as a whole".

The Objective Desire Theory of Reasons (ODR): "agents have reason, or ought, to do or intend just what, given what their circumstances actually are, would best satisfy their strongest, present intrinsic desires taken as a whole".

(Kolodny and Brunero 2016)

To see how a commitment to one or the other of these makes a difference to the implications and plausibility of KR, we can consider the conjunction of these views with KR, which we can represent as KR+SDR and KR+ODR, respectively. At first glance, it may not be clear why it should matter which of these views KR is conjoined with. After all, it doesn't seem to make a difference to the Bank Cases or Train Cases described previously.

However, in other cases, the difference between KR+SDR and KR+ODR emerges. Consider the following variant on the Bank Cases, which Stanley dubs "Ignorant High Stakes":

Ignorant High Stakes

Hannah and her wife Sarah are driving home on a Friday afternoon. They plan to stop at the bank on the way home to deposit their paychecks. Since they have an impending bill coming due, and very little in their account, it is very important that they deposit their paychecks by Saturday. **But neither Hannah nor Sarah is aware of the impending bill, nor of the paucity of available funds.** Looking at the lines, Hannah says to Sarah, "I know the bank will be open tomorrow, since I was there just two weeks ago on Saturday morning. So we can deposit our paychecks tomorrow morning".

(Stanley 2005: 5, emphasis added)

KR+SDR gives a different verdict on this case than KR+ODR. According to KR, Hannah knows that the bank will be open the following day iff it is appropriate for her to treat the proposition that the bank will be open the following day as a reason for action. And, according to TPR, it is appropriate for her to treat that proposition as a reason for action iff she does not have reason to double-check whether it is true. Therefore, Hannah knows that the bank will be open the following day iff she does not have reason to double-check whether the bank will be open the following day. Now, according to SDR, Hannah has reason to do what would best satisfy her strongest present, intrinsic desires taken as a whole, *given what she believes her circumstances to be.* However, in the circumstances that Hannah *believes* herself to be in—circumstances where there is no impending bill and plenty of money in her account—it is not double-checking the bank's hours that would satisfy her strongest, present intrinsic desires, but getting home to a hot meal and a

62 *Anne Baril*

cold beer. Therefore, KR+SDR implies that Hannah doesn't have reason to double-check that the bank will be open the following day, and thus that she knows that the bank will be open the following day. By contrast, according to ODR, Hannah has reason to do what would best satisfy her strongest, present, intrinsic desires taken as a whole, *given what her circumstances actually are*. Given what Hannah's circumstances actually are—circumstances where there is an impending bill and a paucity of available funds—double-checking the bank's hours would best satisfy her strongest, present, intrinsic desires taken as a whole. Therefore, KR+ODR implies that Hannah has reason to double-check whether the bank will be open the following day, and thus that she doesn't know that the bank will be open the following day.

This example illustrates how KR generates different verdicts about cases, depending on the view about the nature and basis of practical reasons with which it is conjoined—not, perhaps, about the original cases that have been taken to provide *prima facie* motivation for KR, but about similar, easily constructed variations on these cases. In his discussion of *Ignorant High Stakes*, Stanley says that "our reaction is that Hannah's utterance of 'I know the bank will be open tomorrow' is false". (Stanley 2005: 5) This intuition will be vindicated by KR+ODR, but not by KR+SDR. The view of reasons KR is conjoined with makes a difference.

4. Pragmatic Encroachment and External Reasons

It may be thought that the previous point is of limited importance, since it is a minority of philosophers who accept either ODR or SDR. But there are other issues about reasons, important issues, on which most philosophers do—perhaps must—take a stance, and which also make a difference to what KR, in conjunction with this stance, implies about different cases. One such issue is whether a person may have "external" reasons for action, or whether they can have only "internal" reasons.

Bernard Williams (1981) introduces the idea of a person's "subjective motivational set", which comprises all of the person's desires, commitments, goals, interests, projects, and so on. According to Williams, S has reason to φ only if φ-ing advances some element in S's subjective motivational set. His view of practical reasons is therefore "internalist", in that practical reasons are "internal" to the motivations of the person who has them. Alternatively, one could be an "externalist" about practical reasons, believing that a person may have practical reasons for action that do not flow from her subjective motivational set. Thus an "externalist" may hold that we have reason to, for example, help others and refrain from harming them, even if we don't have any corresponding desire, commitment, etc.

For our purposes, we may understand these views as follows:[9]

> **Internalism (IR):** S has reason to φ iff φ-ing advances some element in S's subjective motivational set.
> **Externalism (ER):** Internalism is false.

Pragmatic Encroachment and Practical Reasons 63

And we can say that someone has *internal* reason to j iff j—ing advances some element in her subjective motivational set, and that someone has *external reason* to j iff she has reason to j but does not have internal reason to j.

Whether KR is conjoined with IR or ER appears to make no difference to the verdicts KR will generate about the original Bank and Train cases. In Bank Case 2, for example, Hannah presumably cares about the consequences of failing to pay her bills, and so has internal reason to double-check whether the bank will be open the following day, and thus, according to KR+IR, and assuming TPR, doesn't know that the bank is open. But the defender of ER will likely also think that Hannah has reason to double-check whether the bank will be open. She may think that Hannah has good reason to avoid the consequences of failing to pay her bills, whether she cares about these consequences or not. She may also think—as most externalists do—that we often have at least some *prima facie* reason to satisfy the contents of our subjective motivational sets (and so that, in this sense, we have both internal and external reasons). Such theorists would take the fact that Hannah cares about the consequences of failing to pay her bill to provide reason for her to act accordingly (albeit a reason that could be outweighed or undercut by other reasons, including reasons that do not flow from Hannah's subjective motivational set). In either event, the defender of ER will agree with the defender of IR that Hannah has reason to double-check whether the bank will be open, and thus both KR+IR and KR+ER can generate the verdict that Hannah does not know. And likewise for Matt in Train Case 2: both internalists and externalists about reasons will likely agree that Matt has reason to double-check whether the train is an express, and thus both KR+IR and KR+ER can generate the verdict that he does not know.

It has been suggested that defenders of KR may remain neutral on the issue of whether IR or ER is true. Fantl and McGrath, for example, write:

> The apparatus of reasons allows us to stay neutral on debates about the role of preferences and desires in rational action. Humeans will insist that a fact cannot be a reason a person has unless it connects appropriately with some desire or pro-attitude; anti-Humeans will disagree. We don't need to take any stand on the matter.
>
> (Fantl and McGrath 2009: 76)

But we can see how the issue makes a difference to KR by considering situations in which whether the stakes are raised depends on witER IR or ER is true. To illustrate, consider the following example given by Nomy Arpaly:

> [I]magine a group of people . . . eating sushi for the first time. . . . One of them, Todd, contemplates the green stuff on his plate, which is in fact wasabi, and asks, "What's the green stuff?" Jay shrugs and says, "Avocado". Todd goes ahead and eats a spoonful of wasabi; unsurprisingly, this is a very painful experience for him. It is only natural that Todd

64 *Anne Baril*

should feel Jay has shown himself to be a little less than a good person on this occasion. The question he is likely to ask himself is this: Had the wasabi been on Jay's plate rather than on Todd's, would Jay have leapt to his conclusion that it was avocado so quickly? Or would he have been less certain?

(Arpaly 2011: 79)

Imagine that Jay really is so solipsistic as to only care about his own painful taste experiences, and not about Todd's (that there is nothing corresponding in Jay's subjective motivational set). Assuming pragmatic encroachment, it is tempting to say that, when Todd's pain is at stake, the stakes are raised for Jay, such that his belief that the green stuff is avocado cannot be justified or amount to knowledge. But we can say this only if we allow that there are external reasons.

To drive the point home, we can devise cases, modeled on the previous Bank Cases and Train Cases, that will help us illustrate how KR will generate different verdicts about cases depending on whether it is conjoined with IR or ER. Consider first:

Painting Case 1

Amit cares nothing about preserving fine artworks, and only wants to clean junk. One day at the junkyard he finds a painting which he identifies as being mass-produced for IKEA. Amit once heard in a lecture that a safe and effective way to clean paintings is with spit— which is, indeed, true. His friend wonders how they can clean the painting. Amit says, "I know how—we can use spit. I once heard that in a lecture".

Painting Case 2

Amit cares nothing about preserving fine artworks, and only wants to clean junk. One day at the junkyard he finds a painting which he identifies as an Old Master. Amit once heard in a lecture that a safe and effective way to clean paintings is with spit—which is, indeed, true. His friend wonders how they can clean the painting. Amit says, "I know how—we can use spit. I once heard that in a lecture".

Let us grant that Amit really does just care about cleaning junk, and not about preserving fine artworks (or selling them, or impressing people with them, etc.). According to the internalist, then, Amit has no reason to double-check whether it's safe to clean the painting with spit—no reason to do anything other than go ahead and clean the painting with spit—in either case. Thus KR+IR, assuming TPR, will yield the verdict that, in both cases, Amit knows that it's safe to clean the painting with spit. By contrast, the externalist is free to say that Amit has reason to double-check in the second case, and

Pragmatic Encroachment and Practical Reasons 65

the defender of KR+ER is free to say that Amit doesn't know in the second case, even though he thinks he does.

Painting Case 2 give us an example of a case in which KR+IR, but not KR+ER, implies that a subject knows. There are also cases in which KR+IR, but not KR+ER, implies that a subject does *not* know. These are cases in which a person has reason to double-check whether some proposition is true if internalism is true, but not necessarily if externalism is true. Here's an example:

Application Case 1

Brenda is reviewing applications for an administrative position in her department at a public university. After careful consideration of one application, she determines that the applicant is unqualified for the position, and tosses the application on the rejection pile. As she does so, she sees that the Office of Equal Opportunity's questionnaire, which is collected from all applicants, but which is supposed to be removed by the time the applications reach her desk, has accidentally been included in the application. The questionnaire invites individuals to indicate their race/ethnicity, and Brenda sees that the individual has identified as "white". Brenda removes the questionnaire from the application, for the sake of confidentiality, returns the application to the rejection pile, and turns to the next application.

Application Case 2

Brenda is reviewing applications for a position in her department at a public university. After careful consideration of one application, she determines that the applicant is unqualified for the position, and tosses the application on the rejection pile. As she does so, she sees that the Office of Equal Opportunity's questionnaire, which is collected from all applicants, but which is supposed to be removed by the time the applications reach her desk, has accidentally been included in the application. The questionnaire invites individuals to indicate their race/ethnicity, and Brenda sees that the individual has identified as "white". Brenda is deeply racist: she has a profound antipathy towards people of color, and on this basis strongly prefers to work with a white person. Despite having carefully determined a moment ago that the applicant was unqualified, she decides she had better double-check.

Let us assume that in the first case Brenda knows the applicant is unqualified. If we grant that indulging her racist tendencies really would best satisfy the items in Brenda's subjective motivational set—that she really is that deeply racist—then, according to the internalist, Brenda has reason to double-check in the second case; thus KR+IR, assuming TPR, will yield the verdict that Brenda doesn't know the applicant is unqualified in the second

66 *Anne Baril*

case. The externalist, by contrast, is free to deny this—to say that Brenda does not have a genuine reason to double-check whether the applicant is unqualified, even if doing so advances some element in her subjective motivational set—and thus the defender of KR+ER is free to say that Brenda still knows the applicant is unqualified in the second case.[10]

5. Conclusion

The view of practical reasons KR is conjoined with makes a difference to what the defender of KR is able to say about cases. This is important because what the defender of KR is able to say about cases matters for the plausibility of KR. First, many defenders of pragmatic encroachment appeal to our intuitions about the Bank Cases and Train Cases, or others like them, to motivate their views.[11] They must therefore be concerned about whether pragmatic encroachment generates intuitive verdicts about other cases. Second, although some defenders of pragmatic encroachment offer theoretical arguments not based on intuitions in defense of their view,[12] it speaks against a view if it generates counterintuitive verdicts. This, it seems to me, is what KR, in combination with IR, does: it gives the intuitively wrong verdicts about Amit and Brenda. Intuitively, when an Old Master is at stake, rather than a piece of junk, Amit doesn't really know that it is safe to clean a painting with spit, regardless of whether he cares about Old Masters or not. And, intuitively, if Brenda, after careful consideration of an application, knows that the applicant is unqualified, she cannot fail to know this simply because she is racist and the applicant is white. Only KR+ER can vindicate these intuitions.[13]

The view of practical reasons KR is conjoined with, then, makes a difference to the plausibility of KR. Given the centrality of practical reasons to KR, we must evaluate it not in isolation, but in conjunction with answers to our various philosophical questions about the nature and basis of practical reasons. I have focused on KR, but the previous discussion suggests that issues concerning the nature and basis of practical reasons, such as whether internalism or externalism about reasons is true, will also make a difference to principles analogous to KR concerning some other epistemic status, such as justification or warrant.[14] When evaluating any such view, philosophical questions about the nature and basis of practical reasons should not be ignored.

Notes

1. I am grateful to all those who have given me helpful feedback on this chapter, especially to Eric Brown, John Doris, Maria Doulatova, Nicky Drake, Allan Hazlett, Jeremy Henry, Brian Kim, Richard Kim, Micah Lott, Ron Mallon, Matt McGrath, and David Rose.
2. Cf. Kim 2017. Kim understands the category of pragmatic encroachment more broadly, to include positions according to which practical factors are relevant for

determining whether or not a subject believes (which he calls "belief encroachment") and positions according to which practical factors are relevant for determining the meaning of knows in a conversational context (i.e. contextualism).

3. Fantl and McGrath (2002: 67).
4. Consider e.g. "One should act only on what one knows" (Stanley 2005: 9); "One ought only to use that which one knows as a premise in one's deliberations". (Hawthorne 2004: 30) The differences between these formulations and KRN will not make a difference in what follows. See further footnotes 8 and 10.
5. Consider e.g. "If you know that p, then p is warranted enough to be a reason you have to j, for any j" (Fantl and McGrath 2009: 69). The differences between this formulation and KRS will not make a difference in what follows. See further footnotes 8 and 10.
6. Consider e.g. "Where one's choice is p-dependent, it is appropriate to treat the proposition that p as a reason for acting iff you know that p" (Hawthorne and Stanley 2008: 578). I do not think it is necessary to include the caveat that one's choice be p-dependent, and so I do not include it in the KRN principles, but the reader may take it as assumed, if she thinks it is important; it will not make a difference to my argument here.
7. KRN finds further support in the fact that we would challenge someone if they were to treat a proposition as a reason for action without knowing it (e.g. "why did you use that paint for the baby's room if you didn't know it was safe?").
8. I have formulated TPR to facilitate discussion of the KR principles, the formulation of which, in turn, correspond most closely to Hawthorne and Stanley's principle (see footnote 6), but I believe we have no less reason to accept the following variations of TPR, corresponding to the principles defended by Stanley, Hawthorne, and Fantl and McGrath, respectively, cited in footnotes 4 and 5:

> APR: S should act on the proposition that p iff S does not have reason to double-check that p.
> PPR: It is appropriate for S to treat the proposition that p as a premise in one's deliberations iff S does not have reason to double-check that p.
> WPR: p is warranted enough to be a reason S has to j, for any j, iff S does not have reason to double-check that p.

9. This formulation makes externalism, rather than internalism, consistent with skepticism about practical reasons. This will not make a difference to the argument; it is merely to simplify the presentation.
10. In this presentation, I have targeted KR assumed TPR, but the same argument can be given, mutatis mutandis, targeting the principles defended by Stanley, Hawthorne, and Fantl and McGrath, assuming APR, PPR, and WPR, respectively. See footnotes 4, 5, and 8.
11. Stanley (2005), Hawthorne (2004), Hawthorne and Stanley (2008).
12. See Fantl and McGrath (2009, Chapter 3, especially p. 63).
13. Taken in itself, this is a point in favor of KR+ER. However, given the arguments of Williams and others against the existence of external reasons, it may be that KR+ER has other costs, and—given that one must accept either ER or IR—the KR theorist is confronted with a dilemma.
14. E.g. "S is justified in believing that p only if S is rational to act as if p". (Fantl and McGrath 2002: 78).

References

Arpaly, Nomy. (2011). "Open-Mindedness as a Moral Virtue," *American Philosophical Quarterly* 48(1): 75–85.

68 Anne Baril

DeRose, Keith. (1992). "Contextualism and Knowledge Attributions," *Philosophy and Phenomenological Research* 52(4): 913–929.

Fantl, Jeremy and Matthew McGrath. (2002). "Evidence, Pragmatics, and Justification," *Philosophical Review* 111: 67–94.

Fantl, Jeremy and Matthew McGrath. (2007). "On Pragmatic Encroachment in Epistemology," *Philosophy and Phenomenological Research* LXXV(3): 558–589.

Fantl, Jeremy and Matthew McGrath. (2009). *Knowledge in an Uncertain World.* Oxford: Oxford University Press.

Grimm, Stephen R. (2011). "On Intellectualism in Epistemology," *Mind* 120(479): 705–733.

Hawthorne, John. (2004). *Knowledge and Lotteries.* Oxford: Oxford University Press.

Hawthorne, John and Jason Stanley. (2008). "Knowledge and Action," *The Journal of Philosophy* CV(10): 571–590.

Hieronymi, Pamela. (2005). "The Wrong Kind of Reason," *The Journal of Philosophy* CII(9): 437–457.

Hieronymi, Pamela. (2011). "Reasons for Action," *Proceedings of the Aristotelian Society, New Series* 111: 407–427.

Kim, Brian. (2017). "Pragmatic Encroachment in Epistemology," *Philosophy Compass* 12: e12415. doi:10.1111/phc3.12415

Kolodny, Niko and John Brunero. (2016). "Instrumental Rationality," in Edward N. Zalta (ed.) *The Stanford Encyclopedia of Philosophy* (Winter Edition), URL = https://plato.stanford.edu/archives/win2016/entries/rationality-instrumental/

Portmore, Douglas W. (2008). "Are Moral Reasons Morally Overriding?" *Ethical Theory and Moral Practice* 11: 369–388.

Scanlon, Thomas Michael. (1998). *What We Owe to Each Other.* Cambridge, MA: Harvard University Press.

Stanley, Jason. (2005). *Knowledge and Practical Interests.* Oxford: Oxford University Press.

Williams, Bernard. (1981). "Internal and External Reasons," in *Moral Luck.* Cambridge: Cambridge University Press, 101–113.

5 An Externalist Decision Theory for a Pragmatic Epistemology[1]

Brian Kim

Central to epistemological orthodoxy is the tenet that only truth-relevant factors, such as the reliability of belief-forming processes or the counterfactual sensitivity of belief, distinguish knowledge from mere true belief. In recent years, however, this orthodoxy has come under attack. A number of epistemologists have argued in favor of **Pragmatic Encroachment**, which is the view that even if we fix all the truth-relevant factors, varying pragmatic factors can make a difference in determining whether or not a subject's true belief counts as knowledge.[2] Let us call any account that embraces pragmatic encroachment, a **Pragmatic Account of Knowledge**.[3]

The most powerful arguments for pragmatic encroachment appeal to norms that connect knowledge and the practical. Various proponents have converged on some variant of the following principle: S knows that p only if S is justified in taking p for granted in deliberation.[4]

This type of principle along with a suitable pair of cases offers an intuitive argument for pragmatic encroachment. For example, consider Catherine who possesses very strong but inconclusive evidence for her true belief that she was born in New York. We may suppose that she has been told so by her honest and reliable parents. Catherine's true belief appears to be a paradigmatic case of knowledge and if she were filling out an employment form, she would be justified in taking her birthplace for granted. But is Catherine justified in taking for granted that she was born in NY regardless of the practical situation she is in? What if Catherine were caught in a sinister scheme where death would be the punishment for falsely answering a question about her birthplace? In this high-stakes situation, it would be irrational for Catherine to take her birthplace for granted. After all, given the opportunity, she should go and double-check, gathering as much additional evidence as she can. So the epistemic principle connecting knowledge and deliberation along with our intuitions in these cases entails that even though all the truth-relevant factors remain fixed, Catherine's true belief counts as knowledge in the low-stakes scenario but does not count as knowledge in the extreme high-stakes scenario. Most pragmatists also claim that the practical situation of the subject is relevant in a very specific way, by determining the epistemic standards that must be met in order to know. So the reason

70 *Brian Kim*

why Catherine fails to know in the high-stakes scenario is because knowing in this scenario requires that an extremely high standard be met.[5]

My aim in this chapter is not to evaluate the arguments for and against pragmatic encroachment but rather to consider the pragmatic view in more detail. In particular, I want to explore how a pragmatic account of knowledge, which arises from thinking about the relationship between knowledge and action, accounts for the incompatibility of knowledge and epistemic luck. To do so, I will first consider how contemporary pragmatic accounts might address Gettier-style counterexamples. As it stands, proponents of pragmatic encroachment have not discussed these cases in any detail.[6] In section 1, I show that Gettier cases bring to light some problems for and challenges to pragmatic accounts of knowledge. Most importantly, they show that adequate pragmatic theories must appeal to externalist accounts of rational choice. In section 2, I offer one approach to developing an externalist theory of rational choice and on that basis, develop one type of pragmatic account. One upshot of this account is its unique insight into the nature of Gettier cases. In section 4, I conclude by first addressing some potential objections. But more importantly, I show how the proposed framework can be used to explore pragmatic epistemologies by considering some alternatives to the proposed account. My discussion takes on and brings together many different topics (e.g. Gettier cases, skepticism, decision theory, and objective measures of evidential strength). Instead of discussing each issue in careful detail, I shall present, in broad brush strokes, the outlines of a new approach to rational choice. My hope is to show that this approach is particuarly suitable as a foundation for further explorations of pragmatic epistemologies.

1. The Gettier Challenge for Pragmatists

In recent years, a number of pragmatic accounts of knowledge have been offered. Hawthorne and Stanley propose that "where one's choice is p-dependent, it is appropriate to treat the proposition that p as a reason for acting if and only if you know that p".[7] Fantl and McGrath propose that

> you know that p iff: p can be a reason in all three senses—justifying, favoring, and motivating—and it is not a matter of Gettier-like luck that p can be a favoring reason given that it can be a justifying and motivating reason.[8]

Weatherson proposes that "it is legitimate to write something on the decision table . . . iff the decision maker knows it to be true".[9]

Unfortunately, each of these proposals is unsatisfactory. At first glance, both Weatherson's proposal as well as Hawthorne and Stanley's appear to fall prey to Gettier-style counterexamples.[10] Consider a simple Gettier case in which Catherine is told by her very honest and reliable parents that I: she

Decision Theory for a Pragmatic Epistemology   71

will receive a small inheritance when she purchases her first house. Unbeknownst to both her and her parents, her inheritance has been stolen and squandered away by her younger sister. Luckily, a distant relative has set aside an inheritance that will be given to her when she purchases her first home. Intuitively, it seems appropriate for Catherine to treat I as a reason for buying her first house. It also appears legitimate for Catherine to write that she will receive an inheritance as an outcome of buying her first home on the decision table. After all, it's true and she possesses good evidence in favor of its truth. However, since her true belief has been Gettiered, she fails to know in both instances. So each account appears to fall prey to Gettier-style counterexamples.

Of course, a similar reply is available for both accounts. Hawthorne and Stanley can respond by simply insisting that Catherine may not treat I as a reason for acting, and she may not do so because she doesn't know. Similarly, Weatherson can respond by insisting that Catherine's entry in the decision table is illegitimate because she doesn't know. While these replies preserve the extensional adequacy of the two accounts, they undermine their explanatory power. After all, we have no independent account of when one may treat I as a reason or when one may write something on the decision table that explains why we fail to know in Gettier cases. Instead, the lack of knowledge in Gettier cases is used to explain why the proposed conditions for knowing are not met. So we are left with accounts that offer little insight into the nature of knowledge. Instead of gaining understanding about knowledge by appealing to the notion of reasons or a theory of rational decision-making, these accounts provide insight into when one may treat something as a reason or write something on a decision table by considering what we do and do not know.[11]

This latter criticism also applies to Fantl and McGrath's proposal. Since the account appeals to an explicit anti-Gettier condition without any explanation of what it means to meet this condition, we are left with the uninformative claim that Gettiered subjects fail to know because they are in a Gettier case. While their account does connect the concepts of knowledge and reason, we are nevertheless left without a clear account of the type of reason knowledge is.

Gettier cases raise some additional problems that are specific to pragmatic accounts of knowledge. The subject's practical situation is irrelevant to our epistemic evaluations in Gettier cases. When a subject's true belief is Gettiered, she fails to know no matter what practical situation she is in. The irrelevance of practical factors in these cases poses a problem. As previously noted, pragmatic accounts typically claim that the practical situation of the subject determines how strong of an epistemic state the subject must be in if the subject is to be in a position to know. And so they are relevant when we determine whether or not a true belief counts as knowledge.[12] However, in Gettier cases, the subject's epistemic state is not strong enough regardless of what practical situation the subject is in. So our Gettier intuitions appear to

72   Brian Kim

undermine this particular pragmatic claim about what it is to be in a position to know.

The second and more important problem arises from the fact that Gettier cases have taught us that knowledge is incompatible with epistemic luck. And as we have learned, the most plausible anti-luck epistemologies are externalist epistemologies.[13] In order to identify when one is in a position to know, one must account for factors that are external to the subject's internal state. The turn to reason-theoretic analyses could be motivated by the need to provide a pragmatic and externalist account of knowledge.[14] After all, on some views, what counts as a reason is independent of the internal state of the subject.[15] While the appeal to reasons may sometimes be insightful, it does not appear to provide any insight into Gettier cases. As we have seen, reason-theoretic accounts either fall prey to Gettier-style counterexamples or fail to provide accounts with sufficient explanatory power. Unless we have an independent account of the type of reason that knowledge is or provides, the appeal to reasons will be unhelpful.[16] I do not mean to conclude that the reason-theoretic approach cannot work. Rather, I am simply raising an internal challenge for those who adopt the pragmatic viewpoint.[17] We need some explanation of why Gettiered beliefs do not count as knowledge.[18]

The decision-theoretic approach offers an alternative but faces serious problems. Decision theory is typically understood as offering coherentist accounts of rational deliberation and on these accounts, the reasonableness of one's deliberations depends solely on the internal state of the decision maker. So decision theory seems unsuitable as a basis for developing an externalist epistemology. As a result, for pragmatists who are partial to the decision-theoretic apparatus, the challenge is to show how we can develop an anti-luck epistemology within this framework. This is the challenge I hope to address.

In summary, Gettier cases pose two specific challenges for the pragmatic account:

1. We must explain why the practical situation of the subject typically determines the standards required for one's true belief to count as knowledge yet, at the same time, is irrelevant for the assessment of knowledge in Gettier cases.
2. We must show how it is possible to develop an illuminating account of knowledge that both accounts for its practical role and rules out epistemic luck.[19]

On the view I will develop, the practical situation of the subject does typically determine the epistemic standards that must be met for true belief to count as knowledge. However, I will also argue that there is a minimum standard that must be met in any given practical situation and in Gettier cases, the subject fails to meet this minimum standard. As a result, the subject fails to be in a position to know no matter what practical situation

Decision Theory for a Pragmatic Epistemology   73

she is in. As it turns out, in order to articulate an appropriate minimum standard for knowledge, I will need to develop an externalist version of decision theory. This decision theory will take an externalist turn by allowing for external, objective factors to come into play when framing decision problems. This externalist move is motivated by the fact the epistemic evaluation of knowers arises from a third-person, objective point of view. So the externalist revision is required in order for decision theory to provide the appropriate evaluations. Therefore, I will address the first challenge by first addressing the second challenge. On the resulting view, a true belief counts as knowledge just in case, from the externalist, decision-theoretic point of view, the subject's total evidence favors the target proposition and the belief is suitable for rational decision-making.

2. An Externalist Decision-Theoretic Epistemology

In response to Gettier cases, many have amended the justified true belief account of knowledge by replacing the justification condition. I shall adopt this approach by using "warrant" to serve as a placeholder for the new condition, which is sufficient to turn true belief into knowledge.[20] However, given our pragmatic aims, we must replace the purely truth-relevant justification condition with one that accounts for practical factors. So let us use the notion of *pragmatic warrant* as the placeholder for whatever it is, from the pragmatic point of view, that turns true belief into knowledge.

In order to identify the conditions under which a belief is pragmatically warranted, we need to identify the conditions under which it would be appropriate to believe given its practical role. So we should first specify the practical role of belief. Pragmatists have focused on the fact that when you believe that p, you take p for granted when deliberating and deciding what to do.[21] When we engage in belief-based reasoning, we engage in coarse-grained reasoning on the basis of the truth or falsity of propositions without taking into account uncertainties. In general, categorical attitudes play an important role in the lives of bounded agents with limited resources.[22] Beliefs, in particular, simplify one's deliberations by ignoring likelihood and focusing on truth or falsity. So in order to identify the conditions under which a belief is pragmatically warranted, we need to identify the conditions under which it would be reasonable to take a proposition as true in one's deliberation rather than consider the likelihood that a proposition is true.[23] One intuitive proposal is that such a simplification is warranted only if it makes no practical difference to one's deliberations.[24] And such a simplification will make not a practical difference just in case the simplifying effect of that belief does not undermine the rationality of deliberation.

In order to identify when the simplifying effect of a belief does not undermine the rationality of deliberation, we will first need some account of what it means to deliberate in a rational way. For such an account, let's turn to the Bayesian view of rational choice.

74 Brian Kim

2.1 Decision Theory: Part I

Bayesian decision theory (henceforth BDT) articulates what it is to have a coherent standard of evaluation (i.e. a coherent state of mind) for a decision problem. The Bayesian accomplishes this task by first specifying what a decision problem is and identifying the judgments that are relevant for evaluating the choices that one is deliberating between. By then positing a set of coherence constraints governing these judgments, the Bayesian articulates what it is to have a coherent standard of evaluation. And for the Bayesian, a decision maker (henceforth the DM) rationally deliberates just in case she coherently evaluates the choices that are available in a given decision problem.

To introduce the Bayesian view of a decision problem, consider a case where Catherine is deciding how to get home from the museum. The Bayesian assumes that the decision maker (henceforth the DM) identifies a set of *acts* that she is capable of performing and considers worthwhile in evaluating. Catherine considers two acts, taking the train or a cab. Next, it is assumed that the DM has identified the *consequences* these acts will have for each member of a set of mutually exclusive *states*. Here, "states" refer to possible states of the world. For simplicity, let's start with the coarse-grained set of states and consequences summarized in the following decision table (Table 5.1):

Table 5.1 Catherine's Decision Problem

	Traffic	No Traffic
Train	Long Trip, Low Cost	Long Trip, Low Cost
Cab	Long Trip, High Cost	Short Trip, High Cost

In assessing these acts, the Bayesian assumes that the DM's evaluation of her choices is determined by two independent factors, her desire for the consequences and their likelihood. Thus, Catherine's evaluation of the acts depends only on her desire for the consequences and her belief about about the states.[25]

Given this view of decision-making, the Bayesian identifies three types of judgments that are relevant for evaluating a set of acts. Call these *deliberative judgments*. First, the DM must assess the desirability of the consequences using her *deliberative desires*. Next, the DM must assess the likelihood of each state using her *deliberative beliefs*. Finally, the DM must compare acts and specify a set of *deliberative preferences* between them.

The Bayesian offers two logically equivalent ways of articulating the coherence constraints that govern these deliberative judgments. The first way articulates rational constraints on deliberative preferences. One example of

Decision Theory for a Pragmatic Epistemology   75

such a constraint is that rational preferences are transitive. If a DM prefers act A to B and B to C, then the DM should also prefer act A to C. The second way is to identify a class of models that represent every coherent set of deliberative judgments the DM could have about any decision problem that is suitably described. The model-theoretic approach claims that any coherent set of judgments must be representable by the type of model proposed. The Bayesian argues that deliberative beliefs, desires, and preferences are coherent if and only if they are respectively representable by probabilities, utilities, and probability weighted utilities. The probability and utility models function as a regulative ideal for our deliberative judgments since they represent the type of rationally permissible judgments that a DM can have about her decision problem. These two ways of articulating coherence are logically equivalent because it can be shown that the DM has a coherent set of preferences if and only if the DM's deliberative beliefs, desires, and preferences can be represented by probabilities, utilities, and probability weighted utilities.[26]

2.2 Pragmatically Warranted Belief

Now that we have summarized our theory of rational deliberation, we can begin to answer the question with which we started. When is a subject's belief pragmatically warranted? When may a subject take a proposition for granted in her deliberation? Since the standard decision-theoretic framework only deals with graded notions like probability and utility, there is no explicit place for the all-or-nothing beliefs that are typically understood to be necessary for knowledge. However, a natural account can be provided.

Within a well-defined decision problem, a set of coherent preferences is enough to entail that one's beliefs, desires, and preferences are representable as probabilities, utilities, and probability weighted utilities.[27] Call such coherent judgments *ideal* and the set of these coherent judgments a *rational ideal*. Rational ideals function as a rational standard for decision problems.[28] And since the purpose of engaging in practical deliberation is to make a choice, the primary function of a rational ideal is to identify which choices count as rational for a given decision problem. On the Bayesian account, a choice is rational just in case it is amongst the most preferred (i.e., maximizes expected utility). Our intuitive proposal was that a belief is pragmatically warranted only if it makes no difference to one's practical evaluations. If we situate this proposal within the Bayesian view of rational deliberation, we conclude that for a given decision problem, a DM's belief is pragmatically warranted only if her preferences given this belief are *practically coherent* with her ideal preferences. Two sets of preferences are practically coherent just in case they identify the same set of choices as rational. Thus, we have one initial condition governing pragmatically warranted belief: S's belief that p is pragmatically warranted only if S's preferences given her categorical belief that p are practically coherent with S's ideal preferences.[29]

76 *Brian Kim*

This principle proposes that the reasonableness of an all-or-nothing belief depends upon the resulting stability in the evaluation of one's choices. Pragmatically warranted beliefs do not alter what counts as rational relative to our more fine-grained beliefs. To illustrate, suppose Catherine has the following probabilities and utilities (Table 5.2):

Table 5.2 Catherine's Decision Problem With [Probabilities] and (Utilities)

	Traffic [25%]	*No Traffic [75%]*
Train	Long Trip, Low Cost (.5)	Long Trip, Low Cost (.5)
Cab	Long Trip, High Cost (.2)	Short Trip, High Cost (.7)

Calculating expected utilities, $EU(Train) = .5$ and $EU(Cab) = .575$ so taking a cab is ideally preferable to taking the train. Calculating expected utilities conditional on $[\neg T]$ there being no traffic, $EU(Train|\neg T) = .5$ and $EU(Cab|\neg T) = .7$. So even if she believes that there is no traffic, she still prefers the cab. The resulting stability of what Catherine prefers underwrites the rationality of her belief that $\neg T$. Of course, given different probabilities or utilities, she might not be rational taking $\neg T$ for granted. Keeping all else fixed, if a short, high cost trip had a utility of less than .6, $EU(Train) > EU(Cab)$ but $EU(Train|\neg T) < EU(Cab|\neg T)$. Her belief that $\neg T$ would also be unstable if we kept the utilities fixed and $p(T) > .4$. An interesting problem arises in cases of dominance, where the consequences of one choice are always more desirable than the consequences of all the others. No matter what the DM takes for granted, she will always prefer the same choice. The DM would thereby be rational in taking any proposition for granted. However, it is unintuitive to think there are situations in which one may arbitrarily either believe p or believe $\neg$p and be rational in doing so. Believing that p commits the subject to the truth of p. Moreover, truth is an aim and norm of belief.[30] So one ought to have some epistemic reason for believing. We can ensure that the DM's beliefs are not epistemically arbitrary by adding in the minimal condition that the DM must, on the whole, possess evidence that favors p over $\neg$p. So when we evaluate the DM's epistemic state, their total evidence must favor p. While this is a somewhat vague condition, it will do for the moment; I will offer more discussion of this minimal condition in section 3. Thus,

> S's belief that p is pragmatically warranted only if S's preferences given S's belief that p are practically coherent with S's ideal preferences and S's total evidence favors p over $\neg$p.[31]

This latter necessary condition will serve as the minimum epistemic standard for knowledge and failing to meet this standard would mean

Decision Theory for a Pragmatic Epistemology 77

that one's belief is not epistemically motivated. If one's belief fails to be epistemically motivated, then one fails to know in every practical situation. In section 3, I will show that, on the proposed account, Gettier cases lie at a very specific point on the spectrum of epistemically unmotivated beliefs. However, the condition as it has been described so far will not do. After all, subjects do appear to possess evidence that their Gettiered beliefs are true and so they satisfy this minimal condition. What we need is a somewhat specific measure of a subject's strength of evidence. And to develop this, I will outline a decision-theoretic framework that will allow us to measure one's strength of evidence in a way that depends upon what counts as evidence. And by fixing what counts as evidence from an external point of view, we will be able to consider external, "objective" measures of evidential strength when evaluating DM's. And we shall find that from this perspective, Gettiered subjects possess no evidence for or against the target proposition.[32]

2.3 Decision Theory: Part II

So far, our analysis of pragmatically warranted belief has focused on coherent belief. We have proposed that a pragmatically warranted belief must be practically coherent and epistemically motivated. However, if we are to identify the conditions that are both necessary and sufficient for pragmatic warrant, we also need to ensure that pragmatically warranted belief rules out epistemic luck. So pragmatic warrant cannot simply be a matter of internal coherence. The problem is that the Bayesian account of rational deliberation is only concerned with coherence. So let's return to the Bayesian account to see how we might broaden its scope.

Decision theories answer three questions when explicating what it means to have a rational standard of evaluation.

1. What is a decision problem?
2. Which types of judgments are relevant for evaluating choices?
3. What constraints must these judgments meet in order to count as rational?

Decision theorists typically focus on the third question, and there has been a long debate about various coherence constraints on beliefs, desires, and preferences.[33] But how does the Bayesian answer the first two questions? The Bayesian proposes that decision problems can be described by a set of acts, states, and consequences. And the deliberative preferences, beliefs, and desires over these acts, states, and consequences are all that are relevant for evaluating one's choices. Unfortunately, these answers leave us with an incomplete account of rational deliberation. Similarly, suppose one proposed a purely descriptive account of decision-making that focused solely on the evaluative component of choice. This account would be problematic since it would ignore the all important framing component of choice.[34]

78 Brian Kim

2.3.1 Two Limitations of Bayesian Decision Theory

The first problem is that the Bayesian offers no detailed account of how to frame a decision problem.[35] It is simply assumed that there is some way that we can do this. This assumption makes sense when one is choosing between well-defined bets. If I offer you a choice between two bets, one offering $7 if a coin lands heads and nothing otherwise, the other offering $10 if the same coin lands tails and nothing otherwise, the decision table is fixed. The relevant states, which represent possible answers to the question of which side the coin will land, are those that matter for determining the outcome of the bet. The relevant consequences are the monetary prizes. However, when Catherine decides between taking the train or a cab, it is far from obvious what the relevant states and consequences ought to be. When evaluating Catherine's attitudes about her decision problem, how should we frame her decision problem? Should we incorporate into her decision problem considerations about the weather? What about the possibility that the train may derail or that the cab may crash? In order to have a comprehensive account of rational deliberation, we need to answer the framing question: how should the DM's choice problem be framed?

Second, the Bayesian solely focuses on deliberative judgments—those judgments that concern the acts, states, and consequences of a decision problem—and assumes that such judgments are all that matter for characterizing rational deliberation. Viewed as a comprehensive theory, BDT states that so long as a DM deliberates on the basis of any coherent set of beliefs, desires, and preferences, she is free from any rational criticism. This claim to comprehensiveness would only be correct if our deliberative judgments were not based upon any other type of judgment or attitude. However, over the last forty years, an overwhelming amount of research, beginning with the preference reversal experiments of Slovic and Lichtenstein, has slowly undermined this assumption.[36] These experiments show that many of the judgments we use to deliberate are deeply context-dependent, changing from one deliberative context to the next. In reply, many researchers have adopted the methodological assumption that our deliberative judgments are *constructed*. Slovic and Lichenstein write that "the big picture is the overwhelming evidence that people often do not have preexisting preferences but must construct them to fit the situation".[37] If we adopt this constructive point of view, a comprehensive theory of rational deliberation must also account for how our deliberative judgments are constructed in each context. So BDT is incomplete.[38]

In order to address these two limitations, we must add to the Bayesian theory some account of how to frame a decision problem and some account of how DMs construct their deliberative judgments. I will call the resulting theory, a **Constructive Decision Theory**.[39] I call the view constructive to make it explicit that decision problems are not always given and that deliberative judgments do not always pre-exist. Both must sometimes be "constructed".

2.3.2 Constructive Decision Theory

In order to articulate how to frame a decision problem (i.e., demarcate the set of relevant states and consequences), we are guided by the following motto: *what matters in deliberation depends upon what deliberation is for*. And I shall begin our discussion by considering how this might be done from the first-person point of view. We shall later broaden the scope of our inquiry to consider how objective considerations might factor in when we frame the DM's decision problem from the third-person, evaluative perspective.

If we view Table 5.2 as Catherine's own view of her decision problem, then the decision matrix indicates that she restricted the set of relevant consequences to only those that described the time and cost it would take to get home. This is all she took into account and all she cared about. So it seems that only two values were relevant to her deliberation, expediency and thrift. By specifying the relevant values, one can determine the set of relevant consequences. Though it may be a bit strange to suppose that Catherine explicitly judges that these two values are all that matter, it is quite natural to state that she has the goal of getting home in the fastest, most cost-effective way. Goal judgments offer an intuitive way in which the DM demarcates a set of relevant values. Once a goal is set and a set of values is selected as all that matters, the relevant consequences are simply those that describe the outcomes of one's actions relative to these values. So Catherine only needs to describe those consequences of her actions that matter given her concern for the duration and cost of transportation. As a general rule, *the consequences that count as relevant depend upon the values that count as relevant*. What is notable about our goals is that they may change from one deliberative context to the next. In another context, Catherine may have the goal of getting home in the least stressful, most aesthetically pleasing way. This in turn will identify a different set of relevant values. Thus, what deliberation is for is deliberation-specific so the consequences that count as relevant are also deliberation-specific.

Catherine must also demarcate a set of relevant states. I proposed that the only question she considered in her deliberation was whether or not there would be traffic on the streets. Neither the color of the cab, the cleanliness of the train, nor the personality of the cab driver were deemed relevant. Since we have a rule for demarcating the set of relevant consequences, we also need one for our states. What matters must depend upon what deliberation is for and the relevant states are indirectly determined by our goals. Some states matter because their actualization will affect whether one or another of the relevant consequences occur. Catherine recognizes that if there is traffic on the streets, the cab ride may be costly and slow. Since she cares about the cost and duration of the trip, she should consider the possibility of traffic. So the first general rule is that the DM must consider all the states that she thinks will affect whether one or another of the relevant consequences occurs. Call these *consequence-determining states*.

80   Brian Kim

A second set of possibilities matters since their actualization is relevant for assessing the likelihood of the consequence-determining states. Suppose Catherine would find it very likely that there would be traffic if the President were visiting the city. If she judges that the President's presence is relevant for assessing the likelihood of a consequence-determining possibility, Catherine should consider this possibility as well. Call these *evidentially relevant states*.

So one possibility is that the DM herself makes certain judgments, such as goal judgments, that set the parameters for her decision problem. Call these *constructive judgments*, which allow the DM to demarcate a set of relevant consequences and states. These same judgments can also help to construct one's deliberative judgments. They do so by placing constraints on the set of rationally permissible deliberative judgments. For example, the set of relevant values places constraints on the utilities that are rationally permissible. If the cost and duration of the trip are the only values that matter to a deliberation, then a short, low cost trip should be more desirable than a long, high cost trip since the latter outcome is better according to both values.[40]

The type of constructive decision theory that I have so far described is compatible with the Bayesian account. Rational deliberative beliefs, desires, and preferences are still probabilities, utilities, and probability weighted utilities. The only change is that we incorporate how a DM might set the parameters of her deliberation by accounting for constructive judgments within our theory. Though this expands the scope of the types of judgments that are within the purview of our decision theory, it also narrows the scope of the Bayesian coherence constraints.

On one interpretation of BDT, the entirety of one's beliefs, desires, and preferences ought to be representable by a single probability, utility, and probability weighted utility function. So long as there is no change in what the DM believes or desires, these probabilities and utilities should then be used for every decision problem. This interpretation is unrealistic and incomplete since it fails to account for the context-sensitive construction of our deliberative judgments. The constructive account described previously proposes that our deliberative judgments are often constructed on the fly and may vary from one deliberative context to the next. If constructive judgments are deliberation-specific and deliberative judgments are constructed on their basis, the beliefs and desires that count as rational for one deliberation are not necessarily what counts as rational for another. Since the Bayesian principles of rationality explicate what it is for these deliberative judgments to be coherent, they must only apply within a particular deliberative context. So the demand that deliberative beliefs, desires, and preferences be representable by a probability, utility, and probability weighted utility is restricted to the decision problem for which these judgments are constructed.[41]

2.3.3 Beyond Coherence

While the constructive decision theory described in the previous section remains a coherentist and internalist account of rational deliberation, the

Decision Theory for a Pragmatic Epistemology 81

recognition that every comprehensive decision theory must account for how to frame a decision problem opens up the decision-theoretic framework to the development of externalist standards. To do so, we will first show how external, objective factors can be appealed to in setting the parameters of a decision problem. More importantly, these objective factors are relevant when we evaluate DMs from the third-person perspective. And this evaluative use of decision theory is what's relevant for a theory of knowledge. Thus, by appealing to externally framed decision problems, we will be able to develop an externalist, decision-theoretic epistemology.

In order to deal with Gettier cases, we will only need to reconsider how to determine which states are evidentially relevant. When we pick out a set of evidentially relevant states from the third-person perspective, we are demarcating what counts as evidence and how much that evidence counts in the context at hand. This notion of "counting as evidence" is crucial if we, as bounded agents, are to have clear and meaningful measures of evidential support.

For example, suppose we consider a two-sided coin and try to assess the likelihood that it will land heads on the next toss. We know that this coin has been tossed a thousand times, and we can ask anything about these tosses. What sort of information is relevant when assessing the likelihood that coin will land heads on the next toss? This question is relevant if we are to evaluate the strength of a subject's evidence, when the subject possesses information about these previous tosses. The answer to this question depends upon what is taken into account, what information counts as evidence. And what counts as evidence depends upon certain assumptions that must be made for inquiry (or for our purpose, the evaluation of a subject's strength of evidence) to proceed. On the assumption that the coin is fair, no information about the previous tosses counts as evidence for or against. Alternatively, on the assumption that the coin could be biased, information about the proportion of heads to tails in the previous tosses would be relevant. But is the order of the outcomes relevant information? This depends upon whether or not it is assumed that the coin flips are independent. What about the color of the coin? Such information would count as relevant within a context where we consider the possibility that the coin's color could have an effect on its bias. As one can see, such questions could go on forever. Thus, we must restrict what can count as evidence in order to engage in inquiry and to evaluate strength of evidence.

Both subjective factors and objective factors can be used to determine what is evidentially relevant. Suppose Catherine is trying to decide whether to take a cab or the train back home from the museum. And suppose that the only pair of consequence-determining states, from Catherine's points of view, are the ones in which there is or is not traffic on the road. One way to determine the states that are relevant for assessing the probability of these consequence-determining states is to consider Catherine's actual judgments (i.e. what Catherine actually considers). For example, consider the case in which Catherine takes into account the possibility that the President is

82 *Brian Kim*

visiting the city and also judges that this possibility is relevant for assessing the likelihood of traffic. Such a possibility is evidentially relevant and since the explanation of its relevance only appeals to the DM's own judgments about what counts as relevant, it is relevant from the subject's own point of view. So evidentially relevant states can be demarcated in terms of what is subjectively relevant.

Alternatively, we can demarcate what is evidentially relevant from a more objective point of view. For example, consider a case in which there has been an accident on the streets. Catherine is unaware of this fact and has not considered this possibility. Thus, she has not judged the possibility of an accident as being relevant for her deliberation. So from her point of view, information about accidents on the streets are ignored and do not count as evidence. However, there is an intuitive sense in which this possibility ought to be considered. After all, if Catherine had taken it for granted that there had been a car accident, she should have come to a very different assessment of the likelihood of traffic. The intuitive notion of objective relevance comes from the observation that true but unconsidered propositions relevant for assessing the likelihood of any relevant state ought to taken to be account. More on how to interpret "likelihood" in a moment.

To put the point another way, from the third-person point of view, facts about the actual situation determine the space of evidentially relevant possibilities within which one should ideally inquire. And it is relative to this space that we evaluate the strength of a subject's evidence. After all, suppose that Catherine thinks it unlikely that there is traffic since it is fairly late in the evening. Thus, from her point of view, she possesses strong evidence. In contrast, from our perspective, her evidence is much weaker. One way to account for this difference is to incorporate these objectively relevant possibilities into the decision space.[42] And from this new point of view, Catherine's evidence no longer justifies a high degree of confidence.

There are two ways of explaining why, from the third-person perspective, Catherine's strength of evidence is lower once the possibility of an accident is incorporated into the space of possibilities. First, we could counterfactually consider Catherine's rational degree of belief within this broader space. Since Catherine's evidence cannot discriminate between there being an accident or not and since there will almost certainly be traffic if there were an accident, she should be less confident when constructing her probabilities in this broader space of possibilities. Alternatively, we might propose that there is some evidential probability that there is traffic given Catherine's evidence.

I am agnostic between these alternative ways of understanding how changes in the space of possibilities can alter subjective or "objective" probabilities. Thus, I do not have a theory or procedure to identify the set of relevant states from the objective point of view. I am merely relying upon the intuitive idea that when we evaluate a DM's evidence, we do so from the point of view where many true but unconsidered propositions relevant for assessing the likelihood of any relevant state are taken into account.

Decision Theory for a Pragmatic Epistemology 83

Moreover, these possibilities alter the probability by altering what counts as evidence and how much the evidence counts. While I shall rely upon this intuitive characterization, I have included some more discussion of objective relevance in Appendix A to address some questions and problems.[43]

2.4 The Pragmatic Account of Knowledge

We have now seen how both subjective and objective factors can be used to set the parameters of a decision problem. So we can now differentiate various framings of decision problems in terms of the types of parameters they take into account. It should be noted that the use of subjective or objective decision parameters is not mutually exclusive. There are framings that take into account both objective and subjective factors, and there are framings that take into account just one or the other. By adopting the constructive decision-theoretic framework and considering framings of decision problems that incorporate objective parameters, the internalistic view of rational deliberation presented by BDT can be transformed into a view that is friendly to the externalist. And this externalist decision-theoretic framework can be used to evaluate the strength of a subject's evidence from the third-person point of view. As I noted, this more objective measure of a DM's strength of evidence can either be understood as evidential probabilities or the DM's rational degrees of belief relative to the objectively defined set of states. We can thereby appeal to objectively framed decision problems to produce an account of knowledge as pragmatically warranted belief.

> **Pragmatically Warranted Belief:** S's belief that p is pragmatically warranted if and only if, in an objectively framed decision problem, S's preferences given S's belief that p are practically coherent with S's ideal preferences and S's evidence favors p.[44]

3. Gettier Cases

The pragmatic account imposes a minimum standard for knowledge whereby the subject must have favoring evidence from the evaluative, third-person point of view (i.e. relative to objectively framed decision problems). I previously noted that this minimum standard for knowledge would not be met when a subject's belief is Gettiered, and when this minimum standard is not met then the subject fails to know no matter what practical situation she is in. To show this, I will compare and contrast skeptical possibilities and Gettier possibilities. By doing so, we will be able to get a clearer understanding of what it means to evaluate the strength of a subject's epistemic state relative to one or another way of fixing what counts as evidence and how much that evidence counts.

Under normal circumstances, skeptical possibilities, such as brain-in-a-vat possibilities, are ignored. However, it's easy to enter into a context (e.g., a

84 *Brian Kim*

philosophical discussion) where such possibilities are taken seriously. We may do so for the sake of engaging in a certain epistemological project. As Barry Stroud has noted, radical skepticism is closely connected to the epistemological project of trying to ascertain whether we can know anything about a particular domain without presuming any knowledge of that domain.[45] Of course, when this possibility is taken seriously, we cannot assume to possess any evidence for or against any proposition about the external world. For example, perceptual experiences that would normally justify our beliefs that we have hands no longer count as evidence in favor. Thus, in a context where BIV possibilities are deemed serious and relevant, what counts as evidence for or against propositions about the external world changes. And from this perspective where skeptical possibilities are taken seriously, we lack favoring evidence for external world propositions.

In this respect, Gettier possibilities function exactly like skeptical possibilities. Consider Chisholm's case in which you look out at a field and see what looks exactly like a sheep and come to believe that there is a sheep in the field. Unbeknownst to you, the animal you are looking at is a dog, disguised as a sheep. But there is a sheep in the field only behind the hill out of your field of vision. Under normal circumstances, the disguised dog possibility is ignored and not taken seriously. However, suppose that such a possibility were considered. Under those circumstances, your perceptual experience no longer counts as evidence. After all, it is perfectly compatible with the disguised dog possibility. Since the only evidence you possess for the claim that there is a sheep in the field is your perceptual experience, you thereby lack favoring evidence for that claim.

Like skeptical possibilities, Gettier possibilities, when taken seriously, undermine one's evidence. They do so by altering what counts as evidence in favor of certain propositions. In both cases, once certain alternatives are taken seriously, what had previously counted as favoring evidence no longer does so. There are, however, a few differences between radical skeptical hypotheses and Gettier possibilities. First, skeptical possibilities are more general in that they undermine a whole class of potential evidence. In contrast, Gettier possibilities merely undermine the evidence one actually possesses. After all, one could simply walk up to the disguised dog and walk over the hill to see the sheep. Second and more importantly, Gettier possibilities are actual. The animal is a disguised dog. Jones is lying about owning a Ford. The match has impurities. In contrast, there is no presumption that skeptical hypotheses are true. This difference is crucial if my account is to avoid skepticism.

Constructive decision theory is able to capture the context-sensitivity of what counts as favoring evidence by allowing for the set of evidentially relevant states to change from one decision context to next. When this framework is used to evaluate whether subjects know, we must ensure that all true evidentially relevant states are taken into account. This restriction to actualized states is what allows the account to differentiate Gettier possibilities

Decision Theory for a Pragmatic Epistemology   85

from skeptical ones. From the perspective in which Gettier possibilities are taken into account, subjects lack, on the whole, evidence for or against the target proposition. We can thereby conclude that when a subject's belief has been Gettiered, she lacks evidence from this objective, knowledge-evaluating point of view. If she lacks evidence, then she fails to satisfy the minimal epistemic condition required for knowledge. And if she fails to satisfy the minimal condition, then she fails to know in every practical context she could be in.

3.1 The Pragmatic Analysis of Gettier Cases

One may object that I have simply added an externalist and truth-relevant component to the pragmatic account—a component that any good theory of knowledge should have. In addition, it might be thought that the proposed pragmatic account has similarities to both the indefeasibility and relevant alternative analyses of knowledge. So I'd like to make a few remarks about what insight we gain by adopting this pragmatic account. However, before I turn to that task, it is worth reiterating that my primary aim was to address a challenge internal to the pragmatic viewpoint. The challenge was to develop an externalist account of rational deliberation, whether from the reason-theoretic or decision-theoretic perspective, that could provide any explanation as to why Gettiered beliefs do not count as knowledge. After all, previous accounts could offer no such explanation. So I have simply offered one such explanation.

Let us begin by considering the relevant alternatives account of knowledge. This view famously runs into difficulties demarcating the set of alternatives that must be ruled out in order to count as knowing. As is explicit in (Lewis 1996), it is unclear how we can demarcate what counts as a relevant alternative in way that excludes skeptical alternatives but includes Gettier possibilities. The problem in Lewis' account is that it makes an appeal to similarity that is not sufficiently discriminating. The pragmatic notion of objective relevance offers a fairly simple resolution to this problem. First off, the pragmatic account does not talk of ruling out alternatives and instead talks of a space of relevant states or possibilities. Next, the account of relevance is pragmatic in that it ultimately depends upon what is relevant for the decision maker's evaluation of her choices in a decision problem. And I proposed that objectively relevant states are defined in terms of true facts that are evidentially relevant for the assessment of likelihood. As a result, Gettier possibilities count as relevant because they are true while skeptical possibilities do not because they are presumably false.[46] Thus, my pragmatic account acknowledges the similarity between the two types of possibilities while identifying a small but very important discriminating property.[47]

The no defeaters account of knowledge runs into difficulties making sense of a defeater. The problem arises from the need to differentiate misleading from defeating evidence. In the well-known case of Tom Grabit and his

86 Brian Kim

mother, Tom has stolen a book from the library and Smith has seen him do so.[48] However, unbeknownst to Smith, Tom's demented mother has asserted to a friend that Tom was nowhere near the library but Tom's twin John, who is a figment of Mrs. Grabit's imagination, was at the library during the theft. This example posed problems for early indefeasibility accounts. The challenge was to provide an account of a defeater such that Mrs. Grabit's assertion was ruled out and dismissed as a misleading piece of evidence. Though subsequent analyses of defeaters were able to rule these cases out, it became increasingly difficult to imagine that any account could demarcate all true facts into those that were genuine defeaters and those that were misleading.[49]

The most obvious and important thing to note is that the pragmatic account makes no appeal to defeaters. In fact, the account has no use for such a distinction. Instead, the account only relies upon a distinction between relevant and irrelevant states so it does not depend upon any distinction between defeating and misleading facts. In fact, all evidentially relevant facts are taken into consideration from the objective point of view. Let me explain. A particular fact is misleading only if it is taken alone (i.e., if the relevant facts are gerrymandered in the right way). In the case of Demented Mrs. Grabit, the fact that Mrs. Grabit told a friend that Tom's twin and not Tom was at the library is misleading only if it is considered independently of the facts that Mrs. Grabit is a compulsive liar and that Tom has no twin brother. The pragmatic account is happy with so-called misleading facts because it proposes to account for all evidentially relevant possibilities and facts.[50] And the thought is that once all the objectively relevant possibilities are incorporated, no particular fact can be misleading.[51]

Let us conclude by bringing our discussion up to date. In the recent epistemological literature, the two main competitors for explaining why true belief falls short of knowledge in Gettier cases are the ease of error and lack of credit explanations. "According to *Doxastic* Ease of Error Approach, a Gettiered belief that p is one whose subject S could easily have *believed* falsehoods similar to p, in ways similar to how S actually believes p".[52] The most natural way to fill in this account is by appealing to counterfactual properties that a subject's belief must have in order for her true belief to count as knowledge.[53] According to the lack of credit approach, "S's belief B in p is Gettiered iff (B is true and epistemically justified but) B's truth isn't sufficiently creditable to S's cognitive abilities".[54] This account has been explicated by appealing to the explanatory salience of the subject's cognitive abilities as well as the manifestation of the subject's cognitive abilities.[55]

We can better understand the pragmatic account of knowledge by highlighting its alternative explanation of why true belief falls short of knowledge in Gettier cases. Rather than possessing counterfactual properties or manifesting the subject's cognitive abilities, a pragmatically warranted belief is one that is well-formed relative to its function in deliberation and

Decision Theory for a Pragmatic Epistemology   87

the subject's actual situation. The pragmatic account of knowledge focuses on the activity of believing within the broader activity of deliberating. And rational deliberation manifests more than one's cognitive abilities. For example, one may have to evaluate outcomes appropriately relative to one's practical goals. The resulting account proposes that Gettiered beliefs are those that have not been skillfully formed in one's deliberative situation.

The pragmatic account also offers a novel view of the significance of Gettier cases. The minimal epistemic condition that I have been working with is very weak and may have some undesirable consequences. I suggest stronger conditions in section 4.2. However, I started with this condition because it brings to light where, from the pragmatic viewpoint, Gettier cases lie on the spectrum of cases. On the proposed view, there may be contexts in which we know somewhat unlikely propositions (e.g. that a fair coin will land heads on one of two tosses). But Gettier cases are special cases where one lacks favoring evidence for either p or not-p. On one side of Gettier cases are those where one irrationally believes that p even though one possesses, on the whole, varying amounts of favoring evidence for not-p. On the other side of the spectrum are cases where one believes that p and possesses, on the whole, varying amounts of favoring evidence for p.

Since Gettier cases are those in which one possesses neither evidence in favor or against, there is a sense in which, from the third-person point of view, Gettiered belief are true by a matter of pure luck. They are akin to cases in which one thinks that one has all sorts of evidence that a coin toss is biased and will land heads. However, as a matter of fact, the coin is fair and so this evidence does not, in fact, favor that outcome. Cases of pure luck are particularly interesting, because they are the paradigmatic cases in which a successful outcome is not, in any sense, due to the agent's skill. Rather, it's solely a matter of luck. These cases mark an important point in the spectrum of cases in which the agent deserves no credit regardless of the practical situation the agent finds herself in.

4. Exploring Pragmatic Epistemologies

At the outset, I proposed to engage in a broad exploration of pragmatic epistemologies. However, I quickly narrowed in on one type of pragmatic proposal. I did so, in part, because I believe that the proposed account would bring to light an interesting feature of Gettier cases, but I also did so because I believed that this was the best way to introduce the constructive decision-theoretic framework, which I find rich enough for exploring pragmatic epistemologies. So to conclude, I'd like to address some objections to the proposed view. By doing so, we will be able to identify various junctures at which alternatives to the current proposal can be explored. My aim here is to show not only that the current framework is a rich and flexible one, but also to show where exploration might be fruitful.

88 Brian Kim

4.1 Belief, Practical Adequacy and Closure

I considered the following necessary condition on pragmatic warrant: S's belief that p is pragmatically warranted only if S's preferences given her categorical belief that p are practically coherent with S's ideal preferences. This type of condition has been called the practical adequacy condition on knowledge.[56] Call a belief practically adequate just in case it satisfies this necessary condition. Unfortunately, practical adequacy as described is incompatible with certain desirable closure principles on knowledge, such as single-premise closure.[57] I appealed to this practical adequacy principle because it is intuitive and worked for our purposes, but we can explore variations of the principle that preserve single-premise closure.

Consider the strongest belief (the belief that entails all the others) in the set of practically adequate beliefs.[58] We can define *practically adequate** beliefs as any believed proposition that is entailed by this strongest belief. So by brute force, practical adequacy* preserves single-premise closure. Some may find this type of solution ad hoc because it's not clear why the strongest practically adequate belief has any normative significance.

Fortunately, we do have a principled explanation that comes from decision theory, but this requires us to think of categorical belief in a slightly different way. At the beginning of our discussion, I suggested that the practical role of belief was to take a proposition for granted in deliberation. I then explicated this idea within the decision-theoretic framework in terms of ignoring or eliminating columns in a decision table. On this view, the practical role of categorical belief is the following type of simplification. One at first considers an uncertain decision problem in all its complexity, but rather than reason on the basis of all these uncertainties, one simplifies by taking certain propositions as true or false.

There is, however, a slightly different simplifying role that categorical belief can play. On the constructive view of decision-making, beliefs may play a role in framing our decision problems, thereby helping us to demarcate a decision problem and construct the relevant deliberative judgments. If we take this view, when is a belief practically adequate? Here it is useful to borrow some terminology from L.J. Savage. Savage acknowledged that as creatures with bounded resources, we always engage in *small world* decision-making. Here, a world is a particular representation of a decision problem rather than a possible world. While many factors could be relevant to a decision problem, we typically consider very little when thinking about and evaluating our choices. That is, we only consider a restricted set of acts, states, and consequences. Savage never offered a detailed picture of how we select small worlds but he did specify a condition on their selection. He argued that the preferences in a small world must be stable across refinements of that world to larger ones. In layman's terms, one has selected a good perspective on a decision problem only if what counts as rational from that perspective would remain stable when considering more and more possibilities and detail.

Decision Theory for a Pragmatic Epistemology   89

For example, suppose that you believe that it will not rain when deliberating about what to wear for the day. Framing your decision problem on this assumption, you conclude that it is best to wear a light sweater. This is a small world, a world in which one restricts what one considers. For Savage, this world is appropriate for use only if the same choice is best had one considered the likelihood of rain. So, if wearing a light sweater would still count as best from the perspective of the decision problem that accounts for these possibilities, then the original framing could be appropriate. Furthermore, Savage thought that a small world was appropriate only if what counts as rational remains stable across every possible refinement.

On this view, categorical belief does not simplify a decision problem that one has already considered. Rather, beliefs are used to frame a simplified decision problem. Now, appealing to this practical role of belief, we can define a new notion of practical adequacy. Consider the set of all propositions that are relevant to one's decision problem, and define *the smallest world* as the strongest proposition in that set that one may believe when framing one's decision problem such that the set of rational choices would remain stable under every relevant refinement.[59] A belief that p is *practically adequate*** just in case p is entailed by the smallest world. Smallest worlds are the most economical perspectives that one can take on decision problems without sacrificing anything of rational importance.

The two proposals may seem very similar, and it may simply be a matter of aesthetic judgment as to which is more natural. When stability across refinements is the standard for practical adequacy, I do find it natural to prioritize the most coarse-grained decision problem that possesses this property. After all, refinement stability is a counterfactual property and smallest worlds represent an optimal solution. However, when stability across column elimination is the standard for practical adequacy, it's less clear why we should prioritize the largest set of columns we can eliminate. Why isn't every appropriate elimination just as good? Whatever one's preferences between these two approaches, the important point is that the constructive decision-theoretic framework allows us to explore different roles for categorical beliefs and along with these different roles, different notions of practical adequacy.

4.2 Minimal Condition

As I noted previously, the minimal condition that I have considered is very weak. And it may be odd that there are contexts in which we know, for example, that a fair coin will land heads on one of two tosses. Pragmatic epistemologies can certainly allow knowledge to have such features. However, it is also important to note that the proposed account can easily be modified to avoid such consequences. I started with the weakest minimal epistemic condition because that was all that was required to deal with Gettier cases. So I hoped to obey the Peircian creed to not place roadblocks to inquiry. More importantly, by starting with this condition, we gained some interesting insight into the nature of Gettier cases.

Nevertheless, I feel the pull of stronger conditions on knowledge. We could propose that one possess conclusive evidence for p or possess more than mere statistical evidence for p. One can even adopt a pragmatic infallibilism whereby, given what is deemed relevant in a context, one ought to be certain, remove all relevant doubts, or eliminate all alternatives. Thus, the specification of an appropriate minimal condition is another place for further exploration.

My aim here has not been to provide an unobjectionable pragmatic account of knowledge. Rather, I had two goals in mind. First, I wanted to lay out some general challenges for pragmatic epistemologies. Second, I hope to have offered a framework that is rich enough not only to address these particular challenges but many others as well. Thus, I hope to have showed that pragmatists need richer deliberative accounts. And once we appeal to these richer accounts, we will find that there is much more to explore within the pragmatic view of knowledge.

Appendix
Objective Relevance

To offer a more detailed account of objective relevance, let me introduce a distinction and some terminology. From the constructive point of view, there is a difference between bringing a possibility to mind and considering that possibility in one's deliberation.[60] I can bring to mind the possibility that I am a brain-in-a-vat but this does not mean that I have thereby taken this possibility into account when I deliberate. In order to take this skeptical possibility into account, I must construct my beliefs so that they account for this possibility.[61] Just thinking about a possibility does not mean that one has accounted for it.

The notion of objective relevance is meant to capture the idea that there are some actualized states whose consideration would affect the probability of the previously considered states. To capture the idea that probabilities are constructed relative to a space of relevant states, let $p^X(s)$ be the probability of s where $s \in X$ and X is the set of relevant states. Next, we must capture what it would be to take a previously unconsidered state z ($z \notin X$) into account. We can capture this by introducing the concept of refinement. Let me do so informally by way of example. Consider the coarse-grained set of states X = {Rain, No Rain}. We can refine X by taking the possibility of wind into consideration. The result will be the set of states Y = {Rain and Wind, Rain and No Wind, No Rain and Wind, No Rain and No Wind}. So if Y is a refinement of X that takes into account the unconsidered state y, $p^Y(s)$ is the newly constructed probability that has considered both y and $\neg y$. Now we can offer the following definition.

> **Objective Relevance**: A state y is objectively relevant if and only if y is actual, $y \notin X$, and for some $s \in X$ where X is the set of subjectively relevant states and Y is the refinement of X that takes y into consideration, $p^Y(s \mid y) \neq p^X(s)$.

As I noted previously, the probability can either be seen as a counterfactual subjective probability or as an evidential probability. Objectively relevant states are actual states of the world whose consideration as being true would affect probability (in one of these sense) over the set of previously

92 *Brian Kim*

considered states. For Catherine's decision problem, the state of the world in which there is an accident is objectively relevant. There are two competing explanations. It is objectively relevant because there has been an accident and if Catherine considered this possibility and took it for granted that y obtained, the resulting subjective probabilities would be affected. Or it is objectively relevant because there has been an accident and our assessment of Catherine's strength of evidence is affected by taking seriously the possibility that there may or may not have been an accident.

It is important to note that $p^Y(s \mid y) \neq p^X(s)$ does not entail that $p^Y(s \mid \neg y) \neq p^X(s)$.[62] If it did, then every skeptical alternative and its negation might count as objectively relevant leaving us with an unrealistic account of knowledge. A simple example will explain why. Consider a state of the world in which Magneto, the villain of X-Men fame, has held up traffic all over the city. Assuming that such a state obtains, the probability that there is traffic should increase. However, if one takes this possibility seriously but assumes that it does not obtain, one should not be more or less confident that there is traffic on the freeway. When it comes to outlandish possibilities, it does not matter whether they are disregarded or taken for granted that they do not obtain. The probabilities remain the same either way.[63]

One may try to reintroduce skeptical possibilities by conjoining them with true lottery-type possibilities.[64] For example, let y = Magneto has held up traffic or that Bill has not won the lottery. Is this possibility evidentially relevant? Is $p^Y(\text{Traffic} \mid y) \neq p^X(\text{Traffic})$? I can only offer a rough response. My intuitive response is that practically all of the possibilities where y is true are those possibilities where Magneto has not held up traffic and Bill has not won the lottery. And the likelihood of traffic in those possibilities is determined by the likelihood of traffic when those possibilities are ignored.[65] Therefore, since the probabilities are the same when I take these gerrymandered possibilities into account, they are evidentially irrelevant.

In addition, one might think that there are certain types of skeptical possibilities that are in fact true. For example, what about the possibility that someone is dreaming right now rather than the more direct skeptical possibility that I am dreaming. To my mind, possibilities like the former are not genuine skeptical possibilities since they are not perfectly compatible with my evidence. For that reason, it's unclear whether such possibilities are even evidentially relevant. The generic dreaming hypothesis only counts as a genuine skeptical possibility if it were more specific—if someone were dreaming in a way that perfectly matches my current experiences. However, I take it that such a possibility is not actual.

Two additional objections present themselves. First, many objective facts are misleading and in accounting for them, we would have an inaccurate assessment of the DM's epistemic state. For example, if Catherine is unaware that the President is in town, that possibility is nevertheless objectively relevant for Catherine's assessment of the likelihood of traffic. However, it may also turn out that the President's staff has decided not to travel through the

Decision Theory for a Pragmatic Epistemology 93

city in a motorcade, choosing instead to travel by helicopter. In this situation, the initial fact about the President's whereabouts is misleading. And were Catherine to account for only this possibility, her belief that there is no traffic may be weakened enough to undermine her claim to knowledge. In response, it is important to note that such facts are misleading only when considered on their own. And if all the objectively relevant facts are considered, we will be left with an objectively accurate assessment of the DM's epistemic state.

Finally, it may be objected that there are too many objectively relevant facts, resulting in a psychologically unrealistic account of knowledge. This objection does have some intuitive pull. In fact, for subjects who are experts about traffic, a very large number of states may be objectively relevant. After all, epistemically well-positioned subjects should be able to identify evidential connections that others would not be able to recognize. For example, experts may possess statistical information about the relationship between all types of weather and traffic making a multitude of facts about the weather relevant. Though I acknowledge the worry, I am not sure how problematic it is and can only offer a tentative reply. It should be admitted that in most situations, there are a great deal of objectively relevant states whether we interpret probabilities subjectively or evidentially. However, why should we think that there are an unmanageable number of them? Our boundedness as cognitive agents place an upper-bound on the number of evidential connections that we recognize. And if there is an upper-bound on what counts as evidence, there is an upper-bound on the number of objectively relevant states. Moreover, it seems plausible that we can and do make intuitive judgments about how strong a subject's epistemic state is given what is in fact true. It is exactly this type of objective epistemic evaluation that I am trying to capture.

Notes

1. I owe a debt of gratitude to Anubav Vasudevan, Brad Armendt, Declan Smithies, Guillermo Del Pinal, Katie Gasdaglis, Ray VanArragon, and John Collins for their many helpful comments on previous versions of this chapter. I'd also like to thank the audiences at NUS Formal Epistemology Workshop, Oklahoma State University, ASU pragmatic encroachment workshop, and the Midwestern epistemology workshop for their comments and advice.
2. I am following Fantl and McGrath (2009) in the narrow use of this term. However, as they note, the term is sometimes used to refer to any account that allows for pragmatic conditions on knowledge. See (Kim 2017) for a discussion of the varieties of pragmatic encroachment.
3. Pragmatic accounts like those given by Stanley (2005); Hawthorne (2004); Hawthorne and Stanley (2008); Fantl and McGrath (2009); and Weatherson (2012) have been described under the labels "subject-sensitive invariantism", "interest-relative invariantism", "anti-purism", and "anti-intellectualism".
4. Fantl and McGrath (2002) comes closest to this formulation. For ease of explanation, "believing" will be taken to be synonymous with "taking for granted".

5. In general, the standards required to be in a position to know do not always vary when the stakes are raised. To come up with general principles, the notion of risk is more appropriate than the notion of practical stakes.
6. Douven (2005) is an exception but he simply claims that Gettier cases are under-described cases that fail to identify the relevant practical factors.
7. Hawthorne and Stanley (2008, p. 578).
8. Fantl and McGrath (2009, p. 175).
9. Weatherson (2012, p. 77). He also proposes that "it is legitimate to leave a possible state of the world off a decision table iff the decision maker knows it not to obtain".
10. Brown (2008) uses Gettier situations as counterexamples to Hawthorne and Stanley's analysis.
11. While the knowledge-first epistemologist may be happy with this type of analysis, I shall not be discussing this approach.
12. If the belief is false or the subject lacks a belief, then pragmatic factors are obviously irrelevant. However, as noted previously, the pragmatic view concerns the difference between true belief and knowledge, which is accounted for in terms of whether or not the subject is in a position to know.
13. Adopting an infallibilist internalist epistemology, one may be able to rule out luck. However, such a view tends to result in skepticism. See Heller (1999) and Pritchard (2007a) for further discussion.
14. From personal discussions, I have found that the proponents of the reason-theoretic approach are not, in fact, motivated by these concerns. Instead, I believe that the use of a reason-theoretic framework allows one to focus on the relevant aspect of reasonable deliberation without committing oneself to any particular theory of rationality.
15. Finlay and Schroeder (2015).
16. A detailed pragmatic account of knowledge appears to require a detailed account of deliberation. While I am not in principle against the reason-theoretic approach, I am skeptical that such an approach will be fruitful. Reason-theoretic accounts of deliberation tend to be more coarse-grained than their decision-theoretic counterparts. For example, it is hard to talk precisely about the strength of one's reasons in the reason-theoretic framework. However, this simply speaks to the need for richer reason-theoretic accounts.
17. In Kim (2017), I lay out a variety of problems for the pragmatic viewpoint, identifying some as internal to the project and others that are external (i.e., attempt to criticize and undermine the project).
18. Even for those who reject the pragmatic view, there is no agreement as to what the right explanation is. However, the problem with current pragmatic analyses is that they do not appear to offer *any* explanation.
19. In the discussion that follows, I'll argue that Gettier cases are at an interesting point in the spectrum of cases where epistemic luck is involved. And the general framework that I develop leaves open the question of how much epistemic luck is incompatible with knowledge.
20. Warrant is the "elusive quality or quantity enough of which, together with true belief, is sufficient for knowledge" (Plantinga 1993), v.
21. Ganson (2008) defends a view of this kind. However, at the moment there has not been any detailed discussion of what it means to take p for granted in one's practical reasoning. The discussion in the literature assumes that different descriptions of this activity are equivalent for the purposes of the discussion. Some proposals include using p as a premise in reasoning, acting on p, and simplifying one's decision by assuming that p. It's not entirely clear if these are equivalent descriptions. I explore some potential differences in section 4.
22. See Thomason (1986, 2007, 2014).

Decision Theory for a Pragmatic Epistemology 95

23. Locke (2015) offers a similar discussion but focuses on the notion of premising rather than the notion of belief. The discussion there also differs in that the focus is on what is rationally permissible or appropriate rather than on what is warranted.
24. This necessary condition has been helpfully called "practical adequacy" by Anderson and Hawthorne (2019), but it is important to note that this is only a necessary condition for pragmatic warrant. In order to provide necessary and sufficient conditions, we need to account for the externalist component of warrant.
25. Alternatively, we could consider Catherine's belief that there is traffic given a particular act. However, for ease of discussion, I will work within a theory like the one presented in Savage (1972) and only consider examples where both act-state independence and the determinism of consequences holds. While many of the restrictions of Savage's theory are not important to my discussion, I avoid appealing to a theory like the one presented in (Jeffrey 1983) because, to my mind, an account on which belief and desire are separable is more compatible with the constructive approach that shall be offered in the following.
26. Savage (1972) offers the paradigmatic proof.
27. While coherent preferences for any particular problem cannot ensure a unique representation, this will not matter for our purposes. While I will talk about conditional expected utilities in addition to talk about conditional preferences, we could simply use the latter way of speaking. However, for ease of presentation, I will appeal to both locutions.
28. There's an interesting question whether we ought to be coherent across decision problems and if we should, whether this results in a demand to be coherent across every decision problem. I have discussed these issues in Kim (2014).
29. Sets of preference can be practically coherent without producing the same preference ordering. For example, one's unconditional preference ordering may be $A > B > C$ while one's preference ordering given P is $A > C > B$. Thus, there is a question about whether pragmatically warranted belief must also require a stable preference ordering. Since the difference between these two views will not make a difference to my discussion of Gettier cases, I will not consider this issue in any detail.
30. There is a lively debate about what it means for belief to aim at the truth. I do not believe that the point here depends upon any particular interpretation of this platitude. See Chan (2014) for a thorough discussion of the topic.
31. Though Fantl and McGrath (2002) presents a necessary condition for rational belief that is similar, I will develop its connection with knowledge in a way that is very different from their account. In addition, we should read the condition that one must have favoring evidence as a necessary condition for a subject to possess propositional justification. So if I am being careful, I am only proposing an account of when one is in a position to know. To turn such an account into an account of knowledge, one must have a satisfactory account of doxastic justification as well. Finally, on my account, all-or-nothing belief is independently necessary for knowledge. I reject the reduction of all-or-nothing belief to degrees of belief that possess some property. Problems for reductive accounts of rational belief are canvassed in Ross and Schroeder (2012). By requiring that the subject possess a categorical belief, we can avoid some of these problems.
32. Irrelevant possibilities, which are those whose truth or falsity have no relevance for the outcomes of a choice, also pose a problem for the account. After all, if we have favoring evidence for an irrelevant possibility, the account appears to entail that we know that such a possibility obtains. I address this issue in fn. 44.
33. See Gilboa (2009) for a summary of the debate.
34. Tversky and Kahneman (1981); Kahneman and Tversky (1984); Tversky and Kahneman (1986).

96 *Brian Kim*

35. There are, of course, some constraints on what counts as an appropriate framing. For example, the principle of act-state independence is a constraint on how a decision maker models his or her decision problems. However, most decision theorists think that we do not need to provide a comprehensive answer to this question. For example Savage writes, "I believe, and examples have confirmed, that decision situations can be usefully structured in terms of consequences, states, and acts in such a way that the postulates of [Foundations of Statistics] are satisfied. Just how to do that seems to be an art for which I can give no prescription and for which it is perhaps unreasonable to expect one" (Drèze 1990, p. 79).
36. See the essays in section 2 of (Lichtenstein and Slovic 2006).
37. Lichtenstein and Slovic (2006, p. 12).
38. In Kim (2014), I offered a detailed discussion of the challenges raised by choice behavior research for normative decision theory. I also show the constructive framework described here can address these challenges. As I note there, the proposed framework has been heavily influenced by Raiffa and Keeny (1967).
39. Some Bayesians would dismiss such judgments and argue that for a normative decision theory, every state and consequence is taken into account and our attitudes are ideally captured by a single probability and utility function (c.f. Jeffrey 1983). On this view, the only reason we restrict the possibilities we consider comes from the economic costs of taking everything into account. However, for some non-economic reasons for restricting the possibilities that we consider, see Shafer (1986).
40. This merely induces a partial ordering but if we also assume that goals have more structure then we can get more uniqueness. For example, in the extreme case where a goal determines the relative importance of values then we may be left with a utility unique up to positive linear transformation.
41. In Kim (2014), I explore how this very limited interpretation of BDT could be used to account for the more global aspects of instrumental rationality.
42. The set of states is a Boolean algebra so if the possibility of an accident is incorporated then so much the possibility that there is no accident on the streets.
43. My discussion will focus on two problems. The first problem is that almost everything can be relevant. The second problem is that we can gerrymander possibilities so that they are relevant.
44. For our purposes, the decision problem counts as objectively framed if the set of evidentially relevant states accounts for evidentially relevant matters of fact. However, there may be reasons to incorporate other objective parameters into the analysis of pragmatically warranted belief. While it will go beyond the scope of this chapter to discuss other objective decision parameters in any detail, it may be useful to consider another example. Goal judgments are subjective parameters that can be used to identify the relevant consequences. However, if there are objective values or goals that a subject ought to have, then these can be used as objective parameters that demarcate the relevant consequences. These alternative parameters may be relevant for the pragmatic account. Some have criticized pragmatic accounts as presenting a highly unstable account of knowledge. For example, Anderson and Hawthorne (2019) present cases where the option to double-check alters one's epistemic status. We can prevent this type of instability if the set of available actions is fixed from the objective point of view. Either the double-checking option is available or it is not and so considering such an option as available does not change whether or not one knows. If we embrace the full set of objective parameters, there will be a way of framing decision problems such that in the actual world, when we fix facts about both the present and the future, there is a unique decision problem the agent faces. This move, however, would not remove instability across possible worlds. I personally think that there just has not been enough discussion

Decision Theory for a Pragmatic Epistemology 97

about how stable knowledge actually is. For example, the paradoxes present in Kripke (2011) raise fascinating questions about the stability of knowledge. And so I am unsure as to how to evaluate these objections about the instability of knowledge on the pragmatic account. In addition, I raised the problem of irrelevant possibilities in footnote 2 and can appeal to the notion of an objectively framed decision problem to offer a tentative response. Objectively framed decision problems only include relevant possibilities. Since the theory only explains how to evaluate deliberative beliefs (i.e., beliefs within a deliberative context), it is silent on whether we possess knowledge of irrelevant possibilities. While I'm somewhat agnostic about how to fill in this silence, I am partial to a Peircean response. When we attribute knowledge that P to ourselves or others, we are interested in whether the question "P or not-P?" has been adequately resolved by the subject. Within any particular deliberative context, questions about irrelevant possibilities are what Peirce would call fake "paper" questions. And if no question has really been asked, who cares what the supposed answer is.

45. Stroud (2000).
46. Of course, we can adopt an evaluative perspective from which skeptical possibilities are taken seriously. We can do so because the subject herself takes these possibilities seriously or we can do so because we as evaluators take these possibilities seriously.
47. See Appendix for more discussion.
48. Lehrer (1969).
49. See the discussion of defeasibility analyses in Shope (1983).
50. Not all seemingly relevant possibilities are evidentially relevant. Suppose that when Catherine is trying to go home from the museum, a series of incredibly unlikely events prevents an accident. While these events are relevant to the story of why there isn't an accident, they are not relevant to the evaluation of likelihood since $p(\text{Accident}|\text{Unlikely}) = 0$ and $p(\neg \text{Unlikely}) \gg 1$.
51. The current approach is to be distinguished from the no false lemmas for more obvious reasons. The decision-theoretic account of Gettier cases appeals to a particular measure of the subject's strength of evidence and does not appeal to instances of reasoning. Furthermore, the proposed account works equally well even when there are no relevant false beliefs.
52. Coffman (forthcoming, p. 6).
53. See Pritchard (2007b) and Hawthorne and Lasonen-Aarnio (2009) for some proposals.
54. Coffman (forthcoming, p. 11).
55. Greco (2010; Sosa (2010).
56. Anderson and Hawthorne (2019).
57. Hawthorne and Stanley (2008) and Zweber (2016) both discuss this problem.
58. If there isn't a unique strongest belief, then I'll assume that there is some way to select between the set of strongest beliefs.
59. Refinements are relevant just in case we are refining our decision problem with a possibility that is relevant to one's decision problem. If there isn't a unique smallest world, I'll assume that there is some way to select between the set of smallest worlds.
60. This distinction is different from the distinction between updating and imaging. The latter two only apply when the relevant proposition has already been considered.
61. This is not an update and is not equivalent to any type of conditionalization.
62. This means that the types of conditional probabilities that I am considering are different from standard conditional probabilities. After all, typically $p(x|y) \neq p(x)$ if and only if $p(x|\neg y) \neq p(x)$. The reason the two types of conditional probabilities diverge is simple. Conditional probabilities assume that probabilities are defined

98 *Brian Kim*

over what one is conditionalizing upon. However, in the cases I am considering, we are conditionalizing on states that have not yet been considered so no probabilities have been defined (i.e., constructed).

63. Taking the subjective interpretation of probability, there is a simple argument for why the shift from disregarding P or $\neg P$ to believing that $\neg P$ should not always affect one's beliefs. There are a large number of outlandish skeptical possibilities. And if we raised our probabilities for every skeptical possibility (for which we possesses a non-zero confidence) that was assumed not to hold, this would give us an artificial and unreasonable way for us to become extremely confident in contingent propositions.

64. Other gerrymandered possibilities are ruled out for alternative reasons. For example, true lottery propositions conjoined with the target proposition are inappropriate since they could not be used as genuine refinements of the original space of possibilities.

65. Increasing the likelihood of Bill's winning the lottery does not change matters since practically none of Bill's winning scenarios are scenarios where Magneto holds up traffic.

References

Anderson, Charity and John Hawthorne (2019). "Knowledge, practical adequacy, and stakes." In: *Oxford Studies in Epistemology: Volume 6*. Oxford: Oxford University Press.

Brown, Jessica (2008). "Knowledge and practical reason." *Philosophy Compass* 3.6, pp. 1135–1152.

Chan, Timothy Hoo Wai (2014). *The Aim of Belief*. Oxford: Oxford University Press.

Coffman, E.J. (forthcoming). "Three approaches to Gettier Belief." In: *The Gettier Problem*. Ed. by Peter Klein Rodrigo Broges Claudio de Almeida. Oxford: Oxford University Press.

Douven, Igor (2005). "A contextualist solution to the Gettier problem." *Grazer Philosophische Studien* 69.1, pp. 207–228.

Drèze, Jacques H. (1990). *Essays on Economic Decisions Under Uncertainty*. Cambridge: Cambridge University Press.

Fantl, Jeremy and Matthew McGrath (2002). "Evidence, pragmatics, and justifcation." *The Philosophical Review* 111.1, pp. 67–94.

——— (2009). *Knowledge in an Uncertain World*. Oxford: Oxford University Press.

Finlay, Stephen and Mark Schroeder (2015). "Reasons for action: Internal vs. external." In: *The Stanford Encyclopedia of Philosophy*. Ed. by Edward N. Zalta. Winter. Retrieved from https://plato.stanford.edu/entries/reasons-internal-external/.

Ganson, Dorit (2008). "Evidentialism and pragmatic constraints on outright belief." *Philosophical Studies* 139.3, pp. 441–458.

Gilboa, Itzhak (2009). *Theory of Decision Under Uncertainty*. Cambridge Books. Cambridge: Cambridge University Press.

Greco, John (2010). *Achieving Knowledge: A Virtue-Theoretic Account of Epistemic Normativity*. Cambridge: Cambridge University Press.

Hawthorne, John (2004). *Knowledge and Lotteries*. Oxford: Oxford University Press.

Hawthorne, John and Maria Lasonen-Aarnio (2009). "Knowledge and objective chance." *Williamson on Knowledge*, pp. 92–108.

Hawthorne, John and Jason Stanley (2008). "Knowledge and action." *Journal of Philosophy* 105.10, pp. 571–590.

Decision Theory for a Pragmatic Epistemology 99

Heller, M. (1999). "The proper role for contextualism in an anti-luck epistemology." *Noûs* 33, pp. 115–129.

Jeffrey, Richard (1983). *The Logic of Decision*, Second Edition. Chicago: University of Chicago Press.

Kahneman, Daniel and Amos Tversky (1984). "Choices, values, and frames." *American Psychologist* 39.4, p. 341.

Kim, Brian (2014). "The locality and globality of instrumental rationality: The normative significance of preference reversals." *Synthese* 191.18, pp. 4353–4376.

——— (2017). "Pragmatic encroachment in epistemology." *Philosophy Compass* 12.5.

Kripke, Saul A. (2011). "Two paradoxes of knowledge." In: *Philosophical Troubles*. Collected Papers Vol I. Ed. by Saul A. Kripke. Oxford: Oxford University Press.

Lehrer, Keith and Thomas Paxson (1969). "Knowledge: Undefeated justified true belief." *The Journal of Philosophy* 66.8, pp. 225–237.

Lewis, David (1996). "Elusive knowledge." *Australasian Journal of Philosophy* 74, pp. 549–567.

Lichtenstein, Sarah and Paul Slovic (2006). *The Construction of Preference*. Cambridge: Cambridge University Press.

Locke, Dustin (2015). "Practical certainty." *Philosophy and Phenomenological Research* 90.1, pp. 72–95.

Plantinga, Alvin (1993). *Warrant and Proper Function*. Oxford: Oxford University Press.

Pritchard, Duncan (2007a). "Anti-luck epistemology." *Synthese* 158.3, pp. 277–297.

——— (2007b). *Epistemic Luck*. Oxford: Oxford University Press.

Raiffa, Howard and Ralph Keeney (1976). *Decisions With Multiple Objectives: Preferences and Value Tradeoffs*. Wiley.

Ross, Jacob and Mark Schroeder (2012). "Belief, credence, and pragmatic encroachment." *Philosophy and Phenomenological Research* 88, pp. 259–288.

Savage, L.J. (1972). *Foundations of Statistics*. New York: Dover.

Shafer, Glenn (1986). "The construction of probability arguments." *Boston University Law Review* 66.3–4, pp. 799–816.

Shope, Robert K. (1983). *The Analysis of Knowing: A Decade of Research*. Princeton: Princeton University Press.

Sosa, Ernest (2010). *Knowing Full Well*. Princeton: Princeton University Press.

Stanley, Jason (2005). *Knowledge and Practical Interests*. New York: Oxford University Press.

Stroud, Barry (2000). *Understanding Human Knowledge: Philosophical Essays*. New York: Oxford University Press.

Thomason, Richmond (1986). "The context-sensitivity of belief and desire." In: *Reasoning About Actions and Plans*. Ed. by Michael George and Amy Lanksy. Burlington, MA: Morgan Kaufmann Publishers Inc., pp. 341–360.

——— (2007). "Three interactions between context and epistemic locutions." In: *Modeling and Using Context*. Ed. by T.R. Roth-Berghofer, D.C. Richardson and B. Kokinov. Berlin: Springer, pp. 467–481.

——— (2014). "Belief, intention, and practicality: Loosening up agents and their propositional attitudes." In: *Epistemology, Context, and Formalism*. Switzerland: Springer, pp. 169–186.

Tversky, Amos and Daniel Kahneman (1981). "The framing of decisions and the psychology of choice." *Science* 211.4481, pp. 453–458.

100   *Brian Kim*

———— (1986). "Rational choice and the framing of decisions." *Journal of Business* 59.4, pp. S251–S278.

Weatherson, Brian (2012). "Knowledge, bets, and interests." In: *New Essays on Knowledge Ascriptions*. Ed. by Jessica Brown and Mikkel Gerken. Oxford: Oxford University Press.

Zweber, Adam (2016). "Fallibilism, closure, and pragmatic encroachment." *Philosophical Studies* 173.10, pp. 1–13.

6 Pragmatic Encroachment and Having Reasons

Stewart Cohen

Back in the days when I would give talks defending contextualism, I would often hear the following objection:

> Your view has the crazy result that knowledge can come and go very easily and for seemingly irrelevant reasons. You can lose your knowledge even though your evidence remains the same, there are no safety or sensitivity changes, etc.

I would respond that this is indeed a crazy result, but fortunately it is not a result of contextualism. One way of thinking about contextualism is that there are multiple "knowledge" relations. Changing contexts does not change which relations you bear to a proposition. Rather all that changes is which relation is expressed by sentences containing "know" and its cognates.

My interlocutors, by and large, seemed satisfied with this response. But then, as the 21st century approached, a number of philosophers I greatly respect began defending the crazy view. That is, they defended what has come to be known as "pragmatic encroachment" (*PE*)—the view that one's knowledge can come and go as one's practical situation changes.[1] Why were they defending such a view?

Part of the story is that these philosophers were impressed by the data that initially motivated contextualism, viz., the shiftiness of our judgments about when a subject knows. But they were worried about the consequences of treating the shiftiness as a semantic phenomenon. So these philosophers took the shiftiness out of the semantics, and located it instead in the truth-conditions (of a semantically invariant knowledge predicate).

I will argue that the coming and going of knowledge entailed by *PE* remains a serious problem. We can begin by looking at one of the cases used by Fantl and McGrath to motivate *PE*.

> On a hike, you come to a frozen pond. Do you walk across or walk around the frozen pond? Walking around will take a while, but you don't want to fall though the ice. How do you decide? The crucial issue is whether the ice is thick enough to hold you. Suppose you do some

102 Stewart Cohen

checking (you call the park authorities) and come to know that the ice is thick enough. So the ice is thick enough becomes a reason you have to believe other things (e.g. that it is perfectly safe to cross it). It would then be very odd not to allow this knowledge into your practical reasoning.[2]

Typically, we would allow that one can come to know the ice is thick on the basis of the testimony of the park authorities. Fantl and McGrath observe that if this is so, that the ice is thick enough becomes a reason you have to cross the lake. It follows that it is rational for you to cross (barring conflicting reasons).

We can represent Fantl and McGrath's reasoning as follows:

Let *Thick* = the ice is thick enough to hold me.

(1) *Thick* (combined with your total evidence and preference ordering) constitutes a sufficient reason to cross (premise)
(2) You know *Thick* (premise)
(3) *Thick* (combined with your total evidence and preference ordering) constitutes a sufficient reason *you have* to cross (from (1) & (2))
(4) It is rational for you to cross (stipulating you do not have stronger reasons not to cross) (from (3))

But this leads to a problem. For we can stipulate that because of the risk of drowning, the expected utility of crossing the lake is less than the expected utility of walking around the lake. So (4) is false. But if (4) is false, then (3) must be false. It follows that either (1) or (2) is false, or either the inference from (1) and (2) to (3), or the inference from (3) to (4), is false. But (1) is uncontroversial, and both inferences seem unimpeachable. Thus (2) must be false. Given that we would normally allow that you could know (2) on the basis the park authority's testimony, it follows that your practical situation bars you from knowing what you would otherwise know.[3]

Of course, were your practical situation to change, so the expectation for crossing was greater than the expectation for walking around, you would know again. According to *PE*, as your practical situation changes, so does what you know.

A consequence of *PE* is that you can lose any piece of knowledge (short of certainty) simply by being offered a bet with massively asymmetrical payoffs. Suppose I know I am in Tucson. Suppose further that someone offers me a bet that costs me 1 dollar if I am in Tucson, and pays me an arbitrarily large amount if I am not. If I know I am in Tucson, then I possess a good reason to decline the bet. After all, it follows from my being in Tucson, that by accepting the bet, I will lose 1 dollar. Thus it is rational for me to decline the bet. But we can stipulate that the bet has a positive expectation. Even though it is extremely likely I am in Tucson, the payoff, if I am not in

Pragmatic Encroachment and Having Reasons 103

Tucson, is arbitrarily large. Thus, it is rational for me to take the bet. By the logic of the argument we rehearsed for *PE*, after being offered the bet, I do not know I am in Tucson. In fact someone could destroy all my knowledge (short of certainty) by offering me such a bet with respect to anything I know. This is another illustration of how PE allows knowledge to come and go in counterintuitive ways. We would not have thought that what we know can change simply because we have been offered a bet.

I think this result motivates reconsidering the argument for practical encroachment. If we are going to reject pragmatic encroachment, we need to find a way to accept (2), while still denying (4). We cannot deny (1). So if we accept (2) we must reject either the inference from (1) and (2) to (3), or the inference from (3) to (4). Since the latter inference is trivial, that leaves rejecting the former inference—from (1) and (2) to (3). This inference might look trivial as well, but I will argue there are reasons to reject it.

If we reject the inference from (1) and (2) to (3), we must hold you can know *thick* where *thick* is a good reason to cross, without possessing *thick* as a good reason to cross. This position allows that you might possess *thick* as a reason to do other things, e.g., to predict that someone else my weight will make it across. But you cannot possess *thick* as a reason to cross as long as it is not rational for you to cross. That sounds very strange. But, I will argue that we are already forced into endorsing the analogous position in cases of purely epistemic rationality.

Consider a (schematic) epistemic version of the argument for pragmatic encroachment:

(1') p (along with your total evidence) constitutes a sufficient reason to believe q (premise)
(2') You know p (premise)
(3') p (along with your total evidence) constitutes a sufficient reason you have to believe q (from (1') and (2'))
(4') It is rational for you to believe q (stipulating that you possess no defeaters of p) (from (3'))

As in the practical argument, the epistemic version derives (3') from (1') and (2'). But this inference will fail given that evidential support is graded. We can demonstrate this by making the harmless (in this context) assumption that we can model evidential support as a probability. Suppose, where e is my total evidence

$$pr(p|e) < 1 \text{ and } pr(q/p) < 1.$$

Where T is the threshold for rational belief, suppose further

$$pr(q/p) > T \text{ (So (1') is true)}$$
$$pr(p/e) > T \text{ (so (2') can be true, assuming p is true, etc.)}$$

104   *Stewart Cohen*

If pr(p/e) (or pr(q/p)) is close to T, then possibly

pr(q/e) < T.

In a chain of ampliative reasoning, the risk of error accumulates And when the risk accumulates to the point that pr(q/e) < T, (4') is false.

Now we can repeat the reasoning of the practical encroachment argument that led to denying (2). If (4') is false, then (3') is false. So either (1') or (2') must be false. Given that (1') is a stipulation), and that the inferences from (1') and (2') to (3') and (3') to (4') are unimpeachable, we must deny (2').

But this is surely incorrect. For many, if not all, cases where you know p on the basis of e, there will be some q, such that pr(q/p) > T, but pr(q/e) < T.

Suppose it is part of my evidence that it is raining. I infer that the picnic will be canceled. On that basis, I infer that the children will be upset. Suppose that both the probability that the picnic will be canceled given that it is raining, and the probability that the children will be upset given that the picnic is canceled are above T. If either probability is close enough to T, the probability that the children will be upset given that it is raining is less than T. Surely it does not follow from the fact that I cannot rationally believe that the children will be upset on the basis of its raining, that I can not know the picnic will be canceled on the basis of its raining. But that is where the logic of the argument for pragmatic encroachment leads when applied to the epistemic case.

We have been exploring the possibility of denying that in the practical encroachment argument, (1) and (2) together entail (3). The problem is that denying this entailment means that you can know *thick* where *thick* is a good reason to cross, but fail to possess *thick* as a reason to cross. But now we see that we are forced to make the analogous claim in the epistemic version of the argument. We must deny that (1') and (2') together entail (3').

Let *canceled* = the picnic will be canceled.

Then we must hold that you can know *canceled*, where *canceled* is a good reason to believe the children will be upset, but fail to possess *canceled* as a reason to believe the children will be upset. I see no reason why this result should be considered worse in the practical case than in the epistemic case. Indeed we can state the result generally:

RPF (reasons possession failure):

One can know R, where R is a reason to Φ, but fail to possess R as a reason to Φ.

Here, Φ can range over actions as well as beliefs. Again, as we are forced to accept *RPF* in the case where Φ is a belief, I see no objection to accepting it in the case where Φ is an act.

Pragmatic Encroachment and Having Reasons 105

Is there a way to resist accepting *RPF* in the epistemic case? Some views concerning what constitutes your evidence may be seen as problematic for *RPF*. In the case of belief, your reasons consist of your evidence. Consider the view that your evidence is what you know ($E = K$), or what you rationally believe ($E = R$).[4] These views make trouble for *RTF*. If p is known (or rational) on the initial evidence e, then p itself becomes part of your evidence. Since by stipulation $pr(q/p) > T$, it follows that p is evidence (i.e. a reason) for believing q that you possess. This would falsify *RPF*.

But this points to a problem with $E = K/R$. Suppose you infer p from e, and thereby come to know p. If p is a reason to believe q, then you could rationally infer q from p, even though $pr(q/e) < T$. This seems wrong. You cannot make your evidence stronger simply by making inferences from it. If q is not sufficiently probable on your initial evidence e, then it is not rational to believe q even if e supports p and q is sufficiently probable on p. Intuitively, as we reason inductively, the evidential support for our conclusions declines. It is not rational to believe the last member of a long chain of inductive reasoning just because it has a high probability on the penultimate link. Yet this is what $E = K/R$ seems to yield.

We can retain *RPF* while accommodating $E = K/R$ by distinguishing between your basic evidence—your evidence that is not derived from other evidence—and your non-basic evidence. The crucial point is that evidential support is a function of only your basic evidence. We can construe this as a point about updating, *viz.*, you should update only on your basic evidence, not on your non-basic evidence. This blocks the result that if $pr(q/p) > T$, you can rationally believe q, even when $pr(q/e) < T$.

The pragmatic encroachment argument avoids the clearly false conclusion (4) by denying premise (2). But if I am right, there is an epistemic version of the pragmatic encroachment argument. And we cannot avoid conclusion (4') of that argument by denying (2'). In the epistemic version, we can avoid the false conclusion by appealing to *RPF*. I have argued that since we already have to accept *RPF* in the epistemic version, there is no need to deny (2) in the pragmatic version. Rather we can simply appeal to *RPF*. This way of proceeding has two advantages over pragmatic encroachment:

First, by applying *RPF* in both arguments, we obtain a unified solution to both the pragmatic and epistemic versions of the problem. And second, we avoid the problem that one can easily lose one's knowledge for reasons that seem epistemically irrelevant. Surely it is an unwelcome result that although I know I am in Tucson, if I am offered a bet with massively asymmetric pay-offs of the sort described earlier, I will lose my knowledge.

On the *RPF* view, I retain my knowledge that I am in Tucson after being offered the bet. Instead *RPF* allows that I do not possess that I am in Tucson as a reason to decline the bet, despite the fact that I continue to know I am in Tucson. Notice that this is consistent with my possessing that I am in Tucson as a reason to believe some other proposition, e.g., that I am in Arizona. On the *RPF* view, p can be both a good reason to believe q and a good reason to

106   *Stewart Cohen*

believe *r*. Still, if you come to know p, you may possess it as reason to believe *q* without possessing it as reason to believe to believe *r*.

Of course *RPF* is itself an unintuitive result. But given that we cannot avoid accepting *RPF* in the epistemic case, it seems that overall the *RPF* view is superior to the *PE* view.[5]

Notes

1. Jeremy Fantl and Matthew McGrath, *Knowledge in an Uncertain World* (Oxford: OUP) 2009; John Hawthorne, *Knowledge and Lotteries* (Oxford: OUP) 2003; Jason Stanley, *Knowledge and Practical Interests* (Oxford: OUP) 2008.
2. Fantl and McGrath, *ibid*. 73–74.
3. One way of cashing this out is in terms of practical adequacy, Fantl and McGrath, *op. cit*. P is practically adequate when what is rational for you to do is not sensitive to the difference between the actual probability for *p* and probability 1. You do not know *thick* because the difference its actually probability and 1 does make a difference in whether it is rational for you to cross. If you were certain of *thick*, it would be rational for you to cross.
4. For the former, see Timothy Williamson, *Knowledge and its Limits* (Oxford: OUP) 2002. For the latter, see Juan Comesana, "A Pleas for Falsehoods", *Philosophy and Phenomenological Research*, forthcoming. Comesana endorses the restriction I suggest.
5. For comments and criticism, I thank Matt McGrath and especially, Juan Comesana.

7 Pragmatic Encroachment and Closure

Charity Anderson and John Hawthorne

The idea that there is pragmatic encroachment on knowledge has been vigorously explored in recent literature, but what has been rather less explored is how pragmatic encroachment interacts with another important principle about the structure of knowledge, namely, epistemic closure. In this chapter, we plan to go some way toward remedying that. For the purposes of this chapter, we will focus on single-premise closure, which we will understand as the idea that a proposition competently deduced from something one knows (and believed on that basis) is also known.[1]

It is hard to explore the interaction between pragmatic encroachment and closure without some detailed model of how pragmatic encroachment works. To that end, section 1 presents a model for cashing out some standard subject-sensitive ideas. It is a model that we've discussed at length elsewhere,[2] and is built on the idea that one knows p only if the gap between one's strength of epistemic position for p and perfect epistemic position makes no practical difference. In section 2, we explain why that model is antithetical to closure. In section 3, we critically discuss some ways of trying to fix the model so as to restore harmony. In section 4, we discuss the interaction of closure with another idea that is used to motivate pragmatic encroachment, namely the idea that stakes make a difference to whether one knows.

1. Section 1

Pragmatic encroachment is typically motivated by combining a fallibilist view of knowledge—according to which a less than perfect epistemic position may suffice for knowledge in some settings—with the view that a less than perfect epistemic position will be insufficient for knowledge in a setting where the gap between actual and perfect epistemic position makes a decision-theoretic difference.

Following our earlier paper, here is a way to model the view. Let us suppose that strength of epistemic position is thought of as a kind of epistemic probability and is calibrated on a scale of 0–1. (We will assume that one's epistemic probabilities respect the standard probability axioms.) Let rational

108 *Charity Anderson and John Hawthorne*

action be defined in terms of expected utility where the relevant probabilities are the probabilities just alluded to.[3] In this setting, there is a natural way to make precise the idea that the gap between one's actual epistemic position and perfect epistemic position sometimes but not always makes a practical difference. Let's define one's rational preference conditional on p in the following way: one's preferences conditional on p are a matter of what is preferable given one's actual utilities and a probability space that is the result of conditionalizing one's actual probability space on p.

In a situation where one has various options to choose between, the gap makes a practical difference with respect to p if and only if one's actual preference is not the same as one's preference conditional on p.[4] This allows the following precisification of the initial idea: in a decision setting, one knows p only if one's actual preference and one's preference conditional on p match. We will call one's position with respect to p "practically adequate" in such cases.[5] (We admit that there are idealizations built into the model. But as with standard kinds of decision theory there can be all sorts of epistemic illumination provided by a model despite its idealizations.)

2. Section 2

Here we present the sorts of cases that make trouble for reconciling a practical adequacy approach to pragmatic encroachment with closure. The trouble arises when premises for which one is practically adequate and which look otherwise in good epistemic standing entail conclusions for which one is not practically adequate. Given the good epistemic standing of the premise and its passing the practical adequacy test, there will be pressure on the proponent of the view to say that one knows the premise. Given closure, one will then know the conclusion (assuming the story is filled in by supposing that one competently deduces it from the premise). But given practical adequacy failure, one will not know the conclusion. That is to say, there are cases where p is practical adequate, p logically entails q, but q is not practically adequate. Let us illustrate with a few cases.

> Case 1: One wishes to go to Foxboro. One has to choose between train A and train B. One is .95 that train A goes to Foxboro. One is .95 that train B goes to Foxboro. Train B is slightly more comfortable than Train A. As a result, one prefers to get on train B. Consider the conjunctive proposition that train A goes to Foxboro and train B goes to Foxboro. One is practically adequate for this proposition. As things stand one prefers getting on B. Conditional on the conjunctive proposition, one's preferences do not budge. That train A and train B go to Foxboro entails that train A goes to Foxboro. But one is not practically adequate for the proposition that train A goes to Foxboro. Conditional on the proposition that A goes to Foxboro, we have a situation where B is slightly more comfortable, but is also a riskier

Pragmatic Encroachment and Closure 109

option as far as getting to Foxboro is concerned (we assume sufficient probabilistic independence about where the trains go). So long as one is unwilling to risk not making it to Foxboro in order to ride on a slightly more comfortable train, getting on A will be preferable conditional on the proposition that A goes to Foxboro. One will thus fail to be practically adequate for the proposition that A goes to Foxboro.

Case 2: You are need of a clean needle. There are two needles available. You are .98 that needle A is clean and .98 that needle B is clean. (We assume that the probabilities of needles being clean are to some extent independent.) You have a choice between being given one of the needles at random or paying $1 for needle A. As things stand you prefer not to pay. Conditional on the conjunction that needle A is clean and needle B is clean you prefer not to pay. Thus, you are practically adequate for the conjunction. The context is urgent enough that conditional on the proposition that needle A is clean, you prefer to pay $1 to be given needle A. Thus, you fail to be practically adequate with respect to the proposition that needle A is clean.

Case 3: You have the choice between opening door A or staying where you are. If you stay where you are you are certain you will receive a BigMac. If you choose to open door A you are .8 that you'll receive a Whopper, .1 that you will receive Steak Frites (and no Whopper), and .1 that you will receive nothing. Your utilities are as follows: BigMac (100), Whopper (99), Steak Frites (150), and nothing (0). As things stand, you prefer to stay. Conditional on the proposition that there is a Whopper behind door A, you prefer to stay. But conditional on the proposition that there is food behind door A, you'll take door A, since conditionalizing on Food removes the risk of receiving nothing while slightly increasing the prospect of receiving Steak Frites.[6]

In this scenario, you are practically adequate for the proposition that there is a Whopper behind door A, but you fail to be practically adequate for the proposition that there is food behind door A.[7] (Note that if you think .8 is not sufficient for knowledge, it's a trivial matter to change the numbers and maintain the general structure of the example so as to accommodate a higher threshold.) A practical adequacy test on knowledge thus does not fit well with an epistemic closure principle.[8]

3. Section 3

Assuming that one wishes to preserve the principle that knowledge is closed under competent deduction (at least in the single-premise case), there are two obvious fixes for the practical adequacy idea. One fix involves a weakening of the practical adequacy requirement, and one involves a strengthening.

The weakened test requires as a necessary condition for knowledge that p not that one is practically adequate for p, but that one is either (a) practically

110 *Charity Anderson and John Hawthorne*

adequate for p or (b) p is competently deduced from something for which one is practically adequate. Consider someone who stays put in the burger case, explaining their reluctance to open door A by saying, "For all I knew there was no food behind door A". The standard pragmatic encroacher will praise that speech on the grounds that in that practical environment, the strength of epistemic position was insufficient for knowledge. But the new test does not straightforwardly vindicate that attitude, since, while practically inadequate, the proposition that there is food behind door A is entailed by the proposition that there is a Whopper behind door A and one is practically adequate for that proposition. Of course, in some cases a proposition for which one is practically adequate will be entailed by but not competently deduced from various propositions for one is practically adequate. In those cases one will not be able to derive an untoward result from the weakened test. However, practically inadequate propositions are allowed to sneak in as knowledge so long as they happen to be competently deduced from ones for which one is practically adequate.[9]

In general, the weakening may allow lots of beliefs that the pragmatic encroacher doesn't want to count as knowledge to pass the test. Given that the key motivating idea is that practical adequacy is required for knowledge, it would be strange for the pragmatic encroacher to go for this fix. In this way, weakening the practical adequacy test does not look promising.

By contrast, a fix that involves a strengthening of the practical adequacy test looks more plausible. One way to strengthen the test is to require as a necessary condition for knowledge that p not merely that one is practically adequate for p but also that one is practically adequate for every proposition entailed by p.[10] This is indeed a natural reaction to the burger case. The proposition that there is a Whopper entails that there is food.[11] Since one is practically inadequate for the proposition that there is food, one's belief that there is a Whopper fails the strengthened test. The problem with this approach is that it risks making the practical adequacy test so demanding as to yield unwanted skeptical results. Consider the following case.

> Case 4: You are offered a bet on whether it will snow tomorrow in New York. You are .9 that it will snow (SNOW), but the odds of the bet are such that your strength of epistemic position is insufficient to make taking the bet a good idea. Let us suppose that if your strength of epistemic position for SNOW were a bit higher, you would prefer to take the bet. Conditional on SNOW you should take the bet, so you are practically inadequate for SNOW. Consider another proposition for which you are .9 and which is probabilistically independent of SNOW: that your mother will go to Tesco this week (TESCO). Let's suppose you are practically adequate for this proposition. The proposition TESCO entails (TESCO or SNOW). Notice that conditional on that disjunction the probability that it will snow in New York will go up a little bit. This is because if the scenarios are probabilistically independent there will be some part of your epistemic space

Pragmatic Encroachment and Closure 111

where (not-TESCO and not-SNOW). Conditional on the disjunction, the probability of SNOW will go up, and so conditional on the disjunction you'll prefer to take the bet on SNOW. Since you fail to be practically adequate for the disjunction, given the strengthened test you will not only fail to know the disjunction, but also you will fail to know TESCO.

Elsewhere Fantl and McGrath entertain a global infection model according to which if one fails to know something through the damage incurred by pragmatic encroachment then one fails to know any proposition for which one's strength of epistemic position is the same or less.[12] If one learns to live with this, one might think that the result we've just mentioned isn't so bad. However, the damage wrought by the strengthened test cannot in general simply be accommodated by appeal to the global infection model. Change the case so that you are .9 that SNOW and .94 that TESCO. Still, conditionalizing on the disjunction will have the effect of raising the probability of both disjuncts and so you will fail to be practically adequate for the disjunction and, by the strengthened practical adequacy test, will fail to know each disjunct. In this case, although global infection poses no threat for TESCO, the strengthened practical adequacy test delivers the result that you don't know TESCO. Given the strengthened test, failing to know something of probability x doesn't just pose problems for knowing things with probability less than or equal to x. It also poses problems for knowing things with probability greater than x.

4. Section 4

The practical adequacy model is an attempt to systematize the idea that the gap between one's strength of epistemic position and perfect epistemic position destroys knowledge when the gap makes a practical difference. But there are other ideas and slogans associated with pragmatic encroachment that are not directly tied to practical adequacy. One particularly popular idea is that the stakes of a context make a difference: roughly speaking, the idea is that the higher the stakes, the harder it is to know. The literature has not been fully cognizant of the fact that this is not of a piece with the practical adequacy idea—we have argued at length elsewhere that on various natural conceptions of stakes, a stakes-theoretic approach to pragmatic encroachment is not at all the same as a practical adequacy approach.

How then does the stakes idea interact with closure? Once again, we need some moderately rigorous notion of stakes in order to pursue this question. Unfortunately, the literature offers little guidance on how the notion of *stakes* is to be spelled out. In what follows, we shall explore the closure-theoretic ramifications of one quite natural notion of stakes, one that is related to the popular idea that stakes have to do with the "cost of being wrong". We shall call this notion the "p-stakes" of an action. To calculate the p-stakes of an action we compare the expected utility of an

112 *Charity Anderson and John Hawthorne*

action conditional on p and the expected utility of that action conditional on not-p. (One calculates the expected utility of an action conditional on p by conditionalizing one's credences on p and using that updated credence distribution to calculate expected utility.) On this gloss, the larger the gap between these conditional expected utilities, the higher the p-stakes for that action.[13]

The first structural point worth observing is that a low-stakes proposition can entail a high-stakes proposition. Given closure, if one knows the low-stakes proposition one will be in a position to know the high-stakes proposition as well.

> Case 5: One has the option to receive the contents of a box. One is .9 there is a dog in the box (DOG), .09 there is a cat in the box (CAT), and .01 there is an inanimate object with –8000 utility. Let us suppose one likes dogs and cats, but one likes cats an awful lot more than dogs. One's utility for DOG is 100 and one's utility for CAT is 1000.

The expected utility conditional on there being a dog in the box is the same as the expected utility on there not being a dog there. (Since conditional on DOG, one's expected utility is 100, and conditional on not-DOG the expected utility is 100.) Thus, the p-stakes of the proposition that there's a dog in the box are maximally low since the expected utility of DOG and not-DOG are the same.

That there's a dog in the box entails that there's a mammal in the box. But the p-stakes for the proposition that there's a mammal in the box are extremely high. Conditional on not-mammal the expected utility is extremely low whereas conditional on mammal the expected utility is modestly high. So here we have a low-stakes proposition *there's a dog in the box* entailing a high-stakes proposition *there's a mammal in the box*. If one's preferred picture of pragmatic encroachment is one which endorses the "higher the stakes, harder to know" slogan, then the result will be that it is harder to know *there's mammal in the box*, despite the fact that it is entailed by the *there's a dog in the box*.

Consider another case.

> Case 6: One is considering entering a bank. We can imagine this is a paradigm "low-stakes" bank case. Nothing terrible will happen if the tills are closed. Consider the proposition that the tills are open (OPEN). Conditional on OPEN being false, if one walks in one will simply return the next day with little consequence. The differential in expected utility for entering the bank will be roughly the differential induced by the modest cost in energy to make a second trip to the bank.

Now consider the disjunction: either OPEN or it is not the case that if you enter the bank you will be tortured by aliens. This proposition is entailed by

Pragmatic Encroachment and Closure 113

OPEN. But the p-stakes for the disjunction are extraordinarily high. Conditional on the falsity of the disjunction the expected disutility of your action of entering the bank is incredibly high since you will be tortured by aliens. Here again we have the phenomenon of a low-stakes proposition entailing a high-stakes proposition.

How much will this structural fact be damaging for the advocate of pragmatic encroachment who builds his or her position on the ideology of stakes? Let us briefly describe two ways to try to contain the damage. One way is to shift to a maximal gap conception of stakes where the p-stakes of an action are some kind of function of the gaps between (i) the best-case scenario conditional on p and the best-case scenario conditional on not-p and (ii) the worst-case scenario conditional on p and the worst-case scenario conditional on not-p. Regardless of how it interacts with closure, this kind of approach is extremely unpromising since it risks flattening out the stakes difference between paradigmatic high and low-stakes cases. After all, for the fallibilist, there is a small possibility of terrible things occurring even in the "low-stakes bank case" (e.g., being tortured by aliens, the bank falling on your head, etc.) and a small possibility of fantastic things as well (being given millions of dollars by a stranger, etc.).

Of course, we can't preclude the possibility that there is some fairly natural notion of stakes that is in keeping with the ideas in the literature, but which precludes low-stakes propositions entailing high-stakes propositions. We leave it as a challenge to say what that conception is.

There is a second, initially more promising, option. Notice that in Cases 5 and 6 the high-stakes proposition is one for which one has much higher epistemic probability. One might hope that pragmatic encroachment could be developed in such a way that allows one to know a low-stakes proposition in a scenario where it entails high-stakes propositions on account of the fact that the strength of epistemic position for the high-stakes proposition is much stronger. A natural way to develop such a view would be to imagine a sliding scale. When the stakes are maximally low the requirement on knowledge is a relatively low point on a threshold, such as .9. As the stakes increase, the threshold required for knowledge increases with it. In a case where one is .9 in a low-stakes proposition there may be no obstacle to knowing a high-stakes proposition entailed by it so long as the epistemic probability of the high-stakes proposition is suitably higher.

Might one hope to reconcile the stakes idea with closure by some theory spelled out along these lines? A second structural fact is extremely damaging for any such vision. It is this: there are cases where a maximally low-stakes proposition with epistemic probability x entails a significantly high-stakes proposition whose epistemic probability is only slightly higher. We illustrate with this case:

> Case 7: One may open a door. One is .9 that there is a dog behind the door (DOG), .09 that there is a cat behind the door (CAT), and .01

114 *Charity Anderson and John Hawthorne*

that there is something awful behind it (BAD THING). One's utilities are as follows: 100 DOG, 1000 CAT, and –8000 BAD THING. The p-stakes of DOG is maximally low since the expected utility conditional on DOG is 100 and conditional on not-DOG is 100. Consider now the disjunction of (DOG or BAD THING). The epistemic probability of that proposition is only a tiny bit higher than the epistemic probability of DOG—that is, .91. Let us look next at the p-stakes of that proposition. Conditional on it being false, there is a cat behind the door, so the expected utility of opening the door is 1000. Conditional on the disjunction being true, the expected utility is 11. Thus, while the epistemic probability of the (DOG or BAD THING) is only slightly higher, the p-stakes is vastly higher.

When one reminds oneself of cases like this all hope collapses of maintaining our conception of p-stakes and combining it with closure and a sliding scale threshold tied to stakes. Of course, there is an option of formulating a conception of stakes that is more closure-friendly, but we leave it as a challenge to find a notion of stakes that is continuous with the ideas of stakes in the literature and which nicely harmonizes with closure.

We do not take ourselves to have shown that no version of pragmatic encroachment can be harmonized with closure. But we hope we have done enough to show that securing harmony is, at the very least, a difficult task. The discussion here will at least help to illuminate the variety of relevant challenges.[14]

Notes

1. Some qualification is needed to cover cases where one's knowledge of the premise is lost during the reasoning. If a change in practical environment can make knowledge go away (as the pragmatic encroacher thinks), such cases may be more frequent than we have traditionally supposed.
2. See Anderson and Hawthorne (2019).
3. Notice that we are not making assumptions about what actually goes on psychologically when preferences are formed. We do not assume that there are credences corresponding to the epistemic probabilities. And we allow that decisions are often achieved by deploying full beliefs and desires in a way that rarely involves reflecting on the epistemic probabilities.
4. For the purposes of this chapter, the crucial issue is whether one's top ranked preference changes. A more demanding option is to look at the entire ranking and see whether any ordering within the ranking changes. For discussion of this choice point, see Anderson and Hawthorne (2019).
5. Let us say that p is irrelevant to a decision just in case no Jeffrey update on p makes a practical difference. (It should be clear enough how to extend the definition of what is preferable conditional on p to what is preferable conditional on various Jeffrey updates concerning p.) Whenever p is irrelevant to the decision at hand, p is ipso facto practically adequate. Call a decision p-dependent if one's preference condition on p differs from one's preference condition on not-p. In most (but not all cases) where a decision is not p-dependent, p is irrelevant.

Pragmatic Encroachment and Closure 115

(For an exception, consider cases where one has the opportunity to pay a small amount to get the answer to the question whether p. As things stand, it is worth paying. But conditional on p and conditional on not p, one prefers not to pay).

6. See also Case 4 in the next section for another case of the practically adequate entailing the practically inadequate.
7. Note that in this particular example the decision is not p-dependent on the proposition that *there's a Whopper behind door A* (see fn 3 for a definition of p-dependence). However, this fact does not make the challenge to closure go away. In any case, it's easy to tweak the example so that the decision is p-dependent. Assume the choice is between four options: stay and bet on Whopper, stay and bet on not Whopper, open door A and bet on Whopper, open door A and not bet on Whopper, and that the odds of the bet are set in such a way that it is not good to take the bet given the current epistemic probabilities, but that taking the bet is a good idea conditional on the proposition that there is a Whopper.
8. It was brought to our attention at a late stage in the revisions process that Zweber (2016) makes a similar point to the one we advance in this section.
9. Of course, as we noted earlier one might go in for a version of pragmatic encroachment that does not give a starring role to practical adequacy. This is not the place to review the other options.
10. A milder strengthening would be to require that a belief not only be practically adequate but everything competently deduced from that belief be practically adequate as well. Similar points to those made in the following can be made for this version.
11. We may be taking liberties calling this "entailment" but the case can easily be fixed so that the entailment is straightforwardly logical.
12. Fantl and McGrath (2009) chapter 7.
13. In our (2018) we discuss some further potential refinements, as well as some ways to define the notion of the p-stakes of a decision. We will not go over those details here.
14. We are grateful to Juan Comesaña, Cian Dorr, Yoaav Isaacs, Maria Lasonen-Aarnio and Shyam Nair for helpful conversations and comments regarding the issues in this chapter.

References

Anderson, Charity and Hawthorne, John (2019). Knowledge, Practical Adequacy, and Stakes. In *Oxford Studies in Epistemology*, Vol. 6. Oxford.

Fantl, J. and McGrath, M. (2009). *Knowledge in an Uncertain World*. Oxford: Oxford University Press.

Zweber, A. (2016). Fallibilism, Closure, and Pragmatic Encroachment. *Philosophical Studies*, 173(10): 2745–2757.

8 Pragmatic Encroachment on Scientific Knowledge?

Mikkel Gerken

1. Introduction

Pragmatic encroachment theories of knowledge may be characterized as views according to which practical factors may partly determine the truth-value of ascriptions that S knows that p—even though these factors do not partly determine S's belief that p or p itself. The pros and cons of variations of pragmatic encroachment are widely discussed in epistemology. But despite a long pragmatist tradition in the philosophy of science, few efforts have been devoted to relate this particular view to issues in philosophy of science.[1] Consequently, a central aim of the present chapter is to consider how the contemporary debates over pragmatic encroachment connect to philosophy of science. Here is the plot:

In **Section 2**, I provide a general characterization of pragmatic encroachment theories and restrict the discussion to one branch of it.

In **Section 3**, I compare and contrast scientific and non-scientific knowledge and note some *trademark features* of scientific knowledge that will be relevant for the subsequent discussion.

In **Section 4**, I move from exposition to argument by presenting some cases that challenge pragmatic encroachment on scientific knowledge.

In **Section 5**, I argue that a general argument contra pragmatic encroachment theories extends to compromise pragmatic encroachment accounts of scientific knowledge.

In **Section 6**, I consider whether my arguments against pragmatic encroachment may be rebutted by embedding pragmatic encroachment in the anti-realist framework of constructive empiricism.

In **Section 7**, I conclude by arguing that the challenges for pragmatic encroachment on scientific knowledge are grave and that they cast doubt on pragmatic encroachment generally.

2. Pragmatic Encroachment Characterized

Pragmatic encroachment theories come in many forms and shapes. Some of them are metaphysical theories according to which knowledge itself is sensitive to practical factors of, for example, the subject's situation (Hawthorne 2004; Stanley 2005; Fantl and McGrath 2009). Other brands of pragmatic encroachment are semantic theories which claim that practical factors may impact the truth-conditions of knowledge ascriptions. While I will focus on the metaphysical variety, it is worth noting a general characterization (Gerken 2017: Ch. 3.1 for elaboration).

As a general approximation, pragmatic encroachment is the view that knowledge or the truth of knowledge ascriptions depends in part on practical factors and not merely on the subject's beliefs, evidence, epistemic environment and other factors that are, in DeRose's term "truth-relevant" (DeRose 2009: 24; Fantl and McGrath 2009: 178).

Pragmatic encroachment goes beyond the view that practical factors may defeat knowledge by defeating belief. In general, the view goes beyond cases in which practical factors undermine enabling conditions for S's knowledge— for example, by causing the non-existence of S, the truth of the complement clause, etc. The relevant epistemological claim is that someone who continues to believe may cease to know in virtue of a change in (salient) practical factors.

I use the phrase "knowledge ascriptions" and its cognates as shorthand for "assertive utterances" of sentences of the form "S knows that p". Given this terminology, we can state a bi-conditional that characterizes the core of *pragmatic encroachment about knowledge or "knowledge"* (henceforth PEAK):

PEAK

The true theory of knowledge or "knowledge" is a pragmatic encroachment theory if and only if practical factors may partly determine the truth-value of ascriptions that S knows that p—even though they do not partly determine S's belief that p or p itself.

Pragmatic encroachers uphold the right-hand-side of PEAK. Those who reject it are called *strict purists*. Because PEAK's right-hand-side is articulated in terms of truth-values of knowledge ascriptions, it allows for importantly different species of pragmatic encroachers. Pragmatic encroachers may be *metaphysical impurists* and take knowledge itself to be partly, although indirectly, determined by practical factors. Or they may be *semantic impurists* and take the truth-conditions or truth-values of "S knows that p" to be partly determined by practical factors.[2] Consequently, the left-hand side of PEAK is a disjunction since a pragmatic encroacher may either uphold a brand of metaphysical impurism (e.g., interest-relative invariantism) or a brand of semantic impurism (e.g., contextualism or relativism). Thus, "pragmatic encroachment" is a generic label for the family of theories that accept the right-hand side of PEAK. But, as noted, pragmatic encroachment theorists differ radically in their explanations of *why* the right-hand side of PEAK is true.

118   *Mikkel Gerken*

PEAK is more *inclusive* than Stanley's Interest-Relative Invariantism (IRI): "whether or not someone knows that p may be determined in part by practical facts about the subject's environment" (Stanley 2005: 85). This characterization excludes brands of pragmatic encroachment according to which the relevant practical interests are those of someone other than the subject—e.g., the speaker, hearer, community, or evaluator. PEAK is broader since it does not involve requirements pertaining to *whom* the practical factors concern and, as we shall see, this may be an advantage for an extension of the view to scientific knowledge. Moreover, IRI is more restrictive in virtue of being a thesis about knowledge itself, whereas PEAK's right-hand side is compatible with both metaphysical and semantic impurism. Since PEAK is articulated in terms of the truth-*values* of knowledge ascriptions, it allows that the *theoretical explanation* of the alleged truth-value variance turns on the view that knowledge itself is sensitive to practical factors or on the view that "knows" is semantically sensitive to practical factors.

However, while pragmatic encroachment should be characterized in this broad and inclusive manner, I will focus on pragmatic encroachment of the brand that subscribes to *metaphysical* impurism.[3]

3. Non-Scientific and Scientific Knowledge

Since scientific knowledge is a distinctive and important kind of knowledge, it is important to consider whether a pragmatic encroachment theory is plausible of it. Moreover, there are long-standing debates about pragmatism in the philosophy of science (for recent surveys, see Almeder 2007; Kitcher 2012).

To see how debates and theories concerning ordinary knowledge bear on scientific knowledge, we must gain some clarity about their relationship. Of course, this task is complicated by the fact that we do not have an adequate theory of either non-scientific or scientific knowledge. Indeed, the issue of how to distinguish scientific from non-scientific knowledge is not as intensely discussed as the traditional problem of demarcation: the issue concerning how to distinguish science from non-science and, in particular, pseudo-science (Popper 1934/2002; Lakatos 1981; Laudan 1983; Pigliucci and Boudry 2013). However, it is nevertheless possible to pursue some paradigmatic, albeit defeasible, trademarks of scientific and ordinary knowledge, respectively (see also Hoyningen-Huene 2013; Bird forthcoming).

Perhaps the overarching ideal or characteristic of scientific knowledge is that of objectivity. However, it is not clear that the ideal of objectivity may serve as a particularly useful trademark of scientific knowledge. One reason for this is that the ideal is extremely broad and abstract. So, without further specification, it fails to dissociate scientific knowledge from many kinds of ordinary knowledge. Consequently, I will explicate some of the more concrete trademarks of scientific knowledge that exemplify the ideal of objectivity in a more concrete manner.

Following previous work, I will focus on the difference in the *kind* of warrant characteristic of scientific and non-scientific knowledge, respectively (Gerken 2015). I assume pluralism about epistemic warrant in the sense that I assume that a belief may be both justified—i.e., internalistically warranted—and entitled—i.e., externalistically warranted.[4] It is debated how to draw internalist/externalism (justification/entitlement) distinction. Here I assume that that justification depends on the faculty of reason whereas entitlement does not (I argue for this conception in Gerken forthcoming a). Thus, warrants by perception, memory, and testimony are typically entitlements. In contrast, warrants by reasoning and understanding are typically justifications.

Importantly, there are a number of subspecies of justification. For example, accessibilist justification is roughly a warrant that may be reflectively accessed by first-person method. A subspecies of it is *discursive justification* that is, roughly, a warrant that may be *articulated* by the justified individual (Gerken 2012, forthcoming a). This requires but goes beyond first-personal accessibility and is, I suggest, characteristic of scientific warrant. A famous proclamation by Lord Kelvin is illustrative here:

> When you cannot express it in numbers, your knowledge is of a meagre and unsatisfactory kind; it may be the beginning of knowledge, but you have scarcely, in your thoughts, advanced to the stage of *science*, whatever the matter may be.
>
> (Kelvin 1883)

Kelvin's proclamation centers on the importance of numerical measurement. But its broader emphasis is the significance of the ability to express one's grounds for a scientific hypothesis and this is what discursive justification concerns. Science has become an extremely collaborative affair (Hardwig 1985; Wray 2002; Winsberg, Huebner and Kukla 2014; Kitcher 1993; Boyer-Kassem, Mayo-Wilson and Weisberg 2017). Indeed, scientific knowledge is often thought to be characteristically collective knowledge (Wray 2001; Fagan 2012; de Ridder 2014). In consequence, scientists must typically be able to articulate the epistemic reasons for accepting a hypothesis or theory. That is, since science is characteristically collaborative and collective, scientific acceptance characteristically requires an internalist species of warrant—discursive justification.

Elsewhere, I have argued that discursive justification is critical in intra-scientific testimony (Gerken 2013, 2015). Thus, I will consider discursive justification as a kind of warrant that is *characteristic of* scientific knowledge although it may not be strictly required for it. Thus, one trademark of scientific knowledge is the following:

Trademark 1

Scientific knowledge is typically backed by internalist warrants such as, paradigmatically, discursive justification whereas non-scientific knowledge

120 *Mikkel Gerken*

> *is very frequently only backed by externalist warrant (i.e., by various forms of epistemic entitlement).*

Given that scientific knowledge is typically backed by the discursive warrants through a highly systematic process, there is a sense in which it is harder to acquire. Even in cases where non-scientific knowledge is more reliable than scientific knowledge, scientific knowledge may be harder to acquire. This will be the case insofar as systematization marks a central difference between ordinary and scientific knowledge. For example, here is Hoyningen-Huene's central thesis: "*Scientific knowledge differs from other kinds of knowledge, in particular from everyday knowledge, primarily by being more systematic*" (Hoyningen-Huene 2013: 15. See also Bird forthcoming).[5] The assumption that scientific knowledge is highly systematic is connected to the *Trademark 1* in at least two ways. Firstly, because providing discursive justification tends to require a systematic effort in, for example, data collection and analysis and secondly because systematic knowledge requires discursive justification: "the defense of knowledge claims is an absolutely indispensable dimension in science's systematicity" (Hoyningen-Huene 2013: 89).

Thus, an important consequence of the systematic character and the special discursive requirements on scientific knowledge is that it is characteristically more demanding to acquire than ordinary knowledge. We may state this as another trademark of scientific knowledge.

Trademark 2

Scientific knowledge is typically more demanding to acquire than non-scientific knowledge.

Reflection on the scientific ideals of intersubjective replicability and accountability provide further reasons why scientific knowledge is standardly harder to acquire than non-scientific knowledge. The ideal of intersubjective replicability as a key mark of scientific has a long history. Popper provides a clear statement: "the objectivity of scientific statements lies in the fact that they can be inter-subjectively tested" (Popper 1934/2002: 22).

Because scientific knowledge should be replicable where possible, scientists are accountable for setting forth only well-warranted claims in a manner that explicates the warrant as clearly as possible (Kahneman 2012; Winsberg et al. 2014; Gerken 2015). Indeed, part of scientific practice is to present evidence and methodology in accordance with established protocols of one's discipline. So, we may note this as a further contrast between scientific and non-scientific knowledge.

Trademark 3

Scientific knowledge is typically intersubjectively replicable whereas ordinary knowledge is frequently not.

As mentioned, these trademarks may not amount to necessary conditions on scientific knowledge and they are certainly not individually or jointly sufficient for it. Nevertheless, they reflect commonplace characterizations of scientific knowledge that may help illuminate how arguments for and against pragmatic encroachment on non-scientific knowledge bear on scientific knowledge. Consider, for example, Hansson's encyclopedia discussion of demarcation criteria which concludes: "Science is a systematic search for knowledge whose validity does not depend on the particular individual but is open for anyone to check or rediscover" (Hansson 2014).

Although the specifics of Hansson's statement may be challenged, it reflects a commitment to an ideal of replicability that is very widely accepted in the philosophy of science. Note also that this commitment, articulated as *Trademark 3* is closely related to *Trademarks 1* and *2*. For example, replicability tends to require that the justification (such as the data and methodology) for a scientific hypothesis is articulated in *Trademark 1* which in turn helps to explain why scientific knowledge is particularly demanding to acquire *Trademark 2*.[6]

4. Challenges for Pragmatic Encroachment About Scientific Knowledge

A lot of challenges have been raised against pragmatic encroachment theories and, especially, against varieties of metaphysical impurism. In this section, I begin with two cases that target pragmatic encroachment on scientific knowledge specifically. I think that the cases have some force considered on their own. But they are strengthened by reflection on the trademarks of scientific knowledge sketched previously.

4.1 Basic Cases

Let us consider two cases of stakes variation that should make life uncomfortable for pragmatic encroachers about scientific knowledge.

4.1.1 Personal Stakes Variation

The first case that I will consider is one in which two scientists have gathered the exact same amount of evidence for accepting the hypothesis that p although it is extremely important for one scientist but not for the other.

Personal Stakes Variation

Seana has just finished her PhD and she is now applying for academic positions. Unfortunately, her skills are hard to transfer. So, if she does not get an academic position, it will take her years to find a job that will enable her to pay off her significant loans. Seana has gathered very

122   *Mikkel Gerken*

substantive evidence for p and now believes that it is true. So, she considers making p the central hypothesis in her applications since this would strengthen them. However, she is aware that if p turns out to be false, it will eventually be held against her that she made it central and this would likely mean the end of her academic career. As a matter of fact, p is true.

Sean is a full professor late in his career who is now planning to retire. Fortunately, he has saved up for retirement. So, he simply looks forward to finishing his projects in a timely manner. However, he has come across the hypothesis that p which he thinks would be fun to investigate. Sean has gathered very substantive evidence for p and now believes that it is true. He considers making p central in a public lecture instead of merely covering old material. Moreover, he is aware that if p turns out to be false, it would not be held against him or have negative consequences for him given that he is close to retirement. As a matter of fact, p is true.

Since the stakes associated with p are considerably higher for Seana than for Sean, a prominent metaphysical brand of pragmatic encroachment will have it that Seana does not know whereas Sean does. This brand of pragmatic encroachment is one that upholds *subject*-sensitivity according to which it is the practical factors relevant to the subject of a knowledge ascription that partly determines whether she knows. For example, the stakes for Seana are so high that she cannot rationally act on p whereas Sean can rationally act on p (Hawthorne 2004; Stanley 2005; Fantl and McGrath 2009). However, in the context of a scientific investigation, this assumption appears perhaps even more problematic than in the case of ordinary knowledge. For example, it clashes with *Trademark 3* that scientific knowledge should be intersubjectively replicable. Assume, for the sake of the argument, that we ascribe Sean scientific knowledge that p on the basis of *n* trials of some experiment. On a natural understanding of "intersubjective replicability" in *Trademark 3*, any other scientist running *n* trials of the same type of experiment should also be able to acquire scientific knowledge that p on this basis. But according to the version of pragmatic encroachment in question, Seana would not be able to replicate Sean's scientific knowledge by way of *n* trials of the relevant experiment.

This diagnosis runs counter to the overarching idea of scientific objectivity. At least, rejecting this runs the risk of compromising *Trademark 3* according to which scientific knowledge is intersubjectively replicable. More generally, the assumption that subjective stakes are partial determiners of scientific knowledge clashes with the overarching scientific ideal of objectivity.

The case does not make for a knock-down-drag-out argument. For example, it does not show that *no* kinds of practical factors affect the truth-values of knowledge ascriptions.[7] On the other hand, it suggests that in a very central case type pragmatic encroachers are committed to a problematic

Encroachment on Scientific Knowledge   123

consequence given the trademarks of scientific knowledge. Consequently, the case puts pressure on the idea that subjective stakes partly determine whether the subject has acquired scientific knowledge. So, it exemplifies my strategy of abductively compromising pragmatic encroachment from various angles. To this end, let us consider another variety of stakes variation.

4.2.2. General Stakes Variation

Another stakes variation case may reinforce the pressure on pragmatic encroachment on scientific knowledge form another angle. Moreover, this case is more robust against certain responses than the case considered previously.

General Stakes Variation

A scientific hypothesis, H, rests on a set of extraordinarily well warranted propositions, E, and the specific proposition, p. H is extremely important insofar as public policy issues which will affect the lives and deaths of millions of people hinge on whether H is true or false. Consequently, the scientific community has investigated the basis for H and have acquired a compelling set of evidence, E, for p. Now most scientists believe that p is true and accept H.

A scientific hypothesis H*, rests on a set of extraordinarily well warranted propositions, E*, and the specific proposition, p. H* is not important since no public policies are related to H* and nothing of any practical importance seems to hinge on whether p is true or false. Nevertheless, the scientific community has investigated the basis for H* and have acquired a compelling set of evidence, E, for p. Now most scientists believe that p is true and accept H*.

Since the general stakes associated with H are higher than those associated with H*, pragmatic encroachers who are metaphysical impurists appear to be committed to the following assumption: The scientists investigating H do not know that p on the basis of E whereas the scientists investigating H* know that p on the basis of E.

Again, this assumption is in *prima facie* conflict with the scientific ideal of objectivity. More specifically, it does not appear to cohere very well with *Trademark 3*, the ideal of replicability. According to the brand of pragmatic encroachment under consideration, the scientists investigating the low-stakes hypothesis, H*, have scientific knowledge that p. So, it seems odd to deny that they have successfully replicated the scientific knowledge that p. But the group of scientists investigating the high-stakes hypothesis, H, do not have scientific knowledge that p. So, it is not possible to replicate it.

Consider now the scientists investigating the high-stakes hypothesis, H, who are said to lack scientific knowledge that p. Given this assumption, they cannot have replicated the knowledge that p acquired by the scientists

124   *Mikkel Gerken*

investigating the low-stakes hypothesis, H*. But this seems odd since they have obtained type-identical evidence for p as the other group of scientists. Perhaps pragmatic encroachers are willing to bite these bullets or perhaps there is another way out of this conundrum. But the onus is on the pragmatic encroachers to show the way.

Further problems arise once we consider the relationship between scientific knowledge and ordinary knowledge. Consider, for example, the following case:

Lay High/Sci Low

The owner of a dive center, S, is taking a marine biologist, S*, on a tour of a local reef. During the dive, they see a number of white corals and both form the belief that the reef is beginning to suffer from coral bleaching (henceforth p).[8]

If the reef is bleaching, this will have disastrous consequences for S who owns a dive center and whose livelihood depends on a healthy reef. Consequently, S includes the statement that the reef is beginning to suffer from coral bleaching in one of her letters to a local newspaper of the area.

If the reef is bleaching, it will not have any consequences for S* and would not be a discovery of any significance in S*'s scientific community. Nevertheless, S* includes the statement that the reef is beginning to suffer from coral bleaching in one of her scientific articles in a marine biology journal.

In this case, the type of pragmatic encroachment under consideration will have it that the layperson, S, in high stakes does not know that the reef is beginning to suffer from coral bleaching whereas the scientist, S*, in low-stakes does know. However, they both have the exact same evidence and that it is evidence of a type (unsystematic visual perception) that may be assessed without scientific expertise. So, it appears problematic to ascribe scientific knowledge to S* and deny that S possesses ordinary knowledge. The *Trademarks 1* and *2* reinforce the impression that S* should not be ascribed scientific knowledge on the basis of unsystematic perceptual evidence in cases where ordinary knowledge (on the basis of such evidence) is denied.

According to *Trademark 1*, scientific knowledge typically requires *discursive justification* of which S* has very little. Indeed, it would seem that for us to ascribe scientific knowledge to S* that the reef is bleaching, evidence would have to be gathered and analyzed in a systematic manner that S* could cite as reasons in favor of her hypothesis. Moreover, according to *Trademark 2*, scientific knowledge is typically harder to acquire than ordinary knowledge. But pragmatic encroachment on scientific knowledge appears to be committed to the claim that S* has acquired scientific knowledge on a basis that is insufficient for ordinary knowledge.

Consequently, ascribing scientific knowledge for one person and rejecting ordinary knowledge for another although they are in the same epistemic position is highly problematic. We may call this problem for the pragmatic encroacher *"the problem of demanding knowledge"*. The present version of the problem is particularly pressing for pragmatic encroachment about *scientific* knowledge because it arises from reflection about what is characteristic about scientific knowledge.

5. Extending the Argument Argument

As mentioned, pragmatic encroachment has seen its fair share of case-based and principled objections (Neta 2007; Blome-Tillmann 2009). Here I will consider an argument against pragmatic encroachment that I have given elsewhere (Gerken 2017) and argue that it extends to the case of pragmatic encroachment on scientific knowledge. The basic of the argument is that if practical factors even indirectly and partly determined the truth-values of knowledge ascriptions, it should be natural to appeal to them as reasons in *arguments* for and, more straightforwardly, against knowledge ascriptions. But this is far from natural. I call the argument the Argument Argument and here is an instance of it applied to scientific knowledge:

The Argument Argument

A1. The true theory of scientific knowledge or "scientific knowledge" is a pragmatic encroachment theory only if practical factors may partly determine the truth-value of scientific knowledge ascriptions.

[By PEAK]

A2. If practical factors may partly determine the truth-value of scientific knowledge ascriptions, then ((reasonably) believed) practical factors can be good partial epistemic reasons to ascribe/deny scientific knowledge.

A3. It is not part of our reason-giving practices to cite ((reasonably) believed) practical factors as partial epistemic reasons in arguments for ascribing/denying scientific knowledge.

A4. If it is not part of our reason-giving practices to cite ((reasonably) believed) practical factors as partial epistemic reasons in arguments for ascribing/denying scientific knowledge, then ((reasonably) believed) practical factors cannot be good partial epistemic reasons to ascribe/deny scientific knowledge.

A5. ((Reasonably) believed) practical factors cannot be good partial epistemic reasons to ascribe/deny scientific knowledge.

[A3, A4, MP]

A6. Practical factors may not partly determine the truth-value of scientific knowledge ascriptions.

[A2, A5, MT]

126 *Mikkel Gerken*

A7. The true theory of scientific knowledge or "scientific knowledge" is not a pragmatic encroachment theory.

[A1, A6, MT]

I have specified the original Argument Argument to concern scientific knowledge and "scientific knowledge". Thus, A1 is an instance the left-to-right direction PEAK sketched in the preceding. Likewise, the motivation for A2 is similar to the motivation that I have articulated in some detail elsewhere (Gerken 2017). The basic idea underlying A2 is that a factor that bears (even partly and indirectly) on some claim may be cited as a reason for and, more easily, against that claim in an explicit argument. Thus a scientist may naturally say:

(i) There could be water on Planet X. But we do not at present have any evidence for the hypothesis. Therefore, we do not know that there is water on Planet X.

Given a conversational setting where all other necessary conditions on scientific knowledge are presupposed to be met, a scientist may even say:

(ii) After years of investigation, we have now found a wide array of excellent evidence that there is ice on Mars. Therefore, we now know that there is ice on Mars.

In contrast, it is not part of scientists' practice to cite practical factors in arguments concluding that some scientific hypothesis is known. To see this, consider, in contrast with (i) and (ii), the following:

(iii) Our lab will be defunded if it is false that rising ocean temperatures contribute to bleaching of coral reefs. Therefore, we do not know that rising ocean temperatures contribute to bleaching of coral reefs.

Likewise, a scientist with limited evidence that molecules X and Y bind will have a short career if she argues for this claim as follows:

(iv) It turns out that it does not matter to us or anyone else if molecules X and Y bind. Therefore, we know that molecules X and Y bind.

Given the infelicity of (iii) and (iv), A3 is plausible even though the unqualified "knowledge" is replaced with "scientific knowledge". A4 is motivated by the assumption that ordinary and scientific reason-giving in overt arguments is at least *prima facie* evidence for what is and is not a good epistemic reason (see Gerken 2017: Ch. 4.3 for the full story). Indeed, to insist that scientists are misguided in not citing practical factors in arguments for or against scientific knowledge ascriptions would appear to amount to an error-theory of scientific practice.

Thus, the *Argument Argument* appears to generalize to compromise the idea of pragmatic encroachment on scientific knowledge. In fact, the argument might be even stronger with regard to scientific knowledge. After all, citing highly contingent practical factors as reasons in arguments for regarding some scientific hypothesis as scientific knowledge flies in the fact of the overarching scientific value of intersubjective objectivity.

Before moving on, it should be noted that the conclusion is entirely compatible with assuming that scientists may be influence by practical factors in choosing which theory to *accept* in the sense of adopting as a working hypothesis for practical purposes or further research (Douglas 2009; Brown 2013; Elliott and McKaughan 2014; Miller 2014). Likewise, the conclusion is compatible with the idea that practical factors bear on whether it is appropriate to provide scientific expert testimony concerning a scientific theory or hypothesis (Steele 2012. See also Author forthcoming b). The argument only concerns scientific knowledge and the sort of arguments scientists give for ascribing or denying it.

6. Pragmatic Encroachment and the Scientific Realism/Anti-Realism Debate

The arguments given so far may appear to presuppose a framework of scientific realism. After all, they appeal to the overarching ideal of objectivity and make realistically flavored claims about, for example, the nature of evidence and the aim of scientific theories. Moreover, Roush has suggested that realist theories cannot accommodate the idea that practical factors can bear on theory acceptance. Specifically, she suggests that the realist

> can never get to the point where other reasons become legitimate positive reasons for acceptance. This is because if the realist ever got to the point where she had discharged her epistemic duty, there would be only one theory left to choose from.
>
> (Roush 2007: 182)

Consequently, it is important to consider whether the case against pragmatic encroachment is most plausibly embedded in a framework of scientific anti-realism.

The discussions surrounding scientific realism have many facets—the status of unobservables, laws of nature, scientific explanation, the aim of science etc. In consequence, the present discussion will have to be preliminary. This all the more so because the philosophy of science features substantive debates about how best to characterize scientific realism and scientific anti-realism. Consequently, I will consider a somewhat minimal textbook

128 *Mikkel Gerken*

characterization of scientific realism (e.g., Bird forthcoming; Godfrey-Smith 2009; Chakravartty 2011). According to such a characterization of scientific realism, scientific theories and hypothesis are

>SR 1: evaluable in terms of (approximate) truth of an objective reality.
>SR 2: reasonably aiming at (approximate) truth of an objective reality.

This characterization does not require that scientific theories *be* (approximately) true. Rather, it says simply that they may be *assessed* in terms of truth of an objective reality and, hence, that there is such an objective reality. Standardly, the notion of objectivity is characterized in terms of mind-independence or theory-independence (e.g., Psillos 1999: xix).

Often further conditions are included in the characterization of scientific realism.[9] Such further conditions may include the view that unobservable entities hypothesized by the scientific theories genuinely exist and that true theories explain observable phenomena (e.g., Bird forthcoming; Chakravartty 2011). But I will set aside discussions about unobservable entities and scientific explanation in order to focus on metaphysical scientific anti-realism which rejects SR 1 and pragmatic varieties of constructive empiricism which rejects SR 2.

6.1 Metaphysical Anti-realism

One radical kind of scientific anti-realism rejects SR 1 on metaphysical grounds by rejecting the idea that theories may truly represent an objective reality. Given that scientific theories, according to such an anti-realism, are not truth-evaluable SR 2 is rejected as a consequence. Likewise, further claims associated with scientific realism—such as the existence of unobservable entities—are rejected as a consequence of the rejection of SR 1. Thus, the characteristic feature of such a radical metaphysical anti-realism is the rejection of metaphysical commitment to the existence of an objective (mind or theory independent) reality. Given this stance, the rejection of the rest of the anti-realist commitments ensues.

Given that such a metaphysical anti-realism is hard to square with strict purism about scientific knowledge, one might think that it would be an apt ally for pragmatic encroachment theories about scientific knowledge. After all, if the arguments against pragmatic encroachment on scientific knowledge hinges on a realist assumption such as SR 1, rejecting that assumption would appear to amount to a defense of pragmatic encroachment on scientific knowledge.

However, the putative alliance between metaphysical anti-realism and pragmatic encroachment on scientific knowledge may be untenable for pragmatic encroachers. The reason why is that pragmatic encroachment on scientific knowledge is not clearly coherent with metaphysical anti-realism insofar as the relevant kind of knowledge is presumed to be factive.

Encroachment on Scientific Knowledge 129

Given factivity of scientific knowledge, scientific theories and hypotheses are known only if they are true of their subject matter. But this appears to presuppose that the belief, theory or hypothesis can be evaluated with regard to truth of this subject matter. So, a pragmatic encroacher would at least have to commit to an anti-realist theory of truth. However, pragmatic encroachers do not typically seek to *replace* the traditional truth requirement on knowledge with practical factors or to revise it with an anti-realist account of truth. Rather, the view is typically the much more modest claim that the truth requirement must be supplemented with a pragmatic requirement. Roughly, that knowledge, and *a fortiori* scientific knowledge, requires that the epistemic strength of subject's belief, theory or hypothesis must match a threshold determined in part by practical factors. So, an alliance between pragmatic encroachment theories on scientific knowledge and metaphysical anti-realism runs the risk of abandoning the explanandum of scientific knowledge in the process of defending the pragmatic encroachment theory of it. This may amount to relieving the headache by cutting off the head.

Of course, the matter is complex and I emphasize that I have not sought to argue that all species of pragmatic encroachment on scientific knowledge are incompatible with all species of metaphysical scientific anti-realism. However, an alliance between the two views will at least render pragmatic encroachment theories on scientific knowledge a rather radical view. In consequence, I will consider whether a more moderate scientific anti-realism might be more suitable.

6.2 Constructive Empiricism

The key claims of constructive empiricist views are often regarded as more moderate than the ones that reject SR 1. A characteristic claim of constructivist empiricist brands of scientific anti-realism is the denial of SR 2—the view that scientific theories and hypothesis should aim at truly representing an objective reality. Rather, the aim of scientific theories and hypothesis should aim at being empirically adequate—i.e., compatible with observable data (van Fraassen 1980. See also Monton 2007). Constructive empiricism is compatible with the idea that scientific theories and hypotheses—including those concerning or postulating unobservable entities—may be true and, it in this regard it is not in conflict with the idea that scientific knowledge entails truth. However, it is empirical adequacy rather than truth that is, according to constructive empiricism, the proper aim of scientific theories and hypotheses. Van Fraassen characterizes empirical adequacy as consistency with direct observation and this has led to an extensive discussion about the distinction between observation, detection, and theorizing (Fodor 1984; Churchland 1985; Hacking 1985; Ladyman 2000; Dicken and Lipton 2006; Muller and van Fraassen 2008). While this cluster of issues raises challenges to constructive empiricism that anyone who accepts it must

130   *Mikkel Gerken*

address, I will, for the purposes of focusing the present discussion, set aside these important debates and turn to the issue of theory choice. For it is here pragmatic considerations enter the constructive empiricist framework in a way that might intersect with pragmatic encroachment.

Often multiple empirically adequate theories are available and in consequence constructivist empiricists face the task of choosing between them. Such problems of empirical underdetermination and theory choice are not unique to constructive empiricism. However, the problem of empirical underdetermination is particularly pressing for constructive empiricism since admissible data is restricted to *observable* data. Given this restriction, the range of empirically adequate theories widens. Roush, who pursues constructive empiricism as a framework that can accommodate social values in science, notes this asymmetry between scientific realism and constructive empiricism as follows: "For a given domain, there is only one true theory, whereas there are in general many empirically adequate ones" (Roush 2007: 167).

Van Fraassen addresses the problem of theory choice in two moves. The first move consists in introducing the idea of permissible *acceptance* of a scientific theory or hypothesis. Acceptance differs from belief that the theory is true insofar it only "involves as belief only that it is empirically adequate" (van Fraassen 1980: 12).

The second move requires a little more discussion. It is a pragmatic move that consists in including pragmatic criteria for acceptance of scientific theories and hypotheses: "because the amount of belief involved in acceptance is typically less according to anti-realists, they will tend to make more of the pragmatic aspects" (van Fraassen 1980: 13). For example, van Fraassen takes it to be an advantage of a theory if it is "mathematically elegant, simple, of great scope, complete in certain respects: *also* of wonderful use in unifying our account of hitherto disparate phenomena, and most of all, explanatory" (van Fraassen 1980: 87). Of course, scientific realists may argue that these properties of a theory are truth-relevant and, hence, epistemically beneficial. But van Fraassen argues to the contrary in several cases. For example, he insists that simplicity is not an indicator of truth (van Fraassen 1980: 90). More subtly, van Fraassen argues that explanation is context-dependent and that the contextual variance is what counts as a good explanation (van Fraassen 1977, 1980). In his own words, an explanation is "evaluated vis-à-vis a question, which is a request for information . . . what is requested differs from context to context" (van Fraassen 1980: 156). Moreover, the context is partly determined by the *interests* of those seeking an explanation. So, in the case of scientific explanation, the interests of the scientific community partly determine whether an explanation is good (van Fraassen 1980).[10] So, since the choice of theory or hypothesis depends on its explanatory qualities, such choices also depend on interests and similar practical factors relevant to the scientific community. In consequence, certain practical factors may "provide reasons to prefer the theory independently of questions of truth" (van Fraassen 1980: 88).

Encroachment on Scientific Knowledge   131

One consequence, according to Roush, is that constructive empiricism is distinctively apt to accommodate social values: "For the constructive empiricist, social values can legitimately play a role in grounding choices among theories when these are choices among theories all of which are legitimately believed at a given time to be empirically adequate, because the choice of one among these theories is a pragmatic affair" (Roush 2007: 168). More generally, constructive empiricists may emphasize the usefulness of a theory—for example by its potential to make predictions about the area of reality that matters to the scientific community or, on some varieties of the view, the broader community that it serves. The key point, however, is that practical factors may serve as a "deadlock breaker" when scientists face a choice of accepting one among incompatible theories or hypotheses that are believed to be equally empirically adequate.

Such a pragmatic aspect of constructive empiricism appears to mark an important area of overlap with pragmatic encroachment theories of scientific knowledge. However, before exploring this potential alliance, one issue must be addressed. This is the issue as to whether the notion of acceptance may serve in an account of scientific knowledge as a scientific counterpart of belief in an account of non-scientific knowledge. Although this is a substantive issue, I will for the present purpose assume that an accepted hypothesis may be scientifically known insofar as it is true and other conditions are met. Note that to say that acceptance may serve as a as a scientific counterpart of belief in an account of scientific knowledge is *not* to reject the distinction between belief and acceptance. Rather, what is granted is that another attitude than belief—namely, acceptance—may *replace* the belief-condition in an account of scientific knowledge. Thus, a scientist may be said to know a hypothesis that she does not believe. This assumption is not entirely unmotivated since there is a tradition in the philosophy of science of allowing collective acceptance to replace the relevant analog of belief in an account of scientific knowledge (see Cohen 1989; Wray 2001. See also de Ridder 2014). Yet, this assumption may in some ways be contrary to the spirit of constructive empiricism.[11] But since pragmatic encroachers (of the metaphysical variety) are theorizing about knowledge and typically include a doxastic condition on it, the assumption that acceptance may do the job appears to be required.

Given this assumption, a *variety* of constructive empiricism may emerge as a potential ally for theories postulating pragmatic encroachment on scientific knowledge. This variety is one according to which practical factors partly determine whether scientists are permitted to accept a hypothesis and, consequently, whether the hypothesis may be (scientifically) known. Such a variety of constructive empiricism may appear to provide the right mix between consistency with the very idea of scientific knowledge and pragmatic features that aligns with pragmatic encroachment theories in a principled manner. Thus, it appears that there is an independently motivated framework in the philosophy of science which can naturally harbor pragmatic encroachment theories of scientific knowledge.

132 Mikkel Gerken

Moreover, this combination of views may have some force in responding to cases such as *PERSONAL STAKES VARIATION*. According to this view, neither Seana's nor Sean's personal stakes are determining factors. Rather, the relevant stakes are those which are relevant to the general scientific community and this aspect of the account provides some stabilization. Of course, this response is at odds with specifically *subject*-sensitive brands of pragmatic encroachment (Stanley 2005). However, the response is compatible with the right-hand-side of PEAK which does not specify what the relevant practical factors are and to whom they apply. In fact, pragmatic encroachers of the subject-sensitive variety may say that this is a difference between ordinary and scientific knowledge. Secondly, some pragmatic encroachers have independently sought to "stabilize" stakes variation by invoking community interests instead of individual ones (Grimm 2015; Hannon 2015). So, the combination of this variety of pragmatic encroachment theories of scientific knowledge and the outlined variety of constructive empiricism may form a broader framework that is capable of addressing some specific problems. Indeed, constructive empiricism has been seen as a background framework that best harbors the claim that the value-free ideal of science cannot be upheld. As mentioned, Roush suggests that constructive empiricism "may be the only way to grant a legitimate role to social values in theory choice" (Roush 2007: 166). Thus, it is worth considering whether an alliance between pragmatic encroachment and constructive empiricism may be formed.

6.3 Challenges for the Alliance Between Constructive Empiricism and Pragmatic Encroachment

In the previous section, I have done my best to align pragmatic encroachment theories on scientific knowledge with a variety of a broader and independently motivated (if controversial) framework within the philosophy of science. In this section, I will argue that there are significant costs to such an alliance. Furthermore, some of the fundamental problems for pragmatic encroachment theories of scientific knowledge persist despite it.

One concern is that the practical factors that constructive empiricists typically include in an account of theory *acceptance* are rather different from the sort of practical factors that pragmatic encroachers typically appeal to. The differences pertain both to the substance of the practical factors and the role they play. A substantive difference is that the practical factors involved in choice of acceptance of scientific theory or hypothesis are most naturally seen as pertaining to the *usefulness* of the theories or hypotheses under consideration. In contrast, pragmatic encroachers have often focused on the stakes associated with the complement clause of the knowledge ascription although stakes are often merely indicating actionability (Fantl and McGrath 2009; Gerken 2017: Ch. 12).

Encroachment on Scientific Knowledge   133

However, it is not clear how usefulness and stakes are supposed to be related. This is indicated by reflection on the distinct *roles* that practical factors play in a constructivist account of theory/hypothesis acceptance and in pragmatic encroachment theories of scientific knowledge, respectively. Indeed, these different roles of practical factors may give rise to a little dilemma. On the one hand, if a high-stakes hypothesis is assumed to be one that it is *not* pragmatically useful to accept, it is not clear that the practical factors concerning usefulness may play the role of "deadlock breaker" between incompatible but empirically adequate theories of hypotheses. On the other hand, if a high-stakes hypothesis is assumed to be one that it *is* pragmatically useful to accept, a considerable tension rears its head. For pragmatic encroachers typically have it that the higher the stakes pertaining to p, the harder it is to know that p. But this is contrary to the idea that the higher the stakes are, the easier it is to be rationally permitted to accept a hypothesis and, hence, easier for that hypothesis to be a candidate of scientific knowledge. Naturally, there is amble room for theoretical development here. So, I set forth the dilemma as a principled challenge that must be addressed to bring pragmatic encroachment theories in a mutually supporting alignment with constructive empiricism. In particular, the dilemma may indicate that the differences that pertain to acceptance may run so deep that it endangers any real alliance between pragmatic encroachment and constructive empiricism. So, let us revisit this issue.

Recall that to align pragmatic encroachment theories of scientific *knowledge* with constructive empiricism, we had to assume that acceptance of a hypothesis could meet the doxastic requirement on scientific knowledge. However, according to constructive empiricism, the practical factors only bear on the permissible acceptability of a theory. In contrast, pragmatic encroachment has a further commitment concerning the impact of practical factors. Indeed, pragmatic encroachers are careful to note that their theory does not merely postulate that practical factors may determine whether a subject is inclined to believe that p. Recall that this is reflected in PEAK's right-hand-side according to which "practical factors may partly determine the truth-value of ascriptions that S knows that p—*even though they do not partly determine S's belief that* p" (added emphasis).

Indeed, a stock *objection* to pragmatic encroachment theories of knowledge is that practical factors—such as high stakes—may defeat knowledge by defeating belief but that knowledge is defeated *only* in this type of cases (Bach 2005; Weatherson 2005. But see also Ganson 2008; Nagel 2010). In response, pragmatic encroachers argue that the theory involves the *further* claim that even when the relevant doxastic conditions is met, knowledge may be *epistemically* defeated by practical factors such as high stakes (for elaboration, see Gerken 2017: Ch. 3 and 12). Given this central aspect of pragmatic encroachment, however, the similarity between constructive empiricism and pragmatic encroachment appears to be a superficial one that covers over a deeper difference. For the practical factors are, according to

134 *Mikkel Gerken*

constructivist empiricism bearing on the issue of acceptance whereas pragmatic encroachment is committed to the considerably stronger thesis that practical factors bears on the distinctively *epistemic* status that goes beyond the doxastic requirement on knowledge.

So, even if we have good pragmatic reasons for accepting (in van Fraassen's sense) an empirically adequate theory, this is a far cry from the claim that these pragmatic reasons bear on whether we know the theory in question. In fact, van Fraassen himself appears to reject the latter claim: "pragmatic virtues do not give us any reason over and above the evidence of empirical data, for thinking that a theory is true" (1980: 4). Indeed, he claims that pragmatic reasons for theory acceptance "cannot rationally guide our epistemic attitudes and decisions" (van Fraassen 1980: 87).

Roush is also clear that constructive empiricism only accommodates a limited role for practical factors:

> the choice between two epistemically tied rivals that according to CE we legitimately make after the evidence is in is not a choice about which theory is closer to the truth, is more empirically adequate, or has more evidence in its favor. It is a choice about which theory serves better our practical goals.
>
> (Roush 2007: 177)

Thus, the impact of social values on science that Roush takes constructive empiricism to accommodate is far weaker than pragmatic encroachment on scientific knowledge. Indeed, Roush highlights that the brand of constructive empiricism that she is developing "has the feature that we can acknowledge a legitimate role for social values in theory choice while not admitting that social preferences can be reasons to believe a theory true (or empirically adequate)" (Roush 2007: 180). Thus, both van Fraassen and Roush, who regard constructive empiricism as providing room for social values, are clear that the brand of pragmatism involved in constructive empiricism falls short of what is required for pragmatic encroachment on scientific knowledge.

Once we recognize this point, it may also be recognized that an assumption that I made for the sake of argument is far from benign. This is the assumption that acceptance could serve as the doxastic condition of scientific knowledge. However, it is clear that theory acceptance may be *rationalized* by practical factors in a manner that is fundamentally different from belief that a theory is true (or empirically adequate). Consequently, it is very implausible that a merely accepted theory amount to scientific knowledge in cases of underdetermination of evidence. That is, if an empirically adequate theory A is accepted over an empirically adequate theory B on the basis of practical factors, then both realists and constructive empiricist should reject that theory A is known. After all, theory B is an undefeated defeater to theory A and the practical factors do nothing in defeating it.

Encroachment on Scientific Knowledge 135

Finally, it is important to note that the combination of pragmatic encroachment on scientific knowledge and constructive empiricism does not address all of the problems mounted against the former. For example, the instance of *The Argument Argument* that concerns scientific knowledge remains a challenge. However, there is a *prima facie* conflict between the idea of citing practical factors as reasons for ascriptions/denials of scientific knowledge and the scientific ideal of objectivity. So, responding to the *Argument Argument* is at least as urgent for proponents of pragmatic encroachment on scientific knowledge as it is for proponents of pragmatic encroachment on ordinary knowledge.

Furthermore, while the combination of pragmatic encroachment on scientific knowledge and constructive empiricism may have the resources to address some of the problematic cases, many other challenging cases remain. Consider, for example, the response that consists in changing the relevant stakes from the subject of the ascription of scientific knowledge to the broader scientific community (or the even broader community that it serves). Whereas this response may address cases such as PERSONAL STAKES VARIATION, it does not to address cases such as GENERAL STAKES VARIATION. Thus, the core of the case-based arguments against pragmatic encroachment on scientific knowledge persists. Of course, this is not to say that such arguments are conclusive. But it does indicate that they may not be evaded simply by embedding pragmatic encroachment theories in a constructive empiricist framework. Rather, a principled response—or some bullet biting—is required.

6.4 Concluding Remarks on Anti-Realism as a Framework for Pragmatic Encroachment

In considering whether pragmatic encroachment on scientific knowledge may align with anti-realism, we have identified a number of challenges for such a combination of views. One challenge is that by aligning pragmatic encroachment with metaphysical anti-realist positions according to which scientific theories and hypothesis are not true, the pragmatic encroacher runs the risk of losing the baby of scientific knowledge with the bathwater of epistemic purism. For such anti-realisms appear to be incompatible with the kind of theory of knowledge that pragmatic encroachers typically pursue.

Initially, an alliance between pragmatic encroachment and constructive empiricism seemed far more promising. But on closer examination, there are considerable cracks in such an alliance and some of the most severe challenges for pragmatic encroachment theories persist. So, in conclusion, embracing some form of anti-realism is unlikely to provide a quick response to the challenges for pragmatic encroachment theories of scientific knowledge.

136 *Mikkel Gerken*

7. Concluding Remarks

The aspects of pragmatic encroachment on scientific knowledge considered here suggest that the view faces serious challenges. First of all, the challenges that beset pragmatic encroachment on ordinary knowledge also compromise pragmatic encroachment on scientific knowledge. But, moreover, they appear to be particularly troublesome in the case of scientific knowledge. The noted trademarks of scientific knowledge help explain this. Recall that, according to *Trademark 1* and 2, scientific knowledge tends to be harder to acquire than ordinary knowledge in part because it must typically be acquired in a systematic manner and backed by a demanding internalist species of warrant—discursive justification. Relatedly, *Trademark 3* has it that scientific knowledge is, as opposed to ordinary knowledge, typically intersubjectively replicable. So, given these trademarks of scientific knowledge, it is a *less* likely candidate for pragmatic encroachment than ordinary knowledge. The trademarks reflect the less individualistic and more objective character of scientific knowledge whereas the cases for pragmatic encroachers involve variations in subjective stakes (Stanley 2005; Fantl and McGrath 2009). The same is true of the experimental findings that are cited in support of pragmatic encroachment (Sripada and Stanley 2012; Pinillos 2012).

I considered whether pragmatic encroachment about scientific knowledge might be embedded in an anti-realistic framework. But this too proved to be a challenge. Metaphysically anti-realist frameworks appear to be incompatible with the sort of theories of knowledge that pragmatic encroachers are committed to. Constructive empiricist frameworks appeared to be more promising at first glance. But a closer examination revealed both significant conflicts and substantive problems.

While I have considered the realist/anti-realist debate, it remains to be investigated how other frameworks and discussions in the philosophy of science bear on pragmatic encroachment (see, e.g., Miller 2014). However, the present exploration provides some reasons to assume that there are plenty of challenges ahead for pragmatic encroachment theories about scientific knowledge.[12]

Notes

1. A notable exception is (Miller 2014) who appeals to considerations about the *inductive risk* (cf. Douglas 2009) in an argument for pragmatic encroachment. Since the issue is complex, the argument is best addressed separately.
2. For the distinction between metaphysical and semantic purism (Stanley 2005; Fantl and McGrath 2009; Buckwalter and Schaffer 2015). Metaphysical impurists include Hawthorne (2004), Stanley (2005), Fantl and McGrath (2009). Strict purist invariantists include Bach (2005), Brown (2008), Rysiew (2007), Williamson (2005), Nagel (2008), Gerken (2011, 2017). It can be a hard exegetical question whether contextualists such as DeRose (2009) and Lewis (1996) exemplify semantic impurism. Clearer cases are Greco (2012); Hannon (2013);

Henderson (2009, 2011). Semantic impurists most commonly articulate their view in terms of shifting truth-conditions. However, some semantic impurists articulate it in terms of stable truth-conditions but shifting truth-values (Brogaard 2008; MacFarlane 2005).

3. In Gerken (2017) Ch. 4.3.c I give some reasons to suspect that the arguments extend to semantic impurism.

4. The terminology is from Burge (2003). I will rely on previous work in which I argue that both justification and entitlement may fulfill the warrant requirement on knowledge (Gerken 2013, 2015, forthcoming a).

5. Note that Hoyningen-Huene uses "scientific knowledge" in a non-factive manner (Hoyningen-Huene 2013: 21). It should moreover be noted that the present rationale for *Trademark 1* does not require commitment to the more controversial aspects of Hoyningen-Huene account. The required assumption is merely that scientific knowledge is characteristically based on highly systematic investigation.

6. A referee correctly notes scientists characteristically adopt a fallibilist attitude and that prominent arguments for pragmatic encroachment proceed from fallibilism and knowledge-action principles (e.g., Fantl and McGrath 2009). I will not address such arguments on this occasion but I do by arguing against knowledge-action principles in (Gerken 2017).

7. Thanks to Kareem Khalifa on this point.

8. Coral bleaching is the phenomenon that corals turn white because they expel the symbiotic algae that live in their tissues due to stress of various forms (including, but not restricted to, rising temperature).

9. Some theorists take further conditions to be required because casting the issue in terms of the mere aims of science is taken as too weak insofar as it is consistent with science never achieving these aims (see e.g., Kitcher 1993: 150. This leads to a discussion about whether and that what extend science tracks truth, Kukla 1998; Psillos 1999).

10. One prominent criticism, due to Kitcher and Salmon, is that even if there are contextual constraints on explanation, non-contextual objective factors remain important (Kitcher and Salmon 1987. See also Salmon 1989 for more general criticism of pragmatic theories of explanation). In the present context, however, it is worth noting that pragmatic encroachers on knowledge also admit of objective factors. So, all that is required is that objective (truth-related) factors do not exhaust the determiners of a good explanation but that practical factors are *part* of the story.

11. van Fraassen often prefers to talk about the permissability of committing to a theory.

12. The chapter was presented at a workshop at the University of Southern Denmark in March 2017 and I thank the participants for helpful comments. I'm especially grateful to Kareem Khalifa, Brian Kim, and an anonymous referee for Routledge who all provided me with incisive written comments that led to many substantive and presentational changes.

References

Almeder, R. (2007). Pragmatism and philosophy of science: A critical survey. *International Studies in the Philosophy of Science*, 21(2): 171–195.

Bach, K. (2005). The emperor's new "knows". In G. Preyer and G. Peter (eds.), *Contextualism in Philosophy: Knowledge, Meaning, and Truth*. Oxford: Oxford University Press: 51–89.

Bird, A. (forthcoming). Systematicity, knowledge, and bias. How systematicity made clinical medicine a science. *Synthese*: 1–17.

138 *Mikkel Gerken*

Blome-Tillmann, M. (2009a). Contextualism, subject-sensitive invariantism, and the interaction of "knowledge"-ascriptions with modal and temporal operators. *Philosophy and Phenomenological*, 79(2): 315–331.

Boyer-Kassem, T., Mayo-Wilson, C. and Weisberg, M. (eds.) (2017). *Scientific Collaboration and Collective Knowledge*. New York: Oxford University Press.

Brogaard, B. (2008). In defence of a perspectival semantics for "know". *Australasian Journal of Philosophy*, 86(3): 439–459.

Brown, J. (2008). Subject-sensitive invariantism and the knowledge norm for practical reasoning. *Noûs*, 42(2): 167–189.

Brown, M. (2013). Values in science beyond underdetermination and inductive risk. *Philosophy of Science*, 80(5): 829–839.

Buckwalter, W. and Schaffer, J. (2015). Knowledge, stakes, and mistakes. *Noûs*, 49(2): 201–234.

Burge, T. (2003). Perceptual entitlement. *Philosophy & Phenomenological Research*, 67: 503–548.

Chakravartty, A. (2011). Scientific realism. In *Stanford Encyclopedia of Philosophy*. Retrieved from https://plato.stanford.edu/entries/scientific-realism/.

Churchland, P. M. (1985). The ontological status of observables: In praise of the superempirical virtues. In P. M. Churchland and C. Hooker (eds.), *Images of Science: Essays on Realism and Empiricism With a Reply From Bas C. van Fraassen*. Chicago: University of Chicago Press: 35–47.

Cohen, J. (1989). Belief and acceptance. *Mind*, 98(391): 367–389.

de Ridder, J. (2014). Epistemic dependence and collective scientific knowledge. *Synthese*, 191(1): 1–17.

DeRose, K. (2009). *The Case for Contextualism*. New York: Oxford University Press.

Dicken, P. and Lipton, P. (2006). What can Bas believe? Musgrave and Van Fraassen on observability. *Analysis*, 66(3): 226–233.

Douglas, H. (2009). *Science, Policy, and the Value-Free Ideal*. Pittsburgh: University of Pittsburgh Press.

Elliott, K. and McKaughan, D. (2014). Nonepistemic values and the multiple goals of science. *Philosophy of Science*, 81(1): 1–21.

Fagan, M. (2012). Collective scientific knowledge. *Philosophy Compass*, 7(12): 821–831.

Fantl, J. and McGrath, M. (2009). *Knowledge in an Uncertain World*. Oxford: Oxford University Press.

Fodor, J. (1984). Observation reconsidered. *Philosophy of Science*, 51(1): 23–43.

Ganson, D. (2008). Evidentialism and pragmatic constraints on outright belief. *Philosophical Studies*, 139(3): 441–458.

Gerken, M. (2011). Warrant and action. *Synthese*, 178(3): 529–547.

Gerken, M. (2012). Discursive justification and skepticism. *Synthese*, 189(2): 373–394.

Gerken, M. (2013). Internalism and externalism in the epistemology of testimony. *Philosophy and Phenomenological Research*, 87(3): 532–557.

Gerken, M. (2015). The epistemic norms of intra-scientific testimony. *Philosophy of the Social Sciences*, 45(6): 568–595.

Gerken, M. (2017). *On Folk Epistemology: How We Think and Talk About Knowledge*. Oxford: Oxford University Press.

Gerken, M. (forthcoming a). Epistemic entitlement: Its scope and limits. In P. Graham and N. J. L. L. Pedersen (eds.), *Epistemic Entitlement*. Oxford: Oxford University Press.

Encroachment on Scientific Knowledge 139

Gerken, M. (forthcoming b). Expert trespassing testimony and the ethics of science communication. *Journal for General Philosophy of Science.*

Godfrey-Smith, P. (2009). *Theory and Reality: An Introduction to the Philosophy of Science.* University of Chicago Press: Chicago.

Greco, J. (2012). A (different) virtue epistemology. *Philosophy and Phenomenological Research,* 85(1): 1–26.

Grimm, S. (2015). Knowledge, practical interests, and rising tides. In J. Greco and D. Henderson (eds.), *Epistemic Evaluation: Purposeful Epistemology.* New York: Oxford University Press: 117–137.

Hacking, I. (1985). Do we see through a microscope? In P. M. Churchland and C. Hooker (eds.), *Images of Science: Essays on Realism and Empiricism With a Reply From Bas C. van Fraassen.* Chicago: University of Chicago Press: 132–152.

Hannon, M. (2013). The practical origins of epistemic contextualism. *Erkenntnis,* 78(4): 899–919.

Hannon, M. (2015). Stabilizing knowledge. *Pacific Philosophical Quarterly,* 96(1): 116–139.

Hansson, S. O. (2014). Science and pseudo-science. In E. N. Zelta (ed.), *The Stanford Encyclopedia of Philosophy.* Available at: http://plato.stanford.edu/archives/spr2015/entries/pseudo-science/.

Hardwig, J. (1985). Epistemic dependence. *The Journal of Philosophy,* 82(7): 335–349.

Hawthorne, J. (2004). *Knowledge and Lotteries.* New York: Oxford University Press.

Henderson, D. (2009). Motivated contextualism. *Philosophical Studies,* 142(1): 119–131.

Henderson, D. (2011). Gate-keeping contextualism. *Episteme,* 8(1): 83–98.

Hoyningen-Huene, P. (2013). *Systematicity: The Nature of Science.* New York: Oxford University Press.

Kahneman, D. (2012). A proposal to deal with questions about priming effects. *Nature,* September 26. www.nature.com/polopoly_fs/7.6716.1349271308!/suppinfo File/Kahneman%20Letter.pdf.

Kelvin, W. T. (1883). *Electrical Units of Measurement.* Lecture to the Institution of Civil Engineers on 3 May 1883, reprinted in 1889, *Popular Lectures and Addresses,* Vol. I, London: MacMillan and Co.

Kitcher, P. (1993). *The Advancement of Science: Science Without Legend, Objectivity Without Illusions.* Oxford: Oxford University Press.

Kitcher, P. (2012). Scientific realism: The truth in pragmatism. *Poznan Studies in the Philosophy of the Sciences and the Humanities,* 101(1): 171–189.

Kitcher, P. and Salmon, W. (1987). Van Fraassen on explanation. *Journal of Philosophy,* 84(6): 315–330.

Kukla, A. (1998). *Studies in Scientific Realism.* Oxford: Oxford University Press.

Ladyman, J. (2000). What's really wrong with constructive empiricism? Van Fraassen and the metaphysics of modality. *British Journal for the Philosophy of Science,* 51(4): 837–856.

Lakatos, I. (1981). Science and pseudoscience. In S. Brown et al. (eds.), *Conceptions of Inquiry: A Reader.* London: Methuen: 114–121.

Laudan, L. (1983). The demise of the demarcation problem. In R. S. Cohan and L. Laudan (eds.), *Physics, Philosophy, and Psychoanalysis.* Dordrecht: Reidel: 111–127.

Lewis, D. (1996). Elusive knowledge. *Australian Journal of Philosophy,* 74: 549–567.

140 *Mikkel Gerken*

MacFarlane, J. (2005). The assessment sensitivity of knowledge attributions. In T. Gendler and J. Hawthorne (eds.), *Oxford Studies in Epistemology*, Volume 1. Oxford: Oxford University Press: 197–234.

Miller, B. (2014). Science, values, and pragmatic encroachment on knowledge. *European Journal for Philosophy of Science*, 4(2): 253–270.

Monton, B. (ed.) (2007). *Images of Empiricism: Essays on Science and Stances, With a Reply From Bas C. van Fraassen*. Oxford: Oxford University Press.

Muller, F. A. and Van Fraassen, B. C. (2008). How to talk about unobservables. *Analysis*, 68(299): 197–205.

Nagel, J. (2008). Knowledge ascriptions and the psychological consequences of changing stakes. *Australasian Journal of Philosophy*, 86: 279–294.

Nagel, J. (2010). Epistemic anxiety and adaptive invariantism. *Philosophical Perspectives*, 24(1): 407–435.

Neta, R. (2007). Anti-intellectualism and the knowledge-action principle. *Philosophy and Phenomenological Research*, 75(1): 180–187.

Pigliucci, M. and Boudry, M. (2013). *Philosophy of Pseudoscience: Reconsidering the Demarcation Problem*. Chicago: Chicago University Press.

Pinillos, Á. (2012). Knowledge, experiments, and practical interests. In J. Brown and M. Gerken (eds.), *Knowledge Ascriptions*. Oxford: Oxford University Press: 192–220.

Popper, K. R. (1934 [2002]). *Logik der Forschung*. Berlin: Akademie Verlag. English translation as *The Logic of Scientific Discovery*. London: Routledge.

Psillos, S. (1999). *Scientific Realism: How Science Tracks Truth*. London: Routledge.

Roush, S. (2007). Constructive empiricism and the role of social values in science. In H. Kincaid, J. Dupré and A. Wylie (eds.), *Value-Free Science: Ideal or Illusion?* Oxford: Oxford University Press: 164–187.

Rysiew, P. (2007). Speaking of knowing. *Noûs*, 41(4): 627–662.

Salmon, W. (1989). *Four Decades of Scientific Explanation*. Minneapolis: University of Minnesota Press.

Sripada, C. and Stanley, J. (2012). Empirical tests of interest-relative invariantism. *Episteme*, 9: 3–26.

Stanley, J. (2005). *Knowledge and Practical Interests*. Oxford: Oxford University Press.

Steele, K. (2012). The scientist qua policy advisor makes value judgments. *Philosophy of Science*, 79(5): 893–904.

van Fraassen, B. (1977). The pragmatics of explanation. *American Philosophical Quarterly*, 14(2): 143–150.

van Fraassen, B. (1980). *The Scientific Image*. Oxford: Oxford University Press.

Weatherson, B. (2005). Can we do without pragmatic encroachment? *Philosophical Perspectives*, 19: 417–443.

Williamson, T. (2005). Contextualism, subject-sensitive invariantism and knowledge of knowledge. *Philosophical Quarterly*, 55: 213–235.

Winsberg, E., Huebner, B. and Kukla, R. (2014). Accountability and values in radically collaborative research. *Studies in History and Philosophy of Science Part A*, 46: 16–23.

Wray, K. B. (2001). Collective belief and acceptance. *Synthese*, 129: 319–333.

Wray, K. B. (2002). The epistemic significance of collaborative research. *Philosophy of Science*, 69(1): 150–168.

9 Skepticism and Evolution*

N. Ángel Pinillos

1. Introduction

In the Meditations, Descartes raises the possibility of an evil demon massively deceiving us about the source of our perceptions.[1] As we go through the text, dread (perhaps mixed with intellectual exhilaration) sets in as we realize we may not know many ordinary and commonsense propositions. This is in part why the Meditations makes for such a gripping piece of philosophy.

A lot of epistemology since Descartes has been concerned with showing why this pull towards skepticism is mistaken. Less attention has been paid to the question of why we should feel this pull in the first place. In fact, it doesn't seem at all *useful* to be drawn to skeptical judgments in the face of bizarre evil demon scenarios. It may even be a pernicious disposition insofar as it may cause us to lose confidence about propositions we should be more confident about. And if the disposition to fold (or to nearly fold) under skeptical pressure appears to serve no useful purpose, perhaps there is no deep reason why we should possess it. Perhaps our dispositions to skepticism are just an accidental feature of cognition or, as I will argue, a side effect of some other important cognitive capacity. From the design perspective (on this line of thought), if we were to build an artificial intelligence device with ideal cognitive capacities, nothing important would be left out if we designed it to not be tempted by skepticism.[2]

A number of researchers have sought to provide psychological explanations for the draw of skeptical judgments.[3] Space limitations prevent me from discussing these theories in detail. The perspective I advance is different enough from these accounts in that it focuses on the evolutionary function of denials of knowledge and how these interact with internalized knowledge-action principles of the type defended recently by "pragmatic encroachers" in epistemology.[4]

The approach I explore here is that many skeptical judgments are the output of a special purpose meta-cognitive mechanism.[5] I will argue that this mechanism is an adaptation. Adaptations solve problems for organisms. For example, the adaptation of having legs solves the problem of locomotion

142   N. Ángel Pinillos

and the adaptation of having teeth solves the problem of grinding food for digestion. I submit that the mechanism which leads to skeptical judgments is an adaptation which solves the problem of figuring out what action to take. The mechanism does this by monitoring our reasoning on command and detecting premises which are too hasty and should not be assumed. The system flags them as "not knowledge".

This "skeptical mechanism" produced judgments in cases that mattered for our ancestors. These cases involved useful everyday denials of knowledge. In sharp contrast, judgments about evil demon and brains and vats are esoteric philosophical concoctions. Although they are genuine deployments of the mechanism, they are outliers and fall far outside the conditions which originally gave rise to the mechanism. An interesting further question is whether we can learn anything about the epistemic status of mental states that are the outputs of adaptive mechanisms by learning about the original design conditions for those mechanisms. I think we can. I will argue that the mechanism was not designed for esoteric philosophical scenarios and as a result, we are not justified in believing what it tells us about those scenarios. If these outputs are what give the skeptical arguments their intuitive appeal, then we may very well be able to respond to the skeptic. In particular, we will be able to say that the following premise in the skeptical argument is unjustified: I do not know I am not a brain in a vat. I end the chapter with a brief discussion on this issue.

2. Knowledge-Action Principles

I said previously that a certain propensity to deny that people know things in skeptical pressure cases helps us figure out how to act. But how can that be? What does knowledge have to do with action? In a project pioneered by Fantl and McGrath (2002), a number of researchers have posited principles explicitly connecting knowledge and appropriateness of action. Hawthorne and Stanley (2008) propose the following:

> (KA) Where one's choice is p-dependent, it is appropriate to treat the proposition that p as a reason for acting iff you know that p[6]

One important motivation for this principle is that it helps explain why ordinary people use "knows" to criticize behavior. For example, one can criticize a job candidate for not wearing formal attire: "You knew you would be meeting the dean, why didn't you wear formal attire?" or criticize someone for not bringing a hat: "you knew it would be sunny, why didn't you bring a hat?" These are positive attributions which make sense of the "right-to-left" direction.

The "left-to-right" direction is also supported by folk appraisals. For example, an agent can be criticized by being told that they did not know some relevant proposition. For example, I could reasonably say "Why did you throw away the pizza, you didn't know I wouldn't be back for dinner

Skepticism and Evolution 143

again", or "You shouldn't have bought that expensive bicycle, you don't know that we won't need the money for something else this month". Thus, both directions of (KA) are supported by folk behavior.[7]

The idea that the principle can explain folk behavior suggests that ordinary people accept the principle (or something like it) or are sensitive to it. That is, the principle is not *just* some deep metaphysical fact, an ideal of rationality hidden in Plato's heaven. Rather it, is (in some sense) endorsed by ordinary people.

Despite the plausibility of the principle, it might be too strong. Consider the following potential counter-example (to right-to-left) due to Jessica Brown (2008). A surgeon about to remove a patient's kidney double-checks to see if it really is the left kidney that needs removing. Intuitively, the doctor must already know before the surgery that it is the left kidney that needs removal. Yet, she should still double-check. That is, it is not acceptable for her to use the known proposition that the left kidney needs removal in her practical reasoning (without double-checking). Hence (KA) is incorrect. Jessica Brown also objects to left-to-right direction of (KA). "Gettiered" subjects, she argues, could blamelessly use p in reasoning even though they fail to know p.

Maybe you don't find these counterexamples convincing. It doesn't matter. The point I would like to make is that we don't need a principle that is as strong as (KA) to establish an important connection between knowledge and the normativity of action. A weakened principle that holds ceteris paribus (or in "normal cases") will do.[8] In fact, the principles of folk psychology, which aim to explain and predict rational human behavior are of this weakened form. It would not be at all surprising if the correct knowledge-action principle also had this structure.[9]

3. The Skeptical Mechanism

I said previously that the mechanism which normally produces skeptical judgments is an adaptation. Before I argue for this, I have to say how this mechanism is supposed to function. The workings of this mechanism are not transparent to introspection. It is the sort of process we can understand by inspecting people's judgments across a range of hypothetical cases and noting the patterns that emerge. This can be done informally by theorists surveying their own judgments about cases (as traditional epistemologists do) or more formally using controlled experiments. Not surprisingly, it turns out that work from both traditional and experimental epistemology can give us insight into the process.

What we are interested in here is a cognitive model of the skeptical process. Typically, cognitive models are algorithmic descriptions of information processing mechanisms.[10] Minimally, to construct such a model we need to specify the inputs, outputs, and the computation which turns inputs to outputs. In specifying such a model, there is no assumption made that there is a dedicated component of the mind in charge of carrying out such a computation.

144 N. Ángel Pinillos

That is a further claim, a claim that I will in fact be making about skeptical judgments, but further evidence would need to be brought in.

I will be describing what is surely an oversimplified model of the skeptical process. Suppose we are observing Jon Doe is at a restaurant. Jon Doe, who has properly functioning eyes, makes the true judgment that the couch in front of him is crimson red. There is no funny business going on here and so observers would be happy to say that Jon Doe knows the couch in front of him is crimson red. But now consider a "skeptical pressure case" where observers of Jon Doe are reminded that sometimes restaurants have ambiance lighting, so that a non-crimson red couch may turn out to look crimson red. When we are presented with such a possibility, we are more likely to deny that Jon Doe knows the couch in front of him is crimson red.

This example suggests a simple model with two inputs. (Input 1): Doubt about p—which involves the representation of some specific possibility (or class of possibilities) where p is false. (Input 2): The epistemic position of an agent S with respect to some proposition p (evidence or justification S possesses, how the agent formed the belief that p, etc.).

Here's a description of the computation. The agent determines whether S's epistemic position (Input 2) can *rule out* the specific possibility that p could be false (Input 1). If it is determined that it cannot rule it out, then the process returns "S does not know p" as the output. If it is determined that it does rule it out, then the system is disengaged. For example, in the couch case, Input 2 is Jon Doe's epistemic position (Jon Doe's eyes are working properly, he is standing in front of the couch, etc.). The possibility of error (Input 1) is that the restaurant has weird lighting—which is determined to not be ruled out by the agent's epistemic position. The computation then returns that Jon Doe fails to know the couch is red. The reason why it's determined to not be ruled out is that it is perceived that Jon Doe has not checked for ambiance lighting. If it was noticed that he had checked for tricky lighting, then Jon Doe's epistemic position would be seen to rule out the possibility of error (and the system would disengage).

Is this simple cognitive model realistic? Something like it is assumed in contextualist treatments of knowledge (Cohen 1998; Lewis 1996).[11] And experimental work backs this up. For example, Nagel et al. (2013) gave participants "skeptical pressure" cases like the sofa scenario and found that participants who read those scenarios were more likely to deny knowledge than participants in a control condition where they were not reminded that lighting could be tricky. Similar results were verified by Powell et al. (2015), and Schaffer and Knobe (2012) deploying distinct experimental paradigms.

In the next sections I put some flesh into this model. Space constraints limit detailed discussions on these important points.

3.1 Inputs

(a) Skeptical judgments do not just involve fantastical evil demon type situations. They also involve "local" skeptical scenarios. For example, the "crimson red couch" scenario leads to a denial of knowledge regarding the color of the couch, but not to a denial of all perceptual knowledge (even accepting closure). This is an important point. Cognitively, local skeptical scenarios will be treated in the same way as global skeptical cases. Some of these local skeptical scenarios are known in the literature as "lottery" cases (Kyburg 1961). For example, agents claim to not know they will lose the lottery (even though the probability of losing is extremely high and even though they are willing to say they know a lot of other things which have a higher probability of being false—like knowing the time based on a wristwatch). Another example involves agents claiming to not know that the president hasn't been assassinated a few seconds ago (supposed they haven't checked their smart phones). Even though the chances of this occurring are very low, agents tend to judge they fail to know this. The approach I take here is that, cognitively, these cases trade on the possibility of error being made salient plus the agent's epistemic perceived position not being able to rule out this possibility of error (at least not perceived as being ruled out—see section 3.3). As we will see, all of this leads to denials of knowledge.

Note that the reason why these local skeptical cases are philosophically puzzling is that if we really don't know these things, then (by epistemic closure)[12] it would seem like we fail to know more mundane things we ordinarily take ourselves to know. For example, if I don't know that I will lose the lottery this week, then I also don't know the following: that I will be going grocery shopping this weekend (suppose that I know that if I won the lottery, I would eat out at a restaurant for every meal). But presumably I know that I will be heading to the grocery store this weekend (if someone asks me if I know what I will be doing this weekend, I will mention the trip to the grocery store). Note that I am not saying that epistemically, lottery and global skeptical cases are alike. I am conjecturing that judgments from those domains arise from similar cognitive mechanisms.

The way that skeptical and lottery-type cases are discussed in the philosophical literature, it may be thought that they are contrived cases concocted to make a philosophical point with no application to the "real world". But the cognitive mechanisms that explain these cases are, in my view, also responsible for interesting cases in law.

According to the Wells effect, jurors are less likely to convict on probabilistic evidence that is purely "statistical" as opposed to evidence that seems causally connected to the particular case at hand. In a famous experiment, Wells (1992) described to a mock jury a case where it was alleged that a particular bus company, the Blue Bus Company, harmed a dog. One set of jurors were told that the evidence against the Blue Bus company was that 80% of the buses in town were run by the Blue Bus company ("statistical evidence") and hence there is an 80% chance the Blue Bus company harmed the dog. Another set of participants were presented with an eyewitness who claimed to see a Blue Bus bus harm the dog. The jurors were told that the witness

146   N. Ángel Pinillos

was 80% reliable. In both cases, jurors agree that the chance the Blue Bus company harmed the dog was 80% but nonetheless they were more willing to convict on the eyewitness testimony than on the statistical evidence. In recent work, Friedman and Turri (2014) provided evidence that effect persisted for knowledge attributions. Applied to the Blue Bus case, participants would be less likely to say they know that the blue bus company harmed the dog when the statistical evidence was presented as opposed to the eyewitness case. This is so even though participants would readily admit that in both cases there was an 80% chance of guilt. Interestingly, Turri et al. (2017) gave evidence that judgments about whether the accused was blameworthy were mediated by their attributions of knowledge, indicating the cognitive centrality of knowledge judgments.

The idea that global, local skeptical, lottery, and Wells judgments have a common cognitive etiology is a substantive claim. I will say something in its favor next but note that if we are on the right track, then skeptical judgments may be of interest not only to epistemologists and cognitive scientists but also to legal scholars and advocates of justice.

(b) Some research indicates that along with salience of error, the practical import of the question (or "what is at stake") could also lead to denials of knowledge.[13] But this research is controversial.[14] There is also the question of how practical interests should be incorporated into our model, if they play a role at all. For example, Buckwalter and Schaffer (2015) propose that the practical interest of an issue has an indirect effect on skeptical judgments. They argue that practical interests affect the salience of a possibility of error which in turn leads to knowledge denials. On another model they attribute to Pinillos, stakes play a direct role in knowledge attributions. For the purposes of this chapter, I will leave the issue of practical interests aside.

(c) Not every case where error is raised to salience leads to skeptical denials (even when the hypothesis is not ruled out by the evidence). Consider the following example inspired by John Hawthorne (2004, p. 64): Some friends are watching the movie "The Matrix" (which presumably makes the possibility of massive error salient) and one asks the other whether he *knows* if they put real butter in the popcorn they are sharing. The interlocutor would naturally respond in a way that does not reflect a skeptical perspective. This seems to be a counter-example to the simple picture where salience of error (which cannot be ruled out by evidence) leads to denials of knowledge. We need some way to distinguish this type of case from the scenarios where skeptical judgments do arise.

(d) I said that "doubt" (Input 1) would be represented as a specific possibility of error. But these are different things. A doubt that perhaps the lights above are tricky is not quite a specific representation of a possibility. A more sophisticated model would need to explain how agents get from doubt to the representation of a possibility. I also said that Input

2 specified an agent's epistemic status, but left it wide open how this is represented by the agent. Clearly, more details are needed.

3.2 Outputs

I said previously that the skeptical mechanism produces skeptical judgments which are just denials of knowledge. But there is reason to think that the output of the mechanism yields something weaker, like *an inclination* to judge that one fails to know—as opposed to full blown judgments or beliefs. Imagine a philosopher who is a convinced non-skeptic. Convinced by anti-skeptical arguments, they sincerely judge that they know they are not deceived by an evil demon or that they know they will lose the lottery. Nonetheless, they still find themselves feeling the pull to make the skeptical judgment. This is why philosophers often feel the need to explain the psychological pull for skepticism even after all the arguments against skepticism have been given. The idea that the skeptical pull remains after beliefs are otherwise formed suggests that the skeptical mechanism produces an output that is short of belief. In Fodor's terminology, the output is "shallow" and stops short of a full judgment or belief.[15]

Another piece of evidence that the skeptical pull does not become full belief is that it is forgotten soon after the skeptical episode ends. This general phenomenon was noted by Hume when he wrote "Tis happy, therefore, that nature breaks the force of all skeptical arguments in time, and keeps them from having any considerable influence on the understanding".[16] Here, Hume highlights the impermanence of skeptical judgments or inclinations. Though Hume's remarks suggest not only that skeptical inclinations fall short of being full blown beliefs, but that they are all but forgotten "in time".

3.3 Algorithm

I said that when the mechanism (figure 9.1) determines that X's epistemic position with respect to p (input 2) cannot rule out the possibility of error that p (input 1) the mechanism will return an inclination to judge that X fails to know p. There is a difference between saying that a system *determines* that X's epistemic position rules out a possibility of error and saying that in fact X's epistemic position rules out such a possibility. Perhaps one's epistemic position in fact rules out the possibility of an evil demon deceiving us, but it doesn't follow our system will say that it does. In other words, supposing the mechanism represents part of our folk epistemology, it may be that this part of our folk epistemology succumbs to skepticism even though *we* ought not to succumb to it.

A well-known philosophical approach to deal with skeptical cases appeals to the notion of sensitive belief (a type of "truth-tracking"). An agent's belief that p is sensitive just in case if p were false, the agent would not believe p. Robert Nozick (1981) proposed that a necessary condition for knowing p

148 N. Ángel Pinillos

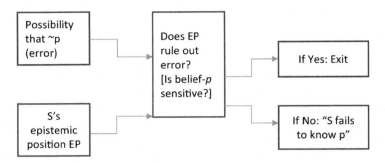

Figure 9.1 Simplified Skeptical Mechanism (SM)

is that the belief that p be sensitive.[17] Take an ordinary case of knowledge, like knowing that you are reading a paper right now. This belief is sensitive since if you weren't reading a paper right now then you would not believe that you were. For example, if you weren't reading a paper right now, maybe you would be making coffee and so you would believe you are making coffee right now (not reading a paper). Hence, sensitivity gets it right in at least some of these ordinary cases of knowledge.[18]

Now consider a global skeptical case. Suppose you believe that you are not a brain in a vat (BIV). This belief is not sensitive: if you were a BIV, you would still believe that you were not a BIV. Accordingly, you don't *know* that you are not a BIV. Similarly, for the lottery cases. Your belief today that you will lose the lottery tomorrow (suppose you own a ticket and have formed the belief that you will lose tomorrow) is not sensitive. If you were to win tomorrow, you would still believe today that you will lose the lottery tomorrow. Enoch et al. (2012) have argued that statistical "Wells effect" cases can also be explained by sensitivity. Suppose you believe on purely statistical evidence that a Blue Bus harmed the dog, then presumably you would still have this belief if it turned out a different bus company harmed the dog. Hence the statistical belief is not sensitive. What about the eyewitness case? Suppose you believe that the Blue Bus Company was responsible on the basis of the eyewitness testimony. Now if the Blue Bus Company weren't responsible, you wouldn't believe this anymore. Presumably, the eyewitness would not have testified. At the very least, it less intuitive that your belief would remain the same in the second case.

Many philosophers doubt that sensitivity is a necessary condition for knowledge. The classic problem with that approach is that (given some plausible assumptions) it requires denying closure for knowledge. As we saw, the account predicts we don't know we are brains in vats (since the corresponding belief is insensitive), but unless we go for global skepticism,

Skepticism and Evolution   149

we should accept that that we know we have hands (which corresponds to a sensitive belief). But the problem is that by closure if I know that I have hands, then I should be able to deduce and come to know that I am not a brain in a vat.

My approach does not say that sensitivity is a necessary condition for knowledge. Rather, I am making the psychological claim that the skeptical judgments are produced by testing for sensitivity. I am not saying anything about what knowledge itself requires.

As a first approximation, what it means for X's epistemic position with respect to p to rule out the possibility of error E is that the following is true: Given X's epistemic position, if E were the case, X would not believe p. For example, let us suppose the possibility of error E^* at issue concerns a deceptive evil demon. Given my epistemic position, if E^* were the case, I would continue to believe that I live in a demon-free world. Hence, my belief that I live in a demon-free world is not sensitive, and so I have the inclination to judge that I fail to know that I live in a demon-free world.

I say that this is an "approximation" because the algorithm would likely involve testing a sample of several nearby-counterfactuals as opposed to relying on a single make or break counterfactual. But for the purposes of this chapter, we will assume a single counterfactual test.

In what follows I will continue to talk about doubt which is not ruled out by an agent's epistemic position or "unresolved doubt". I will leave this at an intuitive level. Readers who find this notion too imprecise may replace it by the notion of insensitivity as described in the previous paragraphs.[19]

4. The Skeptical Mechanism as an Adaptation

We are now ready to consider the hypothesis that the skeptical mechanism (SM) is an adaptation. To say that the SM is an adaptation is to say that it is an adaptation for some function or purpose. I mean to be using teleological terms "function", "for", "purpose" and the like in the sense familiar from the theory of natural selection. This is the sense in which evolutionary biologists say that wings are an adaptation for flying or that hearts are an adaptation for pumping blood.

The notion of an adaptation is a historical-explanatory notion (Williams 1966). Elliot Sober provides the following analysis (1984, p. 208): "A trait T is an adaptation for X in a lineage just in case T evolved in the lineage because there was selection for T and there was selection for T because having T promoted doing X". As such, my claim that "SM is an adaptation for X" or "the function of SM is for X" is really a claim about the historical-explanatory role of SM.[20]

There are other uses of teleological terms not essentially tied with natural selection. For example, the physiologists sense of "function" concerns the

150 N. Ángel Pinillos

role an organ or capacity plays in a complex organism. This is a synchronic ahistorical notion. The synchronic notion often coincides with the historical one. But they can come apart. The appendix presumably has no synchronic function but it has a selection function, for example. To clarify, I will be using "function" and other teleological terms in the historical sense essentially tied to natural selection not the synchronic one.

It is of course, difficult to find direct evidence that SM is an adaptation for X. We can't visually observe the SM or its components, or rely on fossil records. Our evidence will be indirect and highly speculative. As a first step, we need to identify the "X" and give some reason to think it promoted fitness. And here we have our work cut out for us. In many cases, it is easy to at least come up with a plausible story of how a trait helped us survive and reproduce. It doesn't take much imagination to note how having hearts or wings aids fitness. But in the case of SM, it is not at all obvious how it could help us survive or reproduce. (Recall that we started the chapter noting how skeptical judgments seem like a useless feature of our epistemic capacities). So what is the use of SM?

4.1 The Adaptive Function of SM

Let's begin by thinking about a real-world version of the crimson red couch example. Suppose we are walking around the restaurant. A fellow customer says to us: "There is a chance that the lighting here is weird". What should our response be? If it is an otherwise ordinary case and I haven't checked for tricky lighting, surely the fact that this utterance was made raises the likelihood for me that there is in fact tricky lightning and so now I would fail to know the couch is crimson red. After all, why would someone say this if they didn't have good reason to think there is tricky lighting? Similar remarks apply in the third-person. If I am observing someone shopping at the store and this person has not checked for tricky lighting, it would also be reasonable to deny he knows the couch is crimson red (when doubt is raised).

Consider a different case. Suppose I am about to eat some berries I found in the field (I believe they are safe) and a friend tells me that he found similar looking berries that were poisonous. Suppose further that I didn't rule out the possibility of poisonous berries (I didn't check for poison). My friend's utterance would likewise raise the likelihood for me that the berries I am about to eat are poisonous. Perhaps I now do not know that the berries I was about to eat are safe.

What these examples suggest is that there are certain cases where a rational response to somebody raising unresolved doubt *is* to deny knowledge. This is because the raising of unresolved doubt (in these cases) is itself a good indicator that there is evidence against the proposition in question. Let's call these the "good cases". I call these cases "good" because the denials of knowledge seem true.

Now, there are also "bad" cases. One is the brain in a vat scenario. You are a freshman in college and your philosophy professor raises the doubt that you may be a brain in a vat. You run back to your roommate with the bad news that it is all a big con. The possibility of error is unresolved leading you to judge you fail to know ordinary things. Another example is the lottery case where you deny you know you will lose the lottery when considering the possibility that you may win (which is not ruled out). These are "bad" cases because they are problematic in the sense that they lead to epistemic paradoxes (lottery and skepticism). I do not want to assume here that these judgments are necessarily wrong however. By "bad" I do not mean to say that the judgments are false.

The philosophical preoccupation with paradoxical cases has perhaps prevented us from seeing the value of skeptic-type judgments. Focusing on the "good" cases, it is plausible that they are produced by SM (since these are cases in which the raising of unelimated doubt leads to denials of knowledge). And so we can see the function of having the SM: it helps us to correctly detect cases in which an agent fails to know. In other words, the SM is an ignorance detector:

> (Ignorance Detector): The adaptive function of the SM is that it detects failures to know.

Two points of clarification. First, the SM need not get every case right. Wings are for flying but it doesn't follow that birds with wings are able to fly in all weather conditions including heavy rain. The SM gets it right in the sorts of cases that we labeled "good" in the preceding text. I will leave it open for now whether it gets it right in skeptical scenarios (are skeptical cases for SM analogous to heavy rain for wings?). Second, the SM need not be the only way an organism comes to judge that someone fails to know. Opposable thumbs are adaptations for picking up objects, but it doesn't follow that there aren't other ways of picking up objects (we can pick up objects with our mouths, for example).

4.2 Explaining Adaptiveness

We now need to see how detecting ignorance is supposed to be adaptive. Saying that the function of SM is to detect failures to know is not quite to say how it can aid fitness. We need one more step. We need an explanation of how detecting ignorance aids fitness (the analogous case for wings is explaining how flying aids fitness). I will rely on the knowledge-action principles I mentioned earlier. But first let us look at some of the literature on the purpose of knowledge. Edward Craig (1991), Steven Reynolds (2017), and others have argued that knowledge attributions are *for* identifying reliable informants.[21] If I say Fred knows whether the car needs repairing, I am identifying him as a reliable source of information regarding car repairs.

152   N. Ángel Pinillos

If that's the benefit of knowledge attributions, then since SM detects those who fail to know, the benefit of possessing SM is presumably that it helps us detect those individuals that are *not* reliable informants. The idea here would be that early on in evolutionary history, those individuals who possessed SM were better able to weed out bad informants and, as a result, were more likely to survive and pass on their genes.

I don't find this line of reasoning promising. Here's the problem. The SM judgments we discussed previously involved peculiarities concerning specific cases that don't seem to generalize to claims about reliable informants. When I judge (through SM) that my friend doesn't know that the berries are safe to eat, it is not correct to think that he is an unreliable informant about the safety of berries in general. The only thing I can reasonably infer in this regard is that he did not check for poison in these particular berries. And when I judge (through SM) that an agent does not know the couch is crimson red (in the tricky lighting case), it would not be correct for me to infer that the agent is unreliable with respect couch colors. All I can say in this regard is that he failed to check for tricky lighting and so fails to know the color of the couch in this specific instance. More generally, SM judgments involve the processing of specific error scenarios that concern what might have gone wrong in a particular case. The inference to a general reliability claim seems unwarranted (even if we understand this inference as defeasible).[22]

Relatedly, Sinan Dogramaci (2012) has argued that the function of rational assessments of beliefs is to get others to adopt (or reject) the epistemic method which lead to those beliefs—which in turn makes testimony (reliance on the words of others) trustworthy. Dogramaci is explicit that he is concerned with a *sustaining* function of the practice of rational assessments, as opposed to a selection function (which is our present concern). In addition, he is interested in the function of a practice as opposed to the function of a cognitive mechanism. Nonetheless, we might try to extend his ideas to our present concerns (though he might not agree with this extension) by investigating the evolutionary roots of social stigmatization. Let us agree with Dogramaci that when we can call someone "irrational" we are pushing the hearer to reject a certain belief-forming practice. But how does this "pushing" work? What happens if one doesn't go along with the speaker? One possible answer is that there is a threat of stigmatization in cases where the hearer fails to reject the belief-forming practice in question. Now, Kurzban and Leary (2001) have argued that humans possess adaptive mental mechanisms for stigmatizing (as one of a suite of specialized adaptive mechanism for social interaction). The evolutionary benefit of the stigmatization mechanism involves avoiding social partners that would hinder our reproductive or social success (including avoiding uncooperative or pathogen bearing partners). These ideas applied to the SM would be that denials of knowledge are essentially threats. They are threats to reject certain epistemic practices on penalty of being ostracized from the group.

Skepticism and Evolution 153

James Beebe (2012) has proposed another social role for knowledge attributions (or the "knowledge" concept). He argues that knowledge is for distinguishing agents who are most blameworthy due to their un-cooperating behavior. For example, it is useful to detect the agents who are *knowingly* breaking the rules (as opposed to those who are doing so without knowledge that they are breaking the rules). In support of his thesis, Beebe brings up evidence from evolutionary game theory as well as work on the connection between knowledge attributions and blame.

These two social approaches to the function of knowledge are plausible. But they seem to suggest certain peculiar predictions which I am not sure are borne out. If knowledge attributions (or denials) involved threats to ostracize, we would expect to find that agents who make a knowledge attribution will monitor their audience to ensure they end up endorsing the relevant belief-forming method. In case they don't, the speaker should be ready to punish their interlocutor by ostracizing or some other means. Although, we would need to get empirical evidence, it certainly doesn't seem like we monitor our audience in this way today (though maybe things were different in the communities of our ancestors). Regarding Beebe's account, his view seems to predict that knowledge attributions are more reliable in cases that involve cheaters and social norms (in the way that logical reasoning is thought to be more reliable in cheater domains). Again, empirical evidence would need to be brought in, but this is not something that has been noted by epistemologists who are ever so vigilant regarding subtle uses of "knows".

A different and more direct approach appeals to the connection between knowledge and action. We noted that there is an intuitive connection between knowledge and appropriateness of action. According to (KA) (left to right), it is acceptable for X to use p in reasoning only if X knows p. And here we have a possible explanation for how SM can aid fitness. If the principle just mentioned is true and agents accept it, then when SM correctly detects failure to know p, one will be able to correctly deduce that it is not acceptable to use p in reasoning. For example, if my SM correctly detects that Fred fails to know the berries are safe to eat, I will be in a position to correctly judge that it is not acceptable for Fred to rely on the proposition that the berries are safe to eat. That is, he shouldn't assume the berries are safe to eat. Possessing this type of information would give me an evolutionary advantage. If I am Fred, then learning that I shouldn't eat the berries could save my life. If I am considering getting the berries from Fred, then unless I have some further information about the berries, I will also fail to know the berries are safe. And so by the principle, I can judge that I shouldn't assume that the berries are safe (which could save my life). If Fred is my kin, then passing on the information that he shouldn't assume the berries are safe could save his life and help preserve my genes. And in yet other cases, informing others (including Fred) that Fred shouldn't assume the berries are safe can play a beneficial role cooperative strategies.

In the reasoning just rehearsed we used the (KA-left to right) principle. But we could also employ the other direction (right to left) of the principle: If X

154   N. Ángel Pinillos

knows p (and p is relevant), then it is acceptable to use p in reasoning. On this conception, when the SM delivers that X fails to know p, we can't directly infer that it is not acceptable for X to use p. But suppose that prior to activating the SM, you thought that X knew p and then (via KA-right to left) you judged that it is acceptable for X to rely on p. Now when the SM tells you that X doesn't know p after all, you no longer have a reason to think it is acceptable for X to rely on p. So then you stop relying on p. This would be another way in which the SM could be useful.

The argument here depended on an internalized principle connecting knowledge and action. But as discussed earlier, the argument goes through even on a weaker connection between those concepts (principles involving *ceteris paribus* clauses). In addition, our proposal may over-intellectualize meta-cognitive processes. We just imagined our agents helping themselves to an abstract principle connecting the concepts and *deducing* a proposition concerning the appropriateness of action. But the process is likely more reflexive and automatic. What we require is that knowledge denials (or attributes) are deployed to appraise behavior. But we can be neutral about how this is realized in the mind.

Let us put all these strands together. In the "berries" case, we said that the SM could help us avoid eating poisonous berries. The SM tells us X fails to know the berries are safe and so X shouldn't assume the berries are safe. This suggests that the fitness benefits of SM is (excessive) risk avoidance. Whenever a possibility of error concerning p is made salient in a way that cannot be met by evidence, the mechanism tells us to stop relying on p.

I propose the following explanation for why detecting ignorance aids fitness:

> (Risk Avoidance) The explanation for why the SM is adaptive is that it helps the agent avoid excessive risks.

Ignorance Detector tells us the adaptive function of the SM (to detect failures to know), but Risk Avoidance goes a step further. It gives us an explanation for why detecting ignorance should be adaptive in the first place. The hypothesis proposed is then that the SM a meta-cognitive mechanism evolved to help us avoid excessively risky decisions. It monitors reasoning and tells us to not assume p when there is a warning in the environment (i.e., when doubt that p is made salient) and this doubt cannot be ruled out by the agent's evidence or epistemic position.

The SM gives us an advantage but it also comes at a cost. There will be cases in which the SM would needlessly slow us down. Suppose the meat you are preparing is fine to eat but uneliminated doubt tells you, via the SM, that this assumption should not be made. This would lead to an unfortunate delay of your meal (because, for example, you may waste time double-checking the quality of your food). The account I defend assumes, therefore, that the fitness costs of using of SM would be outweighed by the

Skepticism and Evolution 155

fitness benefits. This assumption is highly speculative. But we can reasonably speculate about the steepness of the costs. First, note that when the SM says that an assumption p should not be made, it does not mean that this cannot be reversed by central processing. Second, an agent may revert to reasoning with probabilities. For example, when the SM says you fail to know p, you could still assume that it is probable that p instead of assuming simply p. These considerations suggest that the costs of the SM are mainly loss of speed in decision-making as opposed to missing out entirely on a useful type of reasoning. And so the costs of the SM are somewhat mitigated.

The SM is a sophisticated mechanism. We can imagine a more primitive system (a proto SM) which works by telling us to stop assuming p whenever there is a warning about the correctness of p in the environment (without checking to see if the doubt can be eliminated like in SM). The inability to weed out doubt signals that "should" be ruled out by the agent's evidence would put possessors of this system at a disadvantage. Possessors of this proto-system would presumably be *overly* risk averse. In addition, clever competitors could easily exploit this weakness to gain advantage.

5. Is the Skeptical Mechanism Modular?

In the previous section I gave some reason to think that SM may have afforded our ancestors with an evolutionary advantage. But we want to go beyond a just-so story. What further evidence can we get that the SM was in fact an adaptation?

Natural selection works in a piecemeal fashion. The human body, for instance, did not evolve all at once. Rather, the human body contains organs each with a distinct evolutionary path. What goes for the human body goes for the mind. The visual system, for instance, has a different evolutionary history from the language processing components which is yet (arguably) distinct from our numerical cognitive capacities.

The idea that the mind might have a rich structure populated by mental organs or faculties was all but lost during the reign of behaviorism. It gained currency with Jerry Fodor's influential "The Modularity of Mind".[23] According to Fodor, an important difference between these mental organs or "modules" and bodily organs is that the former process or compute information. As such, many of the features associated with modules are those that help explain the tractability of these computations.

We will begin by looking at some of the features Jerry Fodor proposed were central to modularity. As we will see, this list is perhaps too stringent. Evolutionary psychologists have wanted to relax some of these conditions. A main point of contention between Jerry Fodor and some evolutionary psychologists, for example, is that Fodor thought modules concerned peripheral processing and provided inputs to central processing systems.[24] But this central processing system, with its open-endedness and holistic character,

156   N. Ángel Pinillos

is itself non-modular. Some evolutionary psychologists, on the other hand, hold that central processing is itself populated by multiple modules.[25] The Skeptical Mechanism, if modular, is a part of central processing. It is a meta-cognitive module in charge of monitoring reasoning (which tells us if an assumption is too hasty).[26]

5.1 Domain Specificity

This feature is central to Fodor's conception of modules. Linguistic modules concern language processing and vision module(s) concern visual perception. There some imprecision about this notion however. Jerry Fodor writes that "domain specificity has to do with the range of questions for which a device provides answers (the range of inputs for which it computes analyses)" (p. 103). These ideas in the quote can be separated, however. The range of questions a mechanism answers could be small while the range of inputs could be large. For example, the theory of mind module (if there is one) will answer a narrow range of questions just concerning the mental states of others, but the range of inputs could be quite large if it could include any belief and any desire no matter what the content. And the same could be said about the cheater detector module (if there is one).[27] It is domain-specific in the sense that it is about cheating. Although the range of inputs could be about almost anything (one could cheat "about" anything).

What goes for theory of mind and cheating also goes for the skeptical mechanism. It is certainly domain-specific in that it is just about *knowledge*, but the range of inputs could be quite unconstrained since, for example, doubt (Input 1) could take on any subject matter. So we should count the SM as domain-specific understood in the manner just discussed.

5.2 Information Encapsulation

Modules do not have unfettered access to the agent's beliefs or desires. This is part of what makes computation tractable and fast. A snake detector mechanism (if there is one) should not be free to survey all your random beliefs about reptiles before warning you that you are about to step on a cobra.

In the well-known Müller-Lyer illusion (Figure 9.2), the visual system continues to deliver the representation (and the inclination to judge) that the lines presented are different lengths even after the agent knows fully well that they are the same length (Figure 9.2). This suggests that a perception module does not have access to the belief that the lines are the same length.

Similarly, the SM exhibits information encapsulation. Suppose you believe that skepticism is false. As noted earlier, you still feel the pull to deny you know you are not a brain a in a vat. You still feel the pull to deny you know you will lose the lottery. Many philosophers believe that skepticism is false.

Skepticism and Evolution   157

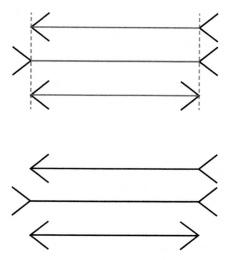

Figure 9.2 Müller-Lyer illusion

But they still feel like they have to explain the psychological pull of skeptical judgments. They try to provide psychological accounts for this pull (see citations in footnote 2). Why should this be? Encapsulation explains this.

Consider other philosophical discoveries. When Saul Kripke (1980) convinced others that there could be a posteriori but necessary truths, there wasn't further work to explain away the psychological pull towards thinking that necessary truths must be a priori. This is because there is no leftover pull towards that thesis after the arguments convince you. Reason is enough to banish any such inclination. Not so for skepticism. Reason is not enough to extinguish the allure of the skeptic. Encapsulation explains this.

5.3 Inaccessibility to Central Processing

This is certainly correct for the grammar module(s). We cannot introspect the descriptive rules of grammar. The typical way to discover those rules is by looking for patterns in our intuitive judgments of acceptability.

This is similar to how we got that sensitivity is the algorithm of the SM. When philosophers introduced sensitivity as requirement for knowledge, it wasn't an introspective report (otherwise, it would have happened a lot sooner). Rather, part of what we do is look at a pattern of judgments and note that sensitivity can explain and predict responses to those cases. Relatedly, there is a debate about whether practical interests play a role in ordinary attributions of knowledge. As we mentioned earlier, some theorists (Buckwalter and Schaffer 2015) hold that it does play a role but only in the following indirect way: when the stakes are high, the possibility of error is

158   N. *Ángel Pinillos*

salient and this leads to a denial of knowledge. Grafting this idea onto our model, practical interests play a role in determining the input to SM, but that's the end of it. Practical interests play no role in the internal algorithm of the system. I do not know whether this is the correct view. But the point is that we cannot settle this by introspection. This is evidence that the inner workings of SM are inaccessible to central processing.

5.4 Mandatory Processing

Modules are mandatorily triggered. An agent does not have to decide to recognize a face or process color. These things just happen. When you hear someone speak in your language, you immediately understand them. You don't have to first *decide* to understand what they are saying. The evolutionary advantage of this feature is clear. Some reactions are too important and time-sensitive to be left up to the agent's central process deliberations.

Unlike language comprehension, which can happen even if one is not attending to someone's speech, SM seems to be only turned on when the agent is attending to practical or theoretical deliberation. Whether or not this means the SM is mandatory, it clearly reflects a good design. If doubt about p is raised about some issue we are not at all interested in, it would be a wasteful use of cognitive resources to execute a function which resolves that we fail to know p. Notice that other cognitive modules share the same feature. Numerical cognition is arguably modular, but we don't just immediately add or subtract numbers when pairs of quantities are presented to us (Mandelbaum 2013). Rather, a precondition for mathematical reasoning is focus on a specific problem.

Eric Mandelbaum (2015) has pointed out that the mandatory feature of modules can be understood in two ways. First it could be understood as meaning "automatic" where this mean that the module will process an input when it is present (regardless of what the agent might be attending to). Second it could be understood as "ballistic", meaning that when the process has started it cannot be stopped. These notions can come apart. Mandelbaum cites a proposal (Crain and Steedman 1985) for a linguistic parser that is automatic but not ballistic. It is not ballistic because the parser halts and goes to check for contextual cues when it is stumped by a garden path sentence. But it is automatic in that it processes speech even when agents are attending to other tasks.

Mandelbaum suggest that the cognitive modules (like our numerical capacities and cheater detectors) are best thought of as ballistic but not automatic. This seems right for SM. SM is only activated when attention is focused on some bit of reasoning. But once the system engages, it delivers the output. So the SM counts as mandatory if the notion is understood in the way just explained.

5.5 Evolutionary Explanation and Innateness

Modules are generally thought to be evolved. As such, they should have an evolutionary function. We saw previously that the evolutionary function of SM is to detect ignorance. In addition, theorists often assume modules have an innate component. This, of course, does not mean that the module does not need to develop and it does not mean that important components of the module are not fixed by the environment. The language modules, for example, develop through childhood and require critical input from the environment.

If the SM is modular, we would expect, for example, characteristic onto-genetic development of the mechanism. Although there is a great deal of research on how children attribute "knows" and "thinks", very little has focused on skeptical judgments. So I will say nothing further about this here.[28]

What about innateness? If the module had an innate component, we would expect some cross-cultural convergence on skeptical judgments. Recent cross-cultural work indicates universality on Gettier judgments, but skeptical judgments haven't been tested.[29] It is plausible that at least some Gettier judgments fail the sensitivity test. I which case, at least some Gettier judgments may be the products of the skeptical module. If so, then the universality of these judgments would add plausibility to the innateness hypothesis.

Turning now to skeptical judgments. If skepticism had an innate component, we would expect it to naturally arise when humans turn to philosophical reflections. Indeed, we find skeptical traditions not just among western thinkers but also in Chinese (Zhunagzi) and Indian thought (Cārvāka).[30] Further textual evidence would need to be uncovered to demonstrate that the way that skepticism is raised in these texts is consistent with the SM posited here.

Finally, I noted that SM is a meta-cognitive process in charge of detecting ignorance. There is now a great deal of evidence that non-human primates possess meta-cognitive mechanisms in charge of detecting uncertainty as well as ignorance. That is, they may be able to detect failures to know.[31] There is then some reason to be optimistic about the existence of further evidence that the SM is an evolved mechanism.

5.6 Functional Dissociability

A key piece of evidence for modularity is the separability of the relevant capacity from the rest of the system. If there is really a module for X, we would expect to have breakdowns of the capacity to X while everything else remains more or less intact. Theorists have argued for the modularity of theory of mind on precisely this ground, for example.[32] Do we have any

160 N. Ángel Pinillos

evidence of an SM deficit? Obsessive Compulsive Disorder is a good candidate. Dubbed as "Foile du doute" or "Madness of Doubt" by the 19th century French psychiatrist Jean Etienne Esquirol, OCD looks like it involves a breakdown of the SM.

Recent cognitive accounts of OCD suggest that OCD is a type of epistemic disorder. It is posited that the failure of a patient to stop checking, washing their hands, and other obsessive behavior is due to "Elevated Evidence Requirements" connected to their appraisal of how personally responsible patients felt for the outcome (including what is at stake). In obsessional cases, the criteria to stop the behavior is more stringent. The criteria includes "objective" epistemic markers like making sure one gathers "more evidence" (checking the door is locked one more time) as well as reaching a subjective "feeling of rightness".[33]

OCD might then involve a dysfunction of the SM mechanism. Possibilities of error that are normally ruled out by evidence are not. According to the SM, this leads to an inclination to judge that you don't know the relevant proposition (i.e., that you locked the door). And via the connection to action, we can no longer help ourselves to that proposition. If the question is important to you, or seems important to you (as it is in virtually all obsessive cases), you will be prone to go out gather get more evidence by re-checking or washing your hands one more time. The SM will then be reactivated.

5.7 Recap

The skeptical mechanism may well be modular. Arguably, it possesses six key characteristics associated with modules.[34] This gives us reason to think that the mechanism, with its stated function, is a product of natural selection.

6. Debunking Skepticism? (Perhaps, but not in the Way You Might Think)

Debunking arguments begin with the claim that some of set of beliefs (the ones to be debunked) are caused (or explained) by factors significantly distinct from what the beliefs are supposedly about. This claim, if accepted, constitutes a defeater for those beliefs. That is, agents who uncover the suspect etiology are no longer justified in having these beliefs. For example, if Joe learns that his belief that the kitchen lights are flickering is caused by a powerful blow to his head, then he is no longer justified in having that belief (assuming he has no other reason to believe the kitchen lights are flickering).

A prominent class of debunking arguments appeal to evolution.[35] The idea here is that some of our beliefs are caused by evolutionary forces instead of their purported subject matter. For example, our moral beliefs are shaped to help us survive and not by some objective moral reality. But if moral beliefs are tied up to commitments to some objective moral reality, then one loses

Skepticism and Evolution 161

justification for those beliefs upon learning that they are not explained by any objective moral realm (or so the account goes).

6.1 First Attempt

In this chapter, I argued that skeptical judgments are shaped by natural selection. A tempting thought is that we have all the ingredients for a debunking argument against those judgments. Insofar as those intuitive judgments are what underwrite the premises in skeptical arguments, then we may have a way to block the skeptical advance.

To construct a debunking argument following the previous blueprint, we need to first show that skeptical judgments are a product of evolution *and* not explained by their purported subject matter. But I do not believe this can be shown. I am in complete agreement that skeptical judgments are a product of evolution, but they are *also* explained by their subject matter. We saw that the Skeptical Mechanism (SM) takes as inputs an agent's epistemic position together with salient doubt. It then tests to see whether the agent's evidence can rule out the raised doubt (by testing for sensitivity). But "checking to see if doubt that p is ruled out by S's evidence" (the SM algorithm) is pretty much the subject matter of judgments of the form "S does not know p". So we cannot say that skeptical judgments are shaped by factors distinct from their subject matter. Now, it may turn out that this isn't a very good algorithm for detecting failures to know. But this would require a more sophisticated argument going beyond the standard debunking move.

The lesson here is that it can be both true that a belief is shaped by evolution and explained by its purported subject matter even when the subject matter is not directly about fitness (this is well-known in the debunking literature). Some beliefs formed through visual perception are like this. They are certainly shaped by evolution but are also appropriately caused by the things the agent is looking at. So just as we do not expect a debunking argument to be successful against perception, we should not expect one to be successful against skeptical judgments—at least not the version just given.

6.2 Towards a Second Attempt

Here's a sketch of a better idea. We begin with the thought that the skeptical mechanism was "designed to function" in real-world conditions where making hasty assumptions would hinder survival or reproduction. Global skeptical cases (involving brains in vats and evil demons), on the other hand, are products of philosophical explorations far removed from those real-world conditions.

From these facts, together with some background conditions which I will try to make explicit in a second, we can infer that we are not justified in believing the outputs of the skeptical mechanism *when it considers global skeptical cases*. That is, we can infer that we are not justified in accepting the

162   N. Ángel Pinillos

skeptical intuitions which underwrite the key premise in the skeptical argument (or at least a leading version of the skeptical argument).

To see this, let us begin with an example from an artificial device. Suppose you buy an ordinary body temperature thermometer and you read in the specs that it is designed to work in the temperature range between 90F and 110F. You read that it was tested to work in that range (you know it wasn't tested in other temperature ranges, suppose) and that it was the intention of the designers to work in that range. Later on you are in need of a meat thermometer. You look everywhere but can only find your body temperature thermometer. You stick it in the roast, wait a few minutes, and take the reading. It says 380F. I think that intuitions are clear that in this case you would not be justified in believing that the meat is 380F or even approximately 380F. This is so even if it turns out that the thermometer reading turned out to be correct and even if the thermometer turned out to be reliable at those high temperatures.

Another example is this. Suppose you take the thermometer to a far away planet where air pressure, temperature, etc. are radically different from the original design conditions of the thermometer. You would also be unjustified in believing the outputs of the thermometer in those conditions.

Why should this be? The following principle seems plausible:

> DEFEAT-ARTIFICIAL With some exceptions E*, knowingly using an artificial device *far outside* its intended conditions renders beliefs in its outputs unjustified.

What are some of these exceptions E*? I can think of at least two. If you have some further reason to think that the device is reliable in those conditions (suppose you tested the thermometer in extreme temperatures) or if you have some other independent way of corroborating the output (suppose you found an additional thermometer designed for those conditions), then you may be justified in believing the outputs after all. But absent these conditions, then I think you would be unjustified in believing the outputs of the device.

I think the general principle extends to natural devices. Of course, here we can't appeal to the *intended conditions* since natural devices were not brought about by anyone's intentions. But intentions are not really doing the explanatory work in DEFEAT-ARTIFICIAL anyways. The intentions of the makers are relevant because they tell us something about the reliability of a device. And they do so by telling us about how the device was made. For example, if the makers of a thermometer intended it to work in a certain temperature range, then they likely tested the thermometer to work in that range. But we can recover reliability information for natural devices by learning about how they were shaped by natural selection. If all we know about thermoreceptor cells on our skin is that they are selected for detecting temperature differences, then we would not be justified in thinking that they would work in conditions far removed from the sorts of conditions under which the receptors evolved. For example, if a scientist were to transplant

Skepticism and Evolution   163

those cells to a device in the lab, they would (absent some further information) not be justified in thinking that the cell receptors would continue to work under extreme temperature conditions, for example. This suggests the following natural analog of our principle:

> DEFEAT-NATURAL With some exceptions E**, knowingly using a natural device *far outside* its natural design conditions renders beliefs in its outputs unjustified.

The exceptions E** are similar to the exceptions E*. If the agent had some independent reason to think that the device was reliable under the unusual conditions or if the agent had some independent reason to think that the specific output of the device was correct, then they would be justified in believing the output of the device in those conditions.

We can apply DEFEAT-NATURAL to the skeptical mechanism (SM). The key assumption (which can certainly be legitimately questioned) is that the global skeptical scenarios (brain in a vat, evil demon etc.) involve situations that are *far outside* the natural design conditions for SM. So we can conclude that, unless the exceptions E** are operative, we are not justified in believing the outputs of the SM applied to global skepticism.

Are the two exceptions E** operative? The first one does not seem operative. We do not seem to have independent reason to think that SM is reliable outside its design range. What about the second exception? Do we have independent reason to think that its output "I do not know that I am not a brain in vat" is true beyond just relying on the intuition that it is true? If there is a further plausible argument for such a proposition (say, the "underdetermination" skeptical argument), then we would need to look carefully at this argument to determine that that its plausibility does not still depend on the outputs of the SM. If it did, then this further argument would not count as an "independent" reason to believe the output of the SM. Hence, the exceptions E** would not be operative and the agent would not be justified in believing the output of SM.

Let us then put these thoughts together. Consider the classical skeptical argument: (Premise 1) I do not know I am not a brain in a vat. (Premise 2) If I know I have hands, I know I am not a brain in a vat. (Conclusion) I do not know I have hands. I find this argument compelling in part because I find Premise 1 intuitive. But now I learn that my intuition for Premise 1 was produced by the SM and that it is operating far outside its design conditions. According to DEFEAT-NATURAL, unless the exceptions E** are operative, I am not justified in trusting this intuition. I am not justified in believing Premise 1. But if the justification in believing the conclusion of the skeptical argument is transmitted from the justification of the premises, then I am not justified in believing the conclusion of the skeptical argument after all. The skeptic is defeated!

Two points about this argument. First, it is an argument that I am not justified in believing the conclusion (and a premise) in the skeptical argument.

164 *N. Ángel Pinillos*

It is not an argument that the conclusion is false. I have not argued that we know we have hands, for example. Second, the lack of justification for believing the conclusion (and Premise 1) does not apply to everyone. It just applies to people who *knowingly* use SM far outside its natural design conditions. But does anyone in fact knowingly use SM far outside its natural conditions? Not at the time of this writing. Before you read this chapter, you probably didn't have any beliefs about SM. The person who is not aware of the claims I made here, for example, will likely still be justified in accepting the conclusion and premises of the skeptical argument. There is nothing too strange about this. This just means that I have argued for something which, if true, is a type of *defeater* for the belief that we do not know we are not brains in vats (Premise 1).[36]

7. Summary

In this chapter, I argued that there is a mechanism SM which produces inclinations to make skeptical judgments. This mechanism takes as inputs (a) doubt concerning p and (b) S's epistemic position with respect to p. The mechanism tests to see if S's belief that p is sensitive. If it is not sensitive, then SM returns an inclination to judge that S does not know p. If it is sensitive, then it disengages. The range of skeptical inclinations produced by the SM run the gamut including global and local skeptical representations, as well as lottery, and statistical representations. I argued that the SM is a product of evolution whose "selection" function is to detect cases where agents fail to know some proposition. This function aids fitness because when an agent fails to know a proposition (it usually means) that the proposition should not be used in reasoning. In short, the SM is a meta-linguistic mechanism which monitors our reasoning for assumptions that are too hasty and, consequently, should not be deployed.

At the end, I suggested (given certain tentative assumptions) that global skeptical beliefs or judgments that arise through SM are unjustified. This is because global skeptical cases are unusual and far different from the sorts of cases that shaped the SM early on our evolutionary history. I indicated how we may exploit this information to undercut at least one version of the skeptical argument.

Notes

* I would like to thank Sinan Dogramaci, Brian Kim, Shyam Nair, Shaun Nichols, Mark Schroeder, and audiences at The University of Buffalo and at Institut Jean Nicod for helpful feedback.
1. Descartes (1996).
2. There is a sense in which contextualists about "knowledge" are also trying to explain why we find skepticism appealing. But their focus is different from the approach I take here which concerns the psychological mechanism which gives rise to our inclinations as well as issue of why we would possess the mechanism in the first place. Their approach, in contrast, is essentially a semantic approach.

Contextualists need not have a theory of why language and "knows" works the way it does.

3. Some recent work: Gerken (2017), Jackson (2015), Hawthorne (2004, p. 164), Nagel (2010), Nichols and Pinillos (forthcoming), Turri (2014), Turri and Friedman (2014), Williamson (2005) and many others.

4. Of course, these other approaches also focus on denials since they concern skepticism.

5. The defense that this system is genuinely "meta-cognitive" is left for another time (Pinillos MS). But readers familiar with that literature will notice the connections. First, the mechanism has essentially a monitor and control flow (monitoring for knowledge following control of our practical reasoning). Second, the algorithm deploys a sensitivity test which is just a counterfactual test directly about mental states (beliefs). Third, the mechanism involves a mix of conscious reflection and implicit inference through an opaque mechanism (think of how "feelings of knowing" arise).

6. See also Ross and Schroeder (2014) and Pinillos (forthcoming).

7. The Knowledge-Action principles are intimately connected with the thesis of pragmatic encroachment. I will not discuss encroachment per se here. See Kim (2017) for an overview.

8. See Pinillos (forthcoming).

9. Philosophers who prefer to think in terms of functions (as opposed to universal principles) might take the folk data cited previously to tell us that the *function of knowledge attributions* is to assess whether a premise is actionable. If this is right, Brown's counterexamples would be less bothersome. Chairs are to sit, but they can be used for other purposes. In this chapter, I will be discussing the evolutionary function of certain cognitive mechanisms which produce inclinations make knowledge-judgments. I will have nothing to say about the function of knowledge *attributions* per se.

10. It should be clear that I am interested here in Marr's algorithmic level of cognitive analysis as opposed to the implementation or computational levels. In other work, (Pinillos MS) I have tried to address the computation or function the agent is trying to approximate when responding in a skeptical pressure case.

11. Contextualist theories are semantic/pragmatic not psychological theories. Some of these theories will tell us, for example, that "X knows P" is false in a context in which the possibility of error is salient (or attention is drawn to the possibility). It won't tell us that in fact people will deny knowledge in those contexts. However, these theorists get their plausibility and motivation from their ability to capture ordinary behavior.

12. There are many formulations of "closure". We need not worry about getting it exactly right here. A plausible enough version says this: If S knows p and correctly deduces q from p, then S is in a position to know q.

13. Pinillos (2012), Sripada and Stanley (2012).

14. Buckwalter and Schaffer (2015) and for a response see Pinillos and Simpson (2014).

15. Fodor (1983).

16. Hume (1968, p. 187).

17. See also Dretske (1971).

18. According to Nozick, Sensitivity plus some other conditions plausibly met in the paper-reading case are sufficient for knowledge.

19. It may be that the mechanism posited serves other functions besides those resulting in denying knowledge. For example, Brian Kim suggests plausibly that it can help us eliminate alternative hypothesis in deliberation.

20. This view is sometimes known as the "Selected Effects Theory of Functions". See, for example, Kraemer (2014), Godfrey-Smith (1994), Griffiths (1993), Millikan (1989), Neander (1991), Wright (1973).

166   N. Ángel Pinillos

21. I am not attributing to Craig or Reynolds claims about evolutionary (selection) functions. They seem to have some other type of teleology in mind. In addition, Craig and Reynolds both talk about the function of knowledge *attributions* (or concepts). In contrast, I am only making a claim about the selection function of a psychological mechanism. Nonetheless, we can try to extend their insights to our present concerns.
22. Nor does it help to say that the agent is unreliable with respect to the specific proposition that *these* berries are safe and *this* crimson couch is red. Whether or not a person is reliable with respect these specific propositions is not very useful information since it is very unlikely that the agents will make a judgment about these particular propositions in the future. What is useful information is whether an agent is reliable with respect to a topic or class of propositions.
23. Fodor (1983).
24. See Carruthers (2003) and the references therein.
25. Carruthers (2006), Carey and Spelke (1994), Cosmides and Tooby (2005), Sperber (1994), Pinker (1997),
26. Finn Spicer (2008) and David Papineau (2000) argue that we have a folk epistemology module which produces positive knowledge judgments. It is important to distinguish this claim from the one I am making here. I am making a specific proposal regarding modularity and a type of knowledge denial. I am neutral about whether other "knowledge" judgments are modular or whether folk epistemology is produced by a module.
27. Cosmides and Tooby (1995).
28. Although developmental work on skepticism is being carried out through the Children's Museum of Phoenix and the Cognition, Computation and Development Lab at Arizona State University.
29. Machery et al. (2016).
30. See Hansen (2017) for an overview of Zhunagzi. See Phillips (2017) for discussion on the Cārvāka school. See the sections on skepticism.
31. Beran et al. (2006), Beran and Smith (2011), Ferrigno et al. (2017), Hampton (2001), Hampton et al. (2004), Kornell et al. (2007), Rosati and Santos (2016).
32. Scholl and Leslie (1999).
33. Salkovskis (1999), Salkovskis et al. (2017), Rachman (2002), Wahl (2008).
34. Jerry Fodor also include "shallow outputs" as part of the criteria for modularity. I argued on 3.2 that the outputs of SM are indeed shallow.
35. See, for example, Street (2006) or Joyce (2006).
36. Brian Kim suggests that a full explanation of the psychological pull concerns why we would generate skeptical hypotheses in the first place. This is correct and I have said nothing about this here. Though an implicit claim being made here is that local skeptical hypotheses naturally arose in our evolutionary history.

References

Beebe, J. (2012). *Social Function of Knowledge Attributions*. Eds. J. Brown and M. Gerken. Oxford: Oxford University Press.

Beran, M.G. and Smith, J.D. (2011). Information seeking by rhesus monkeys (*Macaca mulatta*) and capuchin monkeys (*Cebus apella*). *Cognition*, 120: 90–105.

Beran, M.J., Smith, J.D., Redford, J.S., and Washburn, D.A. (2006). Rhesus macaques (*Macaca mulatta*) monitor uncertainty during numerosity judgments. *Journal of Experimental Psychology: Animal Behavior Processes*, 32: 111–119.

Brown, J. (2008), Knowledge and practical reason. *Philosophy Compass*, 3: 1135–1152.

Buckwalter, W. and Schaffer, J. (2015). Knowledge, stakes, and mistakes. *Noûs*, 49(2): 201–234.

Skepticism and Evolution 167

Carey, S. and Spelke, E. (1994). Domain-specific knowledge and conceptual change. In L. Hirshfeld and S. Gelman (eds.), *Mapping the Mind*. Cambridge: Cambridge University Press.

Carruthers, P. (2003). Moderately massive modularity. *Royal Institute of Philosophy Supplement*, 53: 67–89.

Carruthers, P. (2006). *The Architecture of the Mind: Massive Modularity and the Flexibility of Thought*. Oxford: Oxford University Press.

Cohen, S. (1998). Contextualist solutions to epistemological problems: Scepticism, Gettier, and the lottery. *Australasian Journal of Philosophy*, 76(2): 289–306.

Cosmides, L. and Tooby, J. (1995). Cognitive adaptations for social exchange. In J. Barkow, L. Cosmides, and J. Tooby (eds.), *The Adapted Mind*. Oxford: Oxford University Press.

Cosmides, L. and Tooby, J. (2005). Neurocognitive adaptations designed for social exchange. In D.M. Buss (ed.), *Handbook of Evolutionary Psychology* (pp. 584–627). Hoboken: Wiley.

Craig, E. (1991).*Knowledge and the State of Nature: An Essay in Conceptual Synthesis*. Oxford: Clarendon Press.

Crain, S. and Steedman, M. (1985). On not being led up the garden path: The use of context by the psychological parser. In D. Dowty, L. Karttunen, and A. Zwicky (eds.), *Natural Language Parsing* (pp. 320–358). Cambridge: Cambridge University Press.

Descartes, R. (1996). *Meditations on First Philosophy: With Selections From the Objections and Replies*. Cambridge: Cambridge University Press.

Dogramaci, S. (2012). Reverse engineering epistemic evaluations. *Philosophy and Phenomenological Reasoning*, LXXXIv(3).

Dretske, F. (1971). Conclusive reasons. *Australasian Journal of Philosophy*, 49: 1–22.

Enoch, D., Spectre, L., and Fisher, T. (June 2012). Statistical evidence, sensitivity, and the legal value of knowledge. *Philosophy and Public Affairs*, 40.3: 197–224.

Fantl, J. and McGrath, M. (2002). Evidence, pragmatics, and justification. *Philosophical Review*, 111(1): 67–94.

Ferrigno, S., Kornell, N., and Cantlon, J. (2017). A Metacognitive illusion in monkeys. *Proceedings of the Royal Society B*, 284: 20171541.

Fodor, J.A. (1983). *The Modularity of Mind*. Cambridge, MA: MIT Press.

Friedman, O. and Turri, J. (2014). Is probabilistic evidence a source of knowledge? *Cognitive Science*, 39(5): 1062–1080.

Gerken, M. (2017). *On Folk Epistemology*. Oxford: Oxford University Press.

Godfrey-Smith, P. (1994). A modern history theory of functions. *Noûs*, 28(3): 344–362.

Griffiths, P.E. (1993). Functional analysis and proper functions. *The British Journal for the Philosophy of Science*, 44: 409–422.

Hampton, R.R. (2001). Rhesus monkeys know when they remember. *Proceedings of the National Academy of Sciences of the United States of America*, 98: 5359–5362.

Hampton, R.R., Zivin, A., and Murray, E.A. (2004). Rhesus monkeys (*Macaca mulatta*) discriminate between knowing and not knowing and collect information as needed before acting. *Animal Cognition*, 7: 239–246.

Hansen, C. (2017). Zhuangzi. In E.N. Zalta (ed.),*The Stanford Encyclopedia of Philosophy* (Spring Edition).

Hawthorne, J. (2004). *Knowledge and Lotteries*. Oxford: Clarendon.

Hawthorne, J. and Stanley, J. (2008). Knowledge and action. *Journal of Philosophy*, 105(10): 571–590.

Hume, D. (1968). *Treatise of Human Nature*. Ed. L.A. Selby-Bigge. Oxford: Oxford University Press.

168 N. Ángel Pinillos

Jackson, A. (2015). How you know you are not a brain in a vat. *Philosophical Studies*, 172(10): 2799–2822.

Joyce, R. (2006). *The Evolution of Morality*. Cambridge, MA: MIT Press.

Kim, B. (2017). Pragmatic encroachment. *Philosophy Compass*, 12: 5.

Kornell, N., Son, L.K., and Terrace, H.S. (2007). Transfer of metacognitive skills and hint seeking in monkeys. *Psychological Science*, 18: 64–71.

Kraemer, D.M. (2014). Revisiting recent etiological theories of functions. *Biology and Philosophy*, 29: 747–759.

Kripke, S. (1980). *Naming and Necessity*. Cambridge, MA: Harvard University Press.

Kurzban, R. and Leary, M. (2001). Evolutionary origins of stigmatization: The functions of social exclusion. *Psychological Bulletin*, 127(2): 187–208.

Kyburg, H.E. (1961). *Probability and the Logic of Rational Belief*. Middletown: Wesleyan University Press.

Lewis, D. (1996). Elusive knowledge. *Australasian Journal of Philosophy*, 74(4): 549–567.

Mandelbaum, E. (2013). Numerical architecture. *Topics in Cognitive Science*, 5(1): 367–386.

Mandelbaum, E. (2015). The automatic and the ballistic: Modularity beyond perceptual processes. *Philosophical Psychology*, 28(8): 1147–1156.

Machery, E., Stich, S., Rose, D., Chatterjee, A., Karasawa, K., Struchiner, N., Sirker, S., Usui, N., and Hashimoto, T. (2016). Gettier across cultures. *Noûs*, 50(4).

Millikan, R.G. (1989). In defense of proper functions. *Philosophy of Science*, 56(2): 288–302.

Nagel, J. (2010). Knowledge ascriptions and the psychological consequences of thinking about error. *The Philosophical Quarterly*, 60(239): 286–306.

Nagel, J. (2012). Mindreading in Gettier cases and skeptical pressure cases. In J. Brown and M. Gerken (eds.), *Knowledge Ascriptions*. Oxford: Oxford University Press.

Nagel, J., San Juan, V., and Mar, R.A. (2013). Lay Denial of knowledge for justified true beliefs. *Cognition*, 129(3): 652–661.

Neander, K. (1991). Functions as selected effects: The conceptual analyst's defense. *Philosophy of Science*, 58(2): 168–184.

Nichols, S. and Pinillos, N.Á. (forthcoming). Skepticism and the acquisition of knowledge. *Mind and Language*.

Nozick, R. (1981). *Philosophical Explanations*. Oxford: Oxford University Press.

Papineau, D. (2000). The evolution of knowledge. In P. Carruthers and A. Chamberlain (eds.), *Evolution and the Human Mind* (p. 170). Cambridge: Cambridge University Press.

Phillips, S. (2017). Epistemology in classical Indian philosophy. In E.N. Zalta (ed.), *The Stanford Encyclopedia of Philosophy* (Spring Edition).

Pinillos, N.Á. (MS) *Mind and Doubt*. Manuscript.

Pinillos, N.Á. (2012). Knowledge, experiments, and practical interests. In Jessica Brown and Mikkel Gerken (eds.), *Knowledge Ascriptions* (p. 192). Oxford: Oxford University Press.

Pinillos, N.Á. (forthcoming). Knowledge and the permissibility of action. *Synthese*, 1–23.

Pinillos, N.Á. and Simpson, S. (2014). Experimental evidence in support of anti-intellectualism about knowledge. In J. Beebe (ed.), *Advances in Experimental Epistemology* (pp. 9–44). London: Bloomsbury Academic.

Pinker, S. (1997). *How the Mind Works*. New York: Penguin Press.

Powell, D., Horne, Z., Pinillos, Á., and Holyoak, K. (2015). A Bayesian framework for knowledge attribution: Evidence from semantic integration. *Cognition*, 139: 92–104.

Rachman, S. (2002). A cognitive theory of compulsive checking. *Behaviour Research and Therapy*, 40: 625–639.

Reynolds, S. (2017). *Knowledge as Acceptable Testimony*. Cambridge: Cambridge University Press.

Rosati, A.G. and Santos, L.R. (2016) Spontaneous metacognition in rhesus monkeys. *Psychological Science*, 27: 1181–1191.

Ross, J. and Schroeder, M. (2014). Belief, credence, and pragmatic encroachment. *Philosophy and Phenomenological Research*, 88(2): 259–288.

Salkovskis, P.M. (1999). Understanding and treating obsessive-compulsive disorder. *Behaviour Research and Therapy*, 37: S29–S52.

Salkovskis, P.M. (2017). The termination of checking and the role of just right feelings: A study of obsessional checkers compared with anxious and non-clinical controls. *Behavioural and Cognitive Psychotherapy*, 45(2): 139–155.

Salkovskis, P., Millar, J., Gregory, J., and Wahl, K. (2017). The termination of checking and the role of just right feelings: A Study of Obsessional Checkers Compared with Anxious and Non-clinical Controls. *Behavioural and Cognitive Psychotherapy*, 45(2): 139–155.

Schaffer, J. and Knobe, J. (2012). Contrastive knowledge surveyed. *Noûs*, 46(4): 675–708.

Scholl, B.J. and Leslie, A.M. (1999). Modularity, development and 'theory of mind'. *Mind & Language*, 14: 131–153.

Sober, E. (1984). *The Nature of Selection: Evolutionary Theory in Philosophical Focus*. Cambridge: Bradford/MIT Press.

Sperber, D. (1994). The modularity of thought and the epidemiology of representations. In L. Hirschfeld and S. Gelman (eds.), *Mapping the Mind*. Cambridge: Cambridge University Press.

Spicer, F. (2008). Knowledge and the heuristics of folk epistemology. In V. Hendricks (ed.), *New Waves in Epistemology*. London: Palgrave-Macmillan.

Sripada, C. and Stanley, J. (2012). Empirical tests of interest-relative invariantism. *Episteme*, 9: 3–26.

Street, S. (2006). A Darwinian Dilemma for realist theories of value. *Philosophical Studies*, 127: 109–166.

Turri, J. (2014). Skeptical appeal: The source-content bias. *Cognitive Science*, 38(5): 307–324.

Turri, J. and Friedman, O. (2014). Winners and losers in the Folk epistemology of lotteries. In J. Beebe (ed.), *Advances in Experimental Epistemology*. New York: Bloomsbury Press.

Turri, J., Friedman, O., and Keefner, A. (2017). Knowledge central: A central role for knowledge attributions in social evaluations. *Quarterly Journal of Experimental Psychology*, 70(3): 504–515.

Wahl, K., Salkovskis, P.M., and Cotter, I. (2008). 'I wash until it feels right': The phenomenology of stopping criteria in obsessive-compulsive washing. *Journal of Anxiety Disorders*, 22: 143–161.

Wells, G.L. (1992). Naked statistical evidence of liability: Is subjective probability enough? *Journal of Personality and Social Psychology*, 62(5): 739–752.

Williams, G.C. (1966). *Adaptation and Natural Selection: A Critique of Some Current Evolutionary Thought*. Princeton: Princeton University Press.

Williamson, T. (2005). Contextualism, subject-sensitive invariantism and knowledge of knowledge. *The Philosophical Quarterly*, 55(219): 213–235.

Wright, L. (1973). Functions. *Philosophical Review*, 82(2): 139–168.

10 Deliberation and Pragmatic Belief

Brad Armendt

How do our beliefs interact with our practical interests? Does the practical significance we attach to the truth or falsehood of p sometimes influence how strongly we believe it? If so, when are we more likely to notice the influence, and what can we say about how it happens?

When we deliberate about what to do, our beliefs and our interests interact. Suppose we evaluate our options in light of our expectations about their possible outcomes. Then our beliefs about those outcomes influence our evaluations, and so influence our choice and action.

In the other direction, our comparisons of the competing options influence our beliefs about what we will do, and they sometimes influence our beliefs about what our actions may accomplish. Sometimes a decision does not come quickly, and deliberation takes time. The interactions among all these influences may then take a deliberator through a succession of shifting evaluations and opinions. The theory of *deliberation dynamics* provides ways to model that.

Let us consider the questions raised at the beginning, as they apply to contexts of deliberation, when deliberation stretches over a period of time. The answer to the first question has many parts. Here I mean to pursue one of them, suggested by the second question, namely the possibility that beliefs are sometimes *stake-sensitive*. Might the strength of a deliberator's state of belief vary, depending upon how it matters, upon what she takes to be at stake on the truth of the belief? I have elsewhere discussed at some length the idea that a belief state might be stake-sensitive in this way; here I will be more concise.[1]

1. Stake-Sensitive Belief

You are in a conversation with a student, who asks you: in which part of his chapter on truth and probability did Ramsey give that example about the unwholesome yellow toadstools? After a moment, you reply: in the last section of the chapter, on the "logic of truth". Soon after the student leaves your office, the phone rings. A local radio station invites you to play their quiz game. The prize for a correct answer to their question is valuable, a fabulous overseas trip, and they offer you several subjects to choose among. You pick "Probabilism", and to your amazement, they ask the very same question. Now you think a little longer; it seems like it was the last section of the chapter, but could it have been earlier when Ramsey was talking about beliefs and frequencies?

What, if anything, might be different for you in the two situations? What, if anything, is different about your belief that the yellow toadstool example is in the last section of the chapter? The story is not perfect, but it is intended to bring us to the neighborhood of our topic.[2] To what extent do our beliefs, and how strongly we hold them, depend upon how they matter to us, on what we take to be at stake on them? Might we move from one context to another, remaining in the same doxastic state concerning p, yet believing that p more strongly in the one context than in the other? In order for that to happen, a doxastic state, a belief state, must have a certain sort of complexity, a context-sensitivity that yields, in the presence of one set of stakes, a belief of one strength, and in the presence of different stakes, a belief of a different strength. So the question being asked is about the nature of belief states, as we understand them, or as we think they should be modeled in a theory about them.

If a belief that p is stake-sensitive, then in the absence of contextual stakes, its strength is not definite.[3] It is a persistent doxastic state, let us assume, yet it exerts patterns of influence on choice and inference that vary, when what is understood to be at stake on p varies. Given its persistence, over time we might notice the belief's stake-sensitivity when there is a shift in the pragmatic significance of p. But a change in what is at stake could affect a belief in two ways, only one of which is what I have in mind. My question is whether the strength of a *given* state of belief is sensitive to what is at stake, not on whether *news* of what is at stake leads to *belief change*, from a state of belief in one context, to a different state of belief in another context. No one doubts that our beliefs sometimes change through learning or forgetting; it is less clear that they are sometimes stake-sensitive.

The question is not confined to beliefs that are rational; I am interested in stake-sensitive belief, whether rational or not. For what it's worth, and without argument here, I tend to think that sometimes beliefs are stake-sensitive (in the peculiar way I have described), while also thinking that the ways that may happen are often not rational.

Contexts of deliberation, however, might provide occasions where we find rational stake-sensitive beliefs. Periods of extended, perhaps intermittent, deliberation are in some ways special contexts, to be sure, and my beliefs about what my current deliberation will lead me to do are in some ways special beliefs. But if we seek examples of rational stake-sensitive belief, then contexts of deliberation, special though they may be, are a natural place to look.

172   Brad Armendt

A belief is stake-sensitive when the strength with which you hold it varies in response to variation in how it matters to you, variation in what you take to be at stake on it. One sort of variation is variation in the *size* of the stakes. Sensitivity to the size of the stakes is often raised in pragmatic encroachment discussions, when we consider a believer or knower moving between low-stakes and high-stakes contexts, for example. In previous work on belief I highlighted sensitivity to the sizes of the stakes, as in the previous story of the radio quiz game. Another sort of variation is variation in the *odds* of the stakes, or in the *shape* of the stakes. These variations may occur together. By variation in the odds, I mean variation in the comparative value the believer sees in the truth and in the falsehood of the belief. This might be taken to be the *ratio* of the perceived value of the belief's truth to the perceived value of its falsehood, on some particular value scale. Imagine that in one context you regard p as much better than ~p, but in another context you do not, and in another ~p is better than p. If that is the source of shifts in how strongly you believe that p in each context, then your belief is stake-sensitive.[4]

The question of whether beliefs are stake-sensitive can be raised for full beliefs, for categorical beliefs, and for degrees of belief. Suppose we are talking about action-guiding degrees of belief; a stake-sensitive belief in p could be characterized by a *set* of fair betting quotients, rather than a single one. Which of the fair betting quotients accurately measures the belief could depend on the context, and in particular, on what you then take to be at stake on p. In other words, a stake-sensitive degree of belief in p could have a strength that depends on context, and in particular, on the stakes that you take to actually be in play, as given by valuations you currently attribute to p and to ~p. The current valuations reflect the part that p plays in your current pragmatic interests; the degrees of belief reflect your willingness, in various contexts, to take on new interests and commitments to which p is relevant.[5] In the discussion that follows, let us take beliefs to be degrees of belief; I will assume that rational degrees of belief are subjective probabilities.

If p is one of many members of a partition, it is natural to think of the shape of the stakes on p as comparisons of the value of p to the values of the other members. If you are deliberating among many different options, the shape of the stakes on *A* involves the comparison of its value to the values of the other options *B, C, . . .*[6] Consider, then, in the midst of my deliberation about whether to do *A* or do *B*, my present belief that I will do *A*. This is a belief about the future, perhaps the near future or perhaps a more distant one.[7] The value I attach to the truth of the belief that I (will) do *A* is the value I attach to doing *A*. Similarly, for the rival option *B*. The shape of what is at stake on the truth of *A* involves the pattern of values I attach to *A* and to its rivals. Variation in the shape of the stakes involves variation in the pattern, variation in the relative values I attach to the options.

2. Deliberation and Instability

In the context of extended deliberation, beliefs and evaluations may interact. In some deliberations the interactions are complex, and the process of deliberation delivers contextual changes all by itself; this is particularly so when the decision problem has a form that leads to *decision instability*.

Decision instability can arise in a variety of settings.[8] Allan Gibbard and William Harper illustrated it with the example of the man who met death in Damascus:

> Consider the story of the man who met death in Damascus. Death looked surprised, but then recovered his ghastly composure and said, "I am coming for you tomorrow". The terrified man that night bought a camel and rode to Aleppo. The next day, death knocked on the door of the room where he was hiding and said, "I have come for you".
>
> "But I thought you would be looking for me in Damascus", said the man.
>
> "Not at all", said death "that is why I was surprised to see you yesterday. I knew that today I was to find you in Aleppo".
>
> Now suppose the man knows the following. Death works from an appointment book which states the time and place; a person dies if and only if the book correctly states in what city he will be at the stated time. The book is made up weeks in advance on the basis of highly reliable predictions. An appointment on the next day has been inscribed for him. Suppose, on this basis, the man would take his being in Damascus the next day as strong evidence that his appointment with death is in Damascus, and would take his being in Aleppo the next day as strong evidence that his appointment is in Aleppo.[9]

To find his best option by using causal decision theory, as I will assume he should, the man can use the possible states "Damascus is inscribed" and "Aleppo is inscribed". He takes those states to be outside his causal influence, and they are sufficiently specific, given his present interests, to form a K-partition. Call them K_D and K_A, respectively.

If, for example, he believes the appointment book states Damascus rather than Aleppo, and his belief $pr(K_D)$ is greater than ½, then causal decision theory endorses going to Aleppo.[10] But that decision seems unstable: Since he takes Death's appointment book to be based on reliable predictions, when the man comes to believe he is about to go to Aleppo, he also comes to believe that Aleppo is inscribed after all, so $pr_n(A)$ and $pr_n(K_A)$ are greater than ½, and $pr_n(K_D)$ is less, which makes Damascus the better option. But then the man's preference for Damascus again influences his beliefs; he will probably go there, and Damascus is probably inscribed, $pr_{nn}(D)$ and $pr_{nn}(K_D)$ exceed ½, which makes Aleppo the better option; . . . and so on.

174 *Brad Armendt*

3. Deliberation Dynamics

What should the man do?[11] The sense of instability in problems like *Death in Damascus* arises when he can reevaluate his options in light of the course of his deliberations. This is a good setting for the theory of deliberation dynamics, where your comparisons of your options influence your beliefs about whether you will do them, leading to new evaluations and comparisons of your options, which in turn further influence your beliefs. The theory can be applied to deliberations about many sorts of decision problems, simple and complex.[12]

Deliberation dynamics applies to deliberation that takes place over time. At each moment, your beliefs about states of the world (e.g., Damascus is inscribed) underwrite your current assessments of your options. Those assessments conform, let us suppose, to subjective rational decision theory—throughout this discussion, to causal decision theory. If we assume that the values you attach to outcomes (e.g., life, death) are not shifting, then when your beliefs are stable, so are your assessments of your options. But as in the case of the man who met death, your beliefs may not be stable. At a given moment, your current assessments may influence your beliefs about what you will do, as well as your beliefs about states of the world that matter to the outcome of doing it. Your newly current beliefs then underwrite new assessments, and we can entertain the trajectories of your shifting beliefs and assessments over time. Sometimes those trajectories may display oscillations, as we imagined in the case of the man who met death.[13]

The trajectory of your beliefs will depend on the details of your dynamics. How do your beliefs about what you will do depend on the values you attribute to each option?[14] At time t, you regard one action A as better than its alternative B. (Your $U_t(A)$ is greater than $U_t(B)$ on some specific U_t scale that represents your preferences at t.) How does that influence your belief that you will do A, your $pr_{t+}(A)$, at t_+? The answers to such questions throughout your deliberation might be given by a dynamical rule. Many such rules are possible; among them are rules that *seek the good*, according to which your probabilities that you will perform actions rise exactly when you currently see those actions as better than their alternatives, or more precisely, as better than the *status quo*, which is your current expectation of the outcome of the problem you are deliberating about.[15] If at some moment t your beliefs lead you to regard your options as equally good, then your assessments give you no basis, under dynamics that seek the good, for altering those beliefs and assessments. You are at an *equilibrium* of the dynamics. Since you then regard each action as equally good, to choose one or the other is to break a tie, or "pick" among the tied options.

Returning to Death in Damascus, then, suppose that during his deliberation, the man's evaluations of his options influence his beliefs about what he will soon do, and about what is inscribed in death's appointment book. Suppose that at time t_1 during his deliberation, he regards going to Aleppo

Deliberation and Pragmatic Belief 175

as the better action, so that $U_{t1}(A) > U_{t1}(D)$; this raises his belief that he will go to Aleppo, $pr_{t2}(A) > pr_{t2}(D)$, and also that death will be waiting for him there, $pr_{t2}(K_A) > pr_{t2}(K_D)$.[16] Then, when he reevaluates his options at t_2 with those beliefs, he sees Damascus as the better action, $U_{t2}(D) > U_{t2}(A)$, which influences his beliefs again. Under plausible assumptions, in the Death in Damascus problem, deliberation that seeks the good will eventually lead the man's beliefs to a stable equilibrium, where he sees neither act as better than the other.[17] At that point, his tied evaluations give no basis for further adjustments in the beliefs that underlie them. At the equilibrium state in the original Death in Damascus problem, $pr_{eq}(K_A)$ and $pr_{eq}(K_D)$ are both ½, as are $pr_{eq}(A)$ and $pr_{eq}(D)$. His action will be the outcome of some way of dealing with the tie. So, one rational solution to Death in Damascus is to break a tie between A and D; just pick one of the equally (un)attractive options. Our present focus, however, is on the beliefs at work in rational deliberation, rather than solutions to the problem.

A general feature of equilibrium states, whether your deliberation leads you to them or not, is that you see your available options as equally choiceworthy, as having equal expected utility. It may also happen that you then believe that you are as likely to do one act as the other, but that need not be so in problems that lack the symmetry of Death in Damascus.[18]

Why should the man embark on this deliberative journey? There is at least this reason: a rational choice should be based on all of your relevant beliefs at the time you make it. So, *if* you believe at time t that death is more likely to go to Aleppo than to Damascus, $pr_t(K_A) > pr_t(K_D)$, your evaluations at t of your options, $U_t(A)$ and $U_t(D)$, must use those beliefs. Or, to put it another way, a rational decision theory such as causal decision theory is properly used only when those evaluations do so. What about the beliefs? What sorts of influences on beliefs, what sort of adjustments to beliefs, have we been talking about?

4. Regarding A as Better, and Believing You Will Do It

Consider the man's shifting belief that he will go to Aleppo, $pr_i(A)$, as he deliberates about what to do. At one point, when going to Aleppo looks better, he thinks he will go there; at another point, when it looks worse, he thinks he will not. His state of belief about going to Aleppo appears to be sensitive to the changing shape of the stakes that A carries for him.

Or is it? Is he instead learning new beliefs, stimulated by changes, say, in his belief that "A is better than D"? If learning experiences are revisions that replace old belief states with new ones, then as we noticed earlier, they give no reason to think the states are stake-sensitive. To explore this, we could turn our attention to the rational acquisition and updating of his belief that A is better than D, and others like it. Might *that* belief, if he has it, be sensitive to what is at stake on "A is better than D"? Maybe, but this is getting a bit intricate, and there are other paths of influence to consider.[19]

176 *Brad Armendt*

A deliberator assesses and compares his options; does rationality require that he also maintain up-to-date beliefs about how he assesses them, about how much better he finds one than another? Suppose instead that the shifts in $pr_i(A)$ are directly stimulated by his higher or lower regard for A, rather than by what he believes about that regard. How would his assessments, the shape of the stakes on A, influence his belief? Setting aside learning *via* other beliefs, two possibilities come to mind.

One possibility is that he has *experience* of his comparative regard for his options, and the experience provides grounds for a change of belief about what he will do. Perhaps his current comparative assessments, including that A looks better than D, are sources of experience, akin to perceptual experiences that alter his beliefs in the elements of a Jeffrey-shift (looks like rain), or akin to perceptual experiences endowing him with certainties on which to conditionalize (left knee hurts). If his new belief state replaces his old one, this amounts to a possible way of learning from experience, rather than stake-sensitive belief. That is one possibility. The second is the one we have been pursuing: As his current regard for his options alters the shape of the stakes on A, his stake-sensitive belief that he will go to Aleppo shifts too. The influence is direct, and not mediated by what he believes about his regard for going to Aleppo *vs.* staying in Damascus, nor by an experience of that regard, other than having it.

Either of the two possibilities is compatible with deliberation dynamics, a theory about the rational interaction between your beliefs about what you will do and your assessments of the value of doing it. It takes the influence of your assessments on your beliefs to be systematic, for you, and characterizable by dynamical rules, but it is otherwise silent about the nature of that influence. A dynamical rule is a function from your assessments—of A, for example—to your beliefs about whether you (will) do A. The inputs to the rule are your assessments, not your *beliefs* about your assessments, if you have them. The outputs are your beliefs about what you do.

So it is compatible with deliberation dynamics that the man's belief that he will go to Aleppo is stake-sensitive, and given a reasonable dynamical rule for making such shifts—a rule that seeks the good—there need be nothing irrational about the dependence of that belief on the value of its truth. Here, then, is a scenario for a rational stake-sensitive belief: In extended deliberation, my belief that I will do A sometimes reasonably depends on the shape of what is at stake on its truth.

During our deliberations we sometimes entertain beliefs about, and often have experiences of, assessing and comparing. But how often? To the extent that we suspect that deliberation may at times proceed without them, we leave room for the possibility of rationally stake-sensitive belief. We can investigate whether it is a rational requirement that, throughout your deliberation, you maintain a live stream of beliefs about how you currently evaluate your options, or that you monitor all your evaluations in experience. We can also look for empirical evidence that you do one or the

Deliberation and Pragmatic Belief 177

other whenever you deliberate. The theory of deliberation dynamics neither expects, requires, nor excludes that you do either.

5. Conclusion

I will close with a line of thought about distinguishing among the possibilities; it has to do with the ways rational deliberation may end, in problems like Death in Damascus where deliberation is unstable. We have seen that deliberation may settle into, and remain in, an equilibrium state where going to Aleppo and staying in Damascus are seen as equally good. Given sufficient time, in fact, dynamical rules that seek the good in Death in Damascus are bound to lead to an equilibrium. But time for a given activity, deliberation included, is sometimes in short supply. Before reaching equilibrium, you may get tired, you may have other things to do, or the world may interrupt you. Your deliberation may be truncated for many sorts of reasons.[20]

A question, then: When ongoing deliberation is truncated, why is it truncated where it is? You waver between *A* and *D*; suppose you become tired before reaching the point of thinking the options are equally good, or equally bad. What makes you tired? Is it the effort of evaluating the options yet again, based on your newly adjusted beliefs? Or is it the effort of adjusting beliefs, based on your just-determined values of the options? Perhaps there is no clear answer to the questions. But if the point at which fatigue typically sets in is when yet another utility estimate is called for, that suggests that the adjustments of belief may require less effort, may be more immediate. If on the other hand, fatigue more often leads one to quit at the point of yet another consideration and adjustment of what you will probably do, that suggests the opposite, that the belief adjustments may be less immediate than the revised evaluations. The former case is more favorable to the idea that the belief adjustments arise from stake-sensitivity; the latter case is less so.

Subjective rational decision theory interests us from both third-person and first-person points of view: as a theory that explains the choice-worthiness of actions for a decision maker in light of his relevant beliefs and desires, and as a tool that can help us ascertain what to do, as we reflect on our own relevant beliefs and desires. Insofar as it is easier to notice what occurs in our own deliberations than in the deliberations of others, the questions of the previous paragraph implicitly appeal to what we discern from the perspective of first-person deliberation. Present or future empirical methods for studying the deliberations of others might yield third-person evidence too.

Suppose we had empirical support for the idea that your rational belief about what you will do, during your deliberation, is a stake-sensitive response to your regard for doing it. What, if anything, would that tell us about other beliefs of yours? That surely depends on the nature of the empirical support, but the stake-sensitivity of some rational beliefs would be significant, leading us to wonder whether the means by which it occurs also appear in other situations, affecting other beliefs.

178 *Brad Armendt*

In conclusion, we have seen that extended deliberation is a setting in which some rational beliefs are influenced by what is at stake on their truth. If that influence is direct, and does not destroy and create new belief states, the beliefs are stake-sensitive as well as rational. If influence must always be mediated by other beliefs or by experience, they need not be. The latter alternative seems to me doubtful, but for all I have said, it may be so. Our actual deliberative practices are one source of evidence, among others, that may shed more light on the topic of rational stake-sensitive belief.[21]

Notes

1. See Armendt (2008, 2010, 2013).
2. Since there is little cost to any answer you give, what you say may only loosely indicate how strongly you believe. A better example might have the radio station allow you to bid for a chance to answer the question. The story raises the possibility of stake-sensitive belief, on which I focus here. Elsewhere I consider similar examples and give more attention to other things that may be happening as well, or instead. See Armendt (2008, 2010).
3. This indefiniteness might be seen as a source of imprecision; I have explored that idea elsewhere (Armendt 2013) but do not focus on it here.
4. Your friend offers to place your bet, along with his own, at the racetrack. You tell him to bet \$20 on the horse you like, Apparition. You are anticipating a good race and prospects of victory when your friend returns with your bet on Whirlwind. No doubt this affects your hopes about the outcome of the race; if it also affects your beliefs that Apparition will win, or that Whirlwind will, those beliefs seem sensitive to the shape of the stakes on their truth.
5. Taking on a new commitment, say by accepting a new bet on p at odds that fit your degree of belief in p, would alter the part p plays in your new current interests. That might in turn influence your new degree of belief in p. Does making a bet on p ever lead you to become more confident, or less confident, in the truth of p?
6. There is some abuse of notation here and in the following; I sometimes use A to refer to an action, and sometimes to the proposition "I do A".
7. The offer expires day after tomorrow; the election is on Tuesday; a plan must be in place by next week; I have one minute to make a move . . . Since the time of Richard Jeffrey's development of evidential decision theory (Jeffrey 1965), and before, there have been objections to the idea that I may deliberate about doing A, and simultaneously have some belief about whether I will do A. Evidential decision theory expects an agent to assess A's desirability using conditional beliefs of the form $pr(-/A)$. Without argument, I assume here that present deliberation and present belief about the future action are compatible, and related.
8. Such settings often appear in games among Bayesian players; Battle of the Sexes with a Twin is an example.
9. Gibbard and Harper (1978, pp. 185–186). The story in their example is a variant of one told in W. Somerset Maugham's *Sheppey*, 1933, and alluded to in the title of John O'Hara's *Appointment in Samarra*, 1934; earlier versions of the story are far older, dating to the ninth century and probably earlier; for example, see "When Death Came to Baghdad," in Idries Shah (1967). Different cities appear in various earlier versions of the story.
10. Here I use the K-expectation version of causal decision theory due to Skyrms (1982). Causal decision theory endorses going to Aleppo in the sense that going to Aleppo's expected utility U is maximal, and U represents his preferences. To say that causal decision theory endorses action A is to rely on a principle that endorses actions that maximize U.

Deliberation and Pragmatic Belief 179

11. A plausible answer is toss a coin, or adopt some internal way of performing a mixed act (Harper 1986). However, mixed acts might be ruled out or heavily penalized (Weirich 1985). We might question the legitimacy of such a restriction, but I save that for another occasion. In what follows, I neglect beliefs and assessments concerning mixed acts, but it is straightforward to include them, if a decision maker takes them to be among his options.

12. See Skyrms (1982). In later work, Skyrms (1990) developed an important connection between dynamic deliberation and well-founded solution concepts for noncooperative games among Bayesian players. In decision problems with more than two options, deliberation can be significantly more complex than in Death in Damascus.

13. When you deliberate about different sorts of problems, your shifting beliefs and evaluations follow different sorts of paths. When causal decision theory is used to evaluate your options in a *Newcomb Problem*, for example, deliberation may yield straightforward convergence to high confidence that you will take both boxes, and that the opaque box will be empty, since an increasing confidence that you will take both boxes does not lead you to think it would be better to do otherwise.

    In connection with our larger interests, I do not suggest that all deliberations are clarified by deliberation dynamics; in many deliberations our assessments carry no significant evidence about the state of the world (e.g. what is inscribed). Examples of decision instability such as Death in Damascus provide a setting where beliefs about what you will do matter in deliberation, and the theory of deliberation dynamics gives a framework for saying how they matter, and how they are affected by deliberation.

14. Also, how *much* do your beliefs about what you will do depend on your assessments of those values? An interesting question; here I suppose that the belief shifts are driven only by your shifting assessments of your options.

15. The idea of dynamics that seek the good is Skyrms' (1990, p. 30). Such dynamics must also raise the sum of the probabilities of all the actions better than the *status quo*. Nash, Darwin, and Bayes dynamics are examples of dynamics that seek the good. Dynamics that seek the good may fail to represent the deliberations and actions of some agents. An akratic agent, for example, may have little reason to raise beliefs that at the moment of action he will do what now looks better. (Thanks to Brian Kim here.) A self-destructive agent may have reason to lower those beliefs.

16. The dynamic rule expresses the shift in his beliefs about what he will do, $pr_{t2}(A)$ and $pr_{t2}(D)$. Accompanying shifts in his beliefs about what is inscribed, $pr_{t2}(K_A)$ and $pr_{t2}(K_D)$, will satisfy Jeffrey-conditionalization if his conditional probabilities such as $pr(K_A/A)$ are stable, and there are no further complexities.

17. In general, given sufficient time, we can expect convergence to equilibrium from reasonable starting points. For Death in Damascus, continuous deliberation dynamics that seek the good are guaranteed to converge to equilibrium, but they will not display the oscillations I have described. Discrete-time dynamics that seek the good may well display oscillations; with plausible properties such as a dampening in the learning over time, convergence to equilibrium can also be guaranteed. See Skyrms (1990), Joyce (2012), and William Harper (forthcoming).

18. The original version of Death in Damascus is a symmetric problem, but asymmetric versions are easily given; just add an incentive against travel that makes the outcomes of staying in Damascus a little better than the corresponding outcomes of traveling to Aleppo. Or, imagine that death's appointment book more reliably predicts the traveler's presence when he is in one city than when he is in the other. See Reed Richter (1984).

180 *Brad Armendt*

19. If a belief that A is better than D really plays a part, it could be influenced by A's being seen as better than D in either of the two ways discussed in the next paragraphs. One of the two would be stake-sensitivity.
20. See Armendt (manuscript) for more extensive discussion of truncated dynamical deliberation.
21. Thanks to Brian Kim for his very helpful comments and excellent suggestions for improving this chapter.

References

Armendt, Brad (2008) "Stake-invariant Belief." *Acta Analytica* 23: 29–43.
Armendt, Brad (2010) "Stakes and Beliefs." *Philosophical Studies* 147: 71–87.
Armendt, Brad (2013) "Pragmatic Interests and Imprecise Belief." *Philosophy of Science* 80: 758–768.
Armendt, Brad (manuscript) "Causal Decision Theory and Decision Instability."
Gibbard, Allan and Harper, William (1978) "Counterfactuals and Two Kinds of Expected Utility." In C. Hooker et al. (eds.), *Foundations and Applications of Decision Theory*. Dordrecht: Reidel. Reprinted in W. Harper et al. (eds.), *Ifs*, 153–190. Dordrecht: Reidel.
Harper, William (1986) "Mixed Strategies and Ratifiability in Causal Decision Theory." *Erkenntnis* 24: 25–36.
Harper, William (forthcoming) "Decision Dynamics and Rational Choice." In *Festschrift for Allan Gibbard*.
Jeffrey, Richard C. (1965, 1983) *The Logic of Decision*. Chicago: University of Chicago Press.
Joyce, James M. (2012) "Regret and Instability in Causal Decision Theory." *Synthese* 187: 123–145.
Richter, Reed (1984) "Rationality Revisited." *Australasian Journal of Philosophy* 62: 392–403.
Shah, Idries (Ed.) (1967) *Tales of the Dervishes*. London: Jonathan Cape.
Skyrms, Brian (1982) "Causal Decision Theory." *Journal of Philosophy* 79: 695–711.
Skyrms, Brian (1990) *The Dynamics of Rational Deliberation*. Cambridge, MA: Harvard University Press.
Weirich, Paul (1985) "Decision Instability." *Australasian Journal of Philosophy* 63: 465–472.

11 Doxastic Wronging

Rima Basu and Mark Schroeder

In the Book of Common Prayer's Rite II version of the Eucharist, the congregation confesses, "we have sinned against you in thought, word, and deed".[1] According to this confession we wrong God not just by what we do and what we say, but also by what we think. The idea that we can wrong someone not just by what we do, but by what think or what we believe, is a natural one. It is the kind of wrong we feel when those we love believe the worst about us. And it is one of the salient wrongs of racism and sexism. Yet it is puzzling to many philosophers how we could wrong one another by virtue of what we believe about them. This chapter defends the idea that we can morally wrong one another by what we believe about them from two such puzzles. The first puzzle concerns whether we have the right sort of control over our beliefs for them to be subject to moral evaluation. And the second concerns whether moral wrongs would come into conflict with the distinctively epistemic standards that govern belief. Our answer to both puzzles is that the distinctively epistemic standards governing belief are not independent of moral considerations. This account of moral encroachment explains how epistemic norms governing belief are sensitive to the moral requirements governing belief.

1.1 Doxastic Wronging, What

Our interest in this chapter is in the idea of doxastic wronging. A doxastic wronging happens if one person wrongs another in virtue of what she believes about him. There are three parts of this definition that we want to emphasize. First, doxastic wrongs are directed. When you wrong someone, you don't merely do wrong, you do wrong to them. Second, doxastic wrongs are committed by beliefs. So in particular, the wrong in a doxastic wronging does not lie in what you do, either prior to, or subsequent to, forming a belief, but rather in the belief itself. And third, doxastic wrongs are wrongs in virtue of what is believed. So a belief that is a doxastic wronging does not wrong merely in virtue of its consequences; the wronging lies in the belief, rather than in, or at least, over and above, its effects.

182 *Rima Basu and Mark Schroeder*

It is not obvious to most philosophers that there are any cases of doxastic wronging; indeed whether this is even possible is, we take it, deeply controversial within philosophy, and many philosophers find it to be puzzling. Yet this puzzlement seems to come from theoretical reflection, rather than from ordinary thought. There are many plausible intuitive examples of doxastic wrongs. As we have already noted, one common formulation of the Christian Eucharistic confession appeals to the idea that we can sin against God in thought, as well as in word and in deed. This language is clear that the wrong is a directed one, and the explicit contrast with word and deed makes clear that the wronging lies in the thought, rather than in what we do. As with all doctrinal matters, of course, other interpretations are possible, and will be sought by those who cleave to the view that doxastic wrongs are too philosophically puzzling to be possible. Perhaps the confession does not imply that our beliefs ever wrong God, but only other matters of thought— what we spend time thinking about, for example, or our doubts, rather than our beliefs. But in the absence of some particular reason to think that beliefs cannot wrong, the confession is naturally interpreted as at least suggesting the existence of doxastic wrongs.[2]

Another place to look for doxastic wrongs lies in the feelings we are prone to have when our loved ones believe the worst of us. Just to make the thought vivid, suppose that you have struggled with an alcohol problem for many years, but have been sober for eight months. Tonight you attend a departmental reception for a visiting colloquium speaker, and are proud of withstanding the temptation to have a drink. But when you get home, your spouse smells the wine that the colloquium speaker spilled on your sleeve while gesticulating to make a point, and you can see from her eyes that that she thinks you have fallen off of the wagon. If you are like us, then you will be prone to feel wounded by this. Yes, you have a long history of falling off of the wagon, and yes, there is some evidence that this time is another. You can see how it could be reasonable for someone to draw this conclusion. But it still hurts—not least because in your eyes, tonight was an achievement to stay on the wagon despite adverse circumstances.

The feeling of being wounded is arguably a sign of a directed wrong. If she owes an apology, it is to you, not to anyone else—again the sign of a directed wrong. And it seems to be her belief that you would like an apology for. For example, it would feel insincere and unsatisfying if she apologized for the upstream act of not investigating more carefully before forming this belief, but continued to believe it anyway, or if she apologized for the downstream act of revealing her belief to you by the look in her eyes, but not for the belief itself. Again, in the absence of some particular reason to think that beliefs cannot wrong, this looks to us like a strong prima facie case of a doxastic wrong.

A third, more pervasive place to look for doxastic wrongs lies in the wrongs of racism, sexism, homophobia, and other forms of prejudice. It is important to be clear that there are many harmful consequences of racism (just to focus on one example). But it is also natural to take it that one of the distinctive wrongs committed by a racist lies in what she believes about another human being.[3] The racist is paradigmatically disposed to be influenced by her perceptions of race in the beliefs that she forms about another person—more easily persuaded that someone is dangerous, for example, if they are perceived as black. Racist beliefs are naturally taken not just to be morally problematic, but specifically to wrong their subjects. Moreover, an apology for crossing the street to avoid you by someone who still believes that you are dangerous would strike us as insincere, as would an apology for not checking more carefully before forming this belief, by someone who still holds the belief. So that is again at least some prima facie evidence that at least an important part of the wrong lies in the belief, rather than acts leading up to or subsequent to it. Once more, in the absence of any reason to think that doxastic wrongs are impossible, this looks to us like strong prima facie evidence of a doxastic wronging.

Much more work would be required in order to convince the dogmatic, but it is our belief that prima facie evidence like that assembled here should be taken at face value. All of these cases in which some wrong is committed, and neither apologies for the upstream acts which lead to the belief nor apologies for the downstream acts that are caused by that belief are intuitively satisfactory. This suggests that the real wrong lies somewhere else—neither upstream nor downstream, but in the belief itself, or in its formation. For these reasons, we hold that we do sometimes wrong one another in virtue of what we believe about them, and that an adequate understanding of the morality of interpersonal relationships must take this into account. But in this chapter our purpose is not to offer a positive argument for this conclusion. Rather, it is to make room for this idea, by confronting what we take to be two of the most obvious reasons why the existence of doxastic wrongs might seem to be philosophically puzzling.

1.2 Two Puzzles

As we have been noting, the idea that there are doxastic wrongs is a natural one. Indeed it is, we believe, the position of ordinary common sense. But it has been held by many theorists to be philosophically problematic. Indeed, this idea is so far from being an acceptable one in most mainstream circles in analytic philosophy that intelligent interlocutors often correct us, explaining that we can't really mean what we say we mean when we describe this thesis. There are important puzzles about how we could wrong one another in virtue of what we believe about them, and it is our goal in this chapter to come to grips with two such puzzles: the problem of control and the problem of coordination.

The problem of control is the most familiar such problem. There are a number of ways of trying to press it, but they are all modeled on a familiar challenge to so-called deontological theories of epistemic justification.

184   *Rima Basu and Mark Schroeder*

According to traditional deontological theories, epistemic justification is a matter of what we ought, or are permitted, to believe, or a matter of what is prescribed by certain epistemic rules. Critics object that beliefs cannot be subject to deontological categories like ought, permission, or rules, on the grounds that only behavior over which we have voluntary control can be subject to such categories, and we lack such voluntary control over our beliefs. The problem of control tries to generalize this sort of objection to the idea that there are doxastic wrongs. The idea is that we lack sufficient control over our beliefs to be accountable for them in the way that we would need to be, in order for our beliefs themselves to constitute ways of wronging someone. In contrast, actions are paradigmatically the sort of thing over which we have control, and so, the proponent of this problem alleges, it is much more plausible that we wrong others in virtue of the actions that we take leading up to the formation of some belief, or in the actions that we take on its basis. Hence, proponents of this argument conclude, the apparent wrongs associated with racism, sexism, and so on must all take place either before or after the belief is formed, and cannot be identified with the belief itself. We will respond to the problem of control in sections 2.1 and 2.2.

The problem of coordination, on the other hand, arises because what makes something wrong someone is influenced by moral considerations. But it is generally held that moral considerations are not the sort of consideration that rightly bears on the epistemic matter of what one should believe. And in general, according to popular evidentialist accounts of epistemic rationality, what it is epistemically rational to believe—that is, what is rational in every way that is required for knowledge—depends wholly on whether it is supported by adequate evidence.[4] If moral considerations affect whether something is wrong without affecting the evidence, then nothing will coordinate moral and epistemic standards governing belief. In particular, there may be cases in which a belief wrongs someone even though it is rational in every way required for knowledge—in fact, even if it is knowledge.

But this is puzzling, because in general, we do not wrong someone by doing something for which we have the right sort of adequate justification. If Daniel fails to keep his promise to meet you for lunch because he has been called to his father's deathbed, it may be wise and gracious for him to apologize to you, but he does not owe you an apology. He may harm you by frustrating your expectations for a lunch partner, but that harm is not a wronging. That his father's death was suddenly imminent is an adequate justification for him to break his promise. Similarly, if a belief is rational in every way required for knowledge—or even if it is knowledge—it seems like that ought to be an adequate justification for holding this belief, even if it hurts your feelings. It may be wise or gracious to apologize to each other for our beliefs, on this view, but we surely wouldn't owe apologies. And if this is right, then beliefs do not wrong, if they are epistemically rational. Hence, they cannot wrong at all. We will respond to the problem of coordination in sections 3.1 and 3.2.

Finally, we will conclude in section 4 by gesturing toward an explanation of how it could be true that the epistemic norms governing belief must be sensitive to the moral requirements governing belief. Our strategy will be familiar from the more general literature on pragmatic encroachment in epistemology. Pragmatic encroachment is the thesis that whether someone knows, or whether it is epistemically rational for her to believe, can depend on intuitively practical features of her situation, and not just on the evidence or other truth-related factors.

Because one of the main routes through which the thesis of pragmatic encroachment entered mainstream epistemology was through detailed discussion of intuitions about examples by Jeremy Fantl and Matthew McGrath (2002) and by Jason Stanley (2005), it is often taken to stand or fall on the basis of such intuitive judgments about cases. But Stanley does not claim that the intuitions that support pragmatic encroachment have a role akin to the role of observational data for scientific data. Rather, according to Stanley, these intuitions are intended to reveal in an intuitively compelling way a powerful connection between belief and action that epistemologists had been ignoring.[5] Similarly, we suggest that cases of doxastic wronging are not so much just one more data point. Instead, they are important because they dramatize the role that our beliefs about one another play in constituting our interpersonal relationships—a powerful connection between belief and human sociality.

2.1 The Problem of Control

The first hurdle for establishing the plausibility of doxastic wronging is the intuitively appealing thought that we lack control over our beliefs—that our beliefs are insufficiently voluntary for appropriate ascriptions of praise and blame, and correspondingly for rightness or wrongness, to apply. This problem of control has traditionally been used to establish that beliefs are not subject to distinctively deontological epistemic obligations. That is, there is no sense to be made of the claim that we ought believe or are permitted to believe anything as such terms suggest that we have control over what we believe. Our beliefs, it is argued, are at the mercy of the evidence.[6] That is, there is no interesting sense in which it is up to us what we believe; we lack the necessary voluntary control. Call this the *original* problem of control.

In this section we will show how similar arguments can be extended to argue that beliefs cannot wrong. This version of the problem has seldom been laid out explicitly, in part this is because the thesis that beliefs can wrong has not been given the serious attention it deserves. It is natural to think, however, that the problem of control is at the heart of much of the skepticism towards doxastic wrongs. Call this the *extended* problem of control.

As we will show in this section, there are many places in which the original problem of control goes wrong. As a result, it shouldn't be surprising if those difficulties also extend to the extended problem of control. However,

186 *Rima Basu and Mark Schroeder*

in section 2.2, we will see that this answer is too quick. In fact, more needs to be said to solve the extended problem of control than to solve the original problem of control. Nonetheless, we go on to say it by drawing on one of the main insights of this chapter: that the epistemic standards governing belief are not independent of moral considerations.

The intuitive case for the challenge posed by the problem of control starts by reflecting on instances in which despite feeling wronged, it would be a mistake to say that we are wronged. For example, when your house is destroyed by a tornado, you may very well feel wronged by the tornado. Further, if the tornado destroys only your house, leaving all the other houses on your block untouched, it might even feel like a directed wrong. You might express your frustration at the tornado by turning to the sky and asking why it had to be your house or shaking your fists at the sky demanding an apology for what was done to you. We do not think, however, in such cases that you are wronged by the tornado. Similarly, despite how natural it is to feel wronged by your partner when they believe you've been drinking, perhaps we are just mistaken.

Tornados have no control over whether they form nor what path they take. If there is a thunderstorm with an unstable mix of warm moist air, cool dry air, a change of wind direction, and increase in wind speed, there will be a tornado. Further, once the tornado has formed, there is no interesting sense in which it is up to the tornado whether to turn south or to turn west. Proponents of the problem of control argue that beliefs are, in a way, just like tornados. Just as tornados are at the mercy of instability in the atmosphere and wind shear, our beliefs are similarly at the mercy of the evidence. For example, if you look outside and see drops of water falling from the sky and making the sidewalk wet, you will believe that it is raining outside. On this picture, beliefs are not exercises of agency at all, voluntary or otherwise—they are merely caused in a predictable way by the evidence with which we are presented. Further, just as it is a mistake to think that we are wronged by tornados and other things outside of our control, it is similarly a mistake to think that we are wronged by what others believe of us.

This idea that beliefs are at the mercy of the evidence in the same way tornados are at the mercy of the elements is a widespread sentiment. Consider, for example, the following selection of quotes.

> In saying that his belief is based on particular evidence, we would mean not just that he has the belief and can defend it with the evidence, but that he has the belief just because he has the evidence. This says that if he ceased to believe the evidence, then, other things being equal, he would cease to have that belief.[7]
>
> With respect to almost all normal perceptual, introspective, and memory propositions, it is absurd to think that one has any such control over whether one accepts, rejects, or withholds the proposition. When I look out my window and see rain falling, water dripping off the leaves

Doxastic Wronging 187

of trees, and cars passing by, I no more have immediate control over whether I accept those propositions than I have basic control.[8]

Suppose I am at the grocery store deliberating whether to get lemon sorbet or rocky road ice cream. Suppose I go with lemon sorbet. That was my choice, and thus the decision is mine. It is "up to me". By contrast, suppose I am looking out my window at the sky, and it is raining. I deliberate whether to believe it is raining. I cannot bring myself to believe that it is not raining. It is not up to me what I believe; rather it is up to the evidence. I can't go against definitive evidence that stares me in the face. It is not "up to me" in this way. Belief is not "up to me", but is rationally determined.[9]

Implicit in these quotes is the following thought: for deontological concepts such as obligation or duty to apply in the domain of epistemology, beliefs would have to be different from tornados in the following way. We must be able to choose what to believe; agents need to have control over their beliefs to be responsible for what they believe. We (typically) are not responsible for what is not on our control. Proponents of this original problem of control argue that given that we are no more in control of our beliefs than a tornado is in control of what path it takes, it is just as odd to say that an agent ought believe p as it is to say that a tornado ought take the southeasterly path.

To extend this argument to establish the conclusion that beliefs cannot wrong we can add the following premise that emerges from the tornado analogy: for moral concepts, e.g., wronging, to apply to what an agent believes, agents need to have control over their beliefs. That is, for it to be the case that I can wrong you by what I believe of you, the belief must be in my control. My beliefs, to continue to mix metaphors, cannot be like tornados. It must be up to me whether my belief can turn south or turn west if I am to wrong you given what I believe. In short, we lack sufficient control over our beliefs to be accountable for them in the way that we would need to be in order for our beliefs themselves to constitute ways of wronging someone.

To briefly summarize, our beliefs are psychologically and conceptually limited in a way that makes them more like tornados than something to which deontological or moral concepts apply. With this in hand, we can formulate the two versions of the problem of control we've been discussing as follows.

Original Problem: The Argument Against Deontological Epistemic Obligations

(1) For deontological concepts such as obligation or duty to apply in the domain of epistemology, agents need to have control over their beliefs.
(2) It is not the case that agents have control over their beliefs.
(C) Therefore, deontological concepts do not apply in the domain of epistemology.

188 Rima Basu and Mark Schroeder

Extended Problem: The Argument Against Doxastic Wrongs

(1) For beliefs to wrong, agents need to have control over their beliefs.
(2) It is not the case that agents have control over their beliefs.
(C) Therefore, beliefs cannot wrong.

In the original problem, the two premises—(1) and (2)—have both come under attack for various reasons. Our goal here is not to come down one way or another on which way, in this space of possibilities, is the right way of responding to both versions of this argument. Instead, our goal is to give a sense of the wide space available for objecting to both versions of this argument and convey the point that the argument goes wrong in many places. Further, given that there's more than one place to object to the original problem, it shouldn't be surprising if those objections also apply to the extended problem.

Let us begin with the premise that is most commonly attacked: (2). Shah (2002) argues that a closer examination the connection between deontological concepts and belief reveals an alternative conception of control that is sufficient for deontological concepts to apply in the domain of epistemology. Namely, we have a capacity to be moved by an appreciation of reasons. As a result, Shah rejects (2) on the grounds that we exert control over our beliefs in the following way: through our appreciation of the evidence we are agents with regard to our beliefs and are capable of regulating our beliefs. Steup (2012), in a manner similar to Shah, argues that arguments of the form given previously assume that voluntariness requires responsiveness to practical reasons, but our beliefs are responsive to epistemic reasons and that is the way in which we exercise control over our beliefs. Weatherson (2008) has persuasively argued that this argument relies on too narrow a conception of voluntary. Flowerree (2016) argues that we must be agents with respect to our beliefs if we are to avoid the following reductio that plagues accounts that argue we are not agents with respect to our beliefs: if we are not agents with respect to our beliefs, then we are not agents with respect to our intentions. And Benbaji (2016) argues something even stronger: the argument regarding our lack of control generalizes to show that we're not even agents with respect to our actions.

Resisting (2), however, is not the only strategy. Some philosophers reject the assumption underlying (1) in the original problem: that for deontological concepts to apply in the domain of epistemology control is needed. For example, Hieronymi (2006, 2008) argues that it is not troubling to say that we can no more intend at will than believe at will. Many of our intentions unreliably produce actions, and the unreliability is highly suggestive of a lack of control. For example, consider Janae's intention to drink scotch. Janae would like to one day be the kind of person that can order scotch at a bar and drink it as easily as wine or beer. She did not start out as someone that liked the taste of wine or beer, but over time she has brought herself to

Doxastic Wronging 189

like the taste. There are, however, many items she has failed to bring herself to like. No matter how much she would like to be the kind of person that likes goat cheese, for example, she finds that she cannot stand the taste. It seems that Janae lacks any reliable control over her intentions. Nonetheless, it is not odd to grant that given Janae desires to like goat cheese and drink scotch there is some sense in which Janae ought to like goat cheese and ought to drink scotch, further it is some sort of failing when she does not succeed. Despite the fact that she lacks any reliable kind of control over her intentions, deontological concepts seem to apply. Hieronymi takes these sorts of cases to suggest that control is not central to our notions of responsibility, praise, and blame.[10]

In general, these strategies against the problem of control take the following form. They show that for deontological concepts to apply in the domain of epistemology either we have sufficient control for deontological concepts to apply or there is no control needed for deontological concepts to apply. These strategies all concern different ways of understanding "control" and "sufficiency" and the relationship between "sufficient control" and the applicability of deontological concepts to a domain. Now we must ask whether these arguments might extend to respond to the extended problem of control. Unfortunately, as we will now see, the extended problem of control is more forceful than the original problem. But, we will argue that it can still be answered successfully.

2.2 The Problem of Control, Reconsidered

Let us start by taking a closer look at one of the objections to the original problem of control in order to see why these objections do not automatically transfer to the extended problem of control. Hieronymi (2006) grants that we can exercise a manipulative form of control over our beliefs. For example, we can have extrinsic reasons to produce within ourselves a belief.

> Suppose you can't fall asleep because you are worried about whether your friends arrived safely home through the storm. Wanting sleep, you have an extrinsic reason for the belief that they are safely home. This extrinsic reason gives you reason to produce in yourself a belief. The obvious thing to do, in this case, is to conduct a little investigation: call your friends. If you find them home, you will have brought yourself to the desired belief.[11]

These extrinsic reasons you have, reasons for why the belief is good to have, e.g., you'll be able to fall asleep if you believe your friend arrived safely home through the storm, only support you taking the steps to induce a belief. These reasons, Hieronymi argues, do not bear on the question of whether the belief is true, and as a result cannot support any particular conclusion you might otherwise hope you'd arrive at.

190 *Rima Basu and Mark Schroeder*

According to Hieronymi's answer to the original problem of control, the reason why being at the mercy of the evidence is compatible with epistemic agency is that evidence is the right kind of reason—a constitutive reason—for forming beliefs. So in being led around by the evidence, in being at the mercy of evidence, we are responding to reasons that are paradigmatic of epistemic agency. This objection to the original problem of control does not automatically transfer to the extended problem of control. The latter problem concerns whether moral reasons could be the right kind of reason for or against forming beliefs.

Nevertheless, the structure of Hieronymi's response offers a promising route to an answer to the extended problem of control. What we must show is that evidence is not the only right kind of reason for or against forming beliefs. Once we can show that, we will have opened the door for moral reasons being among the reasons that are active in epistemic agency and have cleared a theoretical hurdle for establishing the possibility of doxastic wrongs.

It seems wrong to us to say that only evidence matters for epistemic agency. On the face of it a lot of things matter. We can find support for this suspicion in an example from Nelson (2010, 87).

> Given the appearance of some distinctive dark, winged shapes, moving across my visual field, what should I believe? That visual evidence, joined with other factors, may license me to believe propositions such as:
>
> 1. There are things moving through the air in front of me.
> 2. There are birds flying in front of me.
> 3. There are jackdaws flying in front of me.
> 4. At least three jackdaws exist.
>
> Which proposition I do believe will depend on, among other things: how my perceptual abilities have developed (e.g. have I learned to discriminate different kinds of bird on the wing?); the background information I happen to have (e.g. do I know what a jackdaw is?); and my particular interests at that moment (e.g. what do I want to know or do now?).[12]

When we ask which proposition we should believe, the answer depends partly on our epistemic situation—in Hieronymi's terms, the constitutive reasons, i.e., the evidence—but also partly on our needs and interests. For example, if Charlie is interested in launching a model airplane, then Charlie should believe 1. But if Zenobia is afraid of birds and wishes to avoid them, then she should believe 2. If D'angelo is conducting a species survey, then depending on the specificity of the survey he should believe either 3 or 4. However, if Diana's interest is to hail a cab, she need not believe either 1–4. The lesson here is that none of Charlie, Zenobia, D'angelo, or Diana are simply being pulled around by the evidence. Given the same evidence—distinctive dark,

Doxastic Wronging 191

winged shapes, moving across their visual field—they are capable of either forming a belief or not. Evidence, then, is not the only thing matters for epistemic agency.

This argument from Nelson shows that we have no trouble not believing things for which we have evidential support. This argument also provides support for thinking that we do respond to a wide variety of considerations that are not just evidence. This picture, however, could be made consistent with the account offered by Hieronymi. Hieronymi offers a two-stage view that can offer a competing diagnosis of each of these cases. For example, although neither Charlie, Zenobia, D'angelo, nor Diana are pulled around by the evidence, how they decide what to believe is settled by what question they ask. When it comes to believing, there are two separate activities answerable to two separate sorts of reasons. First, there is the activity of asking a question, of beginning a course of inquiry. Second, there are the constitutive reasons, i.e., the evidence that is unearthed during the investigation that settles which particular belief we should hold. Hieronymi argues that Charlie, Zenobia, D'angelo, and Diana all exercise managerial control over their beliefs *through* their direct control over the first activity—the question they ask—but with regard to the second activity, their belief, insofar as they are rational, is entirely a matter of the evidence. That is, in the second stage of inquiry they are at the mercy of the evidence.

We can see now see how this two-stage account prevents Hieronymi's objection to the original problem of control argument from automatically transferring to the extended problem of control. For deontological epistemic obligations it is enough that we have managerial control over our beliefs, i.e., control in the first stage of deliberation. For beliefs to wrong, however, it is not enough that we have managerial control over our beliefs. Recall that we are not upset with our spouse because they began an investigation into whether we had been drinking. Although that is another reason we might seek an apology, if that is all that our spouse apologized for her apology would be incomplete. What we seek apology for is what our spouse believes. We seek apology for the second activity, the activity over which Hieronymi argues it is not up to us how we settle the investigation once we begin it. We seem to seek apology for the activity over which Hieronymi argues we lack control. Generally it is thought to be inappropriate, however, to feel wronged by what someone did if what they did was not in their control. This lack of control seems like it could be excusing. If this lack of control is excusing, then we must look elsewhere for an explanation of why we feel wronged by what our spouse believes of us. That is, we need an alternative explanation for what we have been arguing we need doxastic wrongs to explain. That is, we need an explanation for why we might feel wronged by what others believe of us that does not require the controversial assumption that agents have control over their beliefs as the latter seems needed to establish doxastic wrongs.

192   Rima Basu and Mark Schroeder

The two-stage view offers such a debunking argument against doxastic wrongs. This debunking argument starts with a plausible alternative to doxastic wrongs: the observation that in contrast to beliefs, our actions are paradigmatically the sort of thing over which we have control. Given the strong intuitive sway of the idea that we do not control our beliefs, in the way needed for doxastic wrongs, perhaps then it is much more plausible that we wrong others in virtue of the actions that we take leading up to the formation of some belief, or in the actions that we take on its basis. Perhaps, then, the apparent wrongs associated with racism, sexism, and so on must all take place either before or after the belief is formed, and cannot be identified with the belief itself.

There are many reasons to reject this line of reasoning,[13] but as we have focused on in this chapter, an apology that stops at the level of what your partner does or what they reveal about their beliefs feels incomplete. In the example we've been using to motivate doxastic wrongs—wrongs that are directed, wrongs that are committed by beliefs, and wrongs that are wrongs in virtue of what is believed—the apology is not complete until your spouse apologizes for the belief. It is more commonplace than philosophers seem to suggest, given the theoretical pull of the problem of control, to exclaim, "You shouldn't have believed that of me". Thus, in response to this debunking alternative, we suggest that this candidate alternative explanation fails to capture the incompleteness of our spouse's apology. Hence we can reject this alternative explanation and we have good grounds to look back at suggestions made by the two-stage view and figure out where it goes wrong.

To recap, according to the two-stage view, once we get to the second activity, once the investigation is underway, it is no longer up to us what we believe. That is, what we will believe at the conclusion of the investigation is entirely a matter of epistemic considerations, i.e., what the evidence suggests. To answer the two-stage view what we must do is show that we are not at the mercy of the evidence once we consider the evidence. That is, we must that evidence is not the only kind of reason that's the right kind of reason for or against forming beliefs. As we will now go on to show, when it comes to answering a question about the content of a belief, it is often the case that how we answer that question is a matter of our own psychology, and thus up to us.

Consider the following example. Suppose that Neil is ambushed in the street with a bunch of evidence that Taylor Swift has a dog named "Taylor Swift". Managerial control over what he believes has been taken away from him, the question has been asked and the evidence has been presented. Neil, however, does not care at all about Taylor Swift, whether she has a dog or what that dog's name is. Does Neil have any control over what he believes now of Taylor Swift and her dog or is Neil required to believe that Taylor Swift has a dog named "Taylor Swift"? If Neil just doesn't care, it seems odd to say that he is required to believe anything about the name of Taylor Swift's dog. The two-stage view, however, is committed to saying that Neil has no choice in what he believes once the evidence is presented to him. This strikes us as implausible and we think we're in good company in rejecting this consequence of the two-stage view.

Sherlock Holmes for example, as he is presented in Sir Arthur Conan Doyle's work *A Study in Scarlet*, remarks at one point: "there comes a time when for every addition of knowledge you forget something that you knew before. It is of the highest importance, therefore, not have useless facts elbowing out the useful ones".[14] Similarly, the version of Sherlock Holmes that appears in the latest BBC adaption by Stephen Moffat also finds himself chastised by Dr. Watson for being ignorant of Copernican Theory and unaware that the Earth travels around the sun. In *A Study in Scarlet*, when Holmes is similarly chastised in this way he responds, "What the deuce is it to me? [. . .] You say that we go round the sun. If we went round the moon it would not make a pennyworth of difference to me or to my work". Along with the previous examples from Nelson of how evidence underdetermines what we believe, these examples together suggest that we really are capable of responding to a wide variety of considerations that are not just evidence, even once questions have been opened for us. These examples push back against the thought that the problem of control is really a problem. Evidence is not the only thing that matters for epistemic agency, a lot of things matter, and presumably some of those things could be moral reasons. These examples illustrate that we have more control over what we believe than traditionally thought and that when it comes to answering a question about the content of a belief, it is often the case that how we answer that question is a matter of our own psychology, and thus up to us.

Recent work in social psychology further reinforces the picture that we have been sketching concerning belief, apology, interpersonal commitments, and the way in which our interests shape our beliefs. Kruglanski's (2004) work shows that when we choose to settle belief is intimately tied to what he calls our epistemic motivations. The epistemic motivations are goals that we possess with respect to knowledge.[15] He classifies these motivations along two dimensions: closure seeking versus avoidance, and specificity versus nonspecificity. As a result, there are four epistemic motivations explored in Kruglanski's experimental work:

(1) Need for nonspecific closure: you desire a firm answer to a question, but any answer will do
(2) Need to avoid a nonspecific closure: you desire to keep your options open, as a result you are engaging in judgmental noncommitment
(3) Need for specific closure: you are looking for a particular answer to a particular question and it is not the case that you would happy with any

194 *Rima Basu and Mark Schroeder*

answer to the question you are seeking an answer to, your motivations are directionally biased

(4) Need to avoid specific closure: you wish to avoid believing a particular belief

The two-stage view can make sense at most of cases involving the need for nonspecific closure and need to avoid nonspecific closure. This is because in the two-stage view, belief formation decomposes into two separate stages, and all practical considerations matter for is whether to go in for forming a belief at all. They do not matter for which belief you get.

In contrast, there is no way to choose at which stage the need for and need to avoid specific closure could operate. Take some simple cases of the need to avoid specific closure. Tobacco companies have expended considerable money on research investigating whether smoking causes lung cancer. They've avoided coming to the conclusion that it does not by refusing to consider the question at all, but by considering it asymmetrically—applying higher evidential standards to the answer that inconveniences them. The need to avoid specific closure works in just this way at an individual level— allowing even someone who is engaged in considering a question to apply differing standards to each answer.[16]

The way that Kruglanski and his colleagues understand this picture, one's motivation toward closure lies on a spectrum that can be manipulated by a variety of factors, e.g., your need for nonspecific closure can be heightened when you are working towards a deadline. Alternatively you might be tired and given that seeking particular answers to particular questions is taxing, you may instead exhibit more of a need to avoid nonspecific closure. These studies suggest that our belief formation practices are more sensitive to non-evidential considerations and it is unclear whether the two-stage view's limited conception of epistemic agency can accommodate these various epistemic motivations.

When it comes to answering a question about the content of a belief, it is often the case that how we answer that question is a matter of our own psychology, and thus up to us. Evidence is not all that matters for epistemic agency, a lot of things matter and presumably those things could include moral reasons. Hence, there is no problem of control for doxastic wrongs and we've cleared the first theoretical hurdle for establishing the suggestive idea that moral considerations could matter directly for the epistemic rationality of belief.[17]

3.1 The Problem of Coordination, First Pass

So far, we have given our response to the problem of control. The other obstacle to doxastic wrongs arises from the possibility that this leads to a lack of coordination between moral and epistemic standards governing beliefs. The problem is simple: if beliefs can wrong, then there will be non-coordinating epistemic and moral standards governing belief, because while the epistemic standards governing belief depend only on the evidence, whether a belief

Doxastic Wronging   195

wrongs depends instead on moral considerations. And this could easily lead to troubling choices between being rational and being good.

Many authors who are sympathetic to the possibility of doxastic wrongs have described the moral standards governing belief as in conflict with the demands of epistemic rationality. For example, Tamar Gendler (2011, 57) claims that avoiding the doxastic wrongs of racist beliefs requires "explicit irrationality through base-rate neglect". And according to Simon Keller (2004, 329), "a good friendship sometimes requires epistemic irresponsibility".[18] At a first pass, both of these appear to be the claim that there are genuine conflicts of epistemic and moral duties regarding beliefs—cases in which one ought morally to be one way with respect to one's beliefs, but ought epistemically to be a contrary way.

The most natural interpretation of the problem of coordination is that a lack of coordination between moral and epistemic norms governing beliefs is bad, precisely because it would result in such deontic conflicts between epistemic and moral requirements on belief. We reject this interpretation of the problem of coordination, but it is worth taking the time to see why. This first pass articulation of the problem looks like this:

Non-coordination as Conflicts

P1) If there are doxastic wrongs, then there are deontic conflicts between requirements of morality and rational requirements on belief.

P2) If there are deontic conflicts between requirements of morality and rational requirements on belief, then that creates some problem for rational requirements on belief.

P3) There is no problem for rational requirements on belief.

C)   There are no doxastic wrongs.

We'll leave open, here, whether there is a way of making good on an appropriate answer to what would be so bad about deontic conflicts between morality and epistemic rationality that is not bad about deontic conflicts between, for example, prudence, and courage. The main reason why this does not give us a general problem for the idea that there are deontic wrongs is that P1 is false—there could easily be deontic wrongs without any deontic conflicts between moral and epistemic requirements on belief.

If there is to be a deontic conflict between the requirements of morality and the rational requirements on belief, then there must be something, A, which some person X, ought morally to do but ought rationally not to do. So since we are concerned with beliefs, one of the following must be the case, for some proposition p and agent X:

Case 1: X is morally required to believe that p, and X is rationally required not to believe that p.

Case 2: X is morally required not to believe that p, and X is rationally required to believe that p.

The problem for P1 that there can be deontic wrongs without either of these cases ever being possible. The cases of doxastic wrongs that we used to motivate our initial interest in this chapter are cases in which one person wrongs another person by what she *believes* about him—not cases in which someone wrongs another person by what she does *not* believe about him.[19] If there are doxastic wrongs of belief, but no doxastic wrongs of non-belief, then there are *ipso facto* no Case 1 deontic conflicts.

Similarly, in order for there to be Case 2 conflicts, there must be some things that we are epistemically required to believe. But it is not obvious that there are enough things that we are epistemically rationally required to believe, in order to create such conflicts. As we have noted earlier in section 2.2, Mark Nelson (2010) has argued, for example, that there are no positive epistemic duties at all—nothing that anyone is ever epistemically rationally epistemically required to believe at all, only things that it is rationally epistemically irrational to believe. And even if Nelson is wrong and there are some things that we are rationally epistemically required to believe, it is quite plausible that these are going to be insufficiently common, in order to generate conflicts of the required sort. For example, if our only positive epistemic duties are to believe logical truths, then all it takes for there to be doxastic wrongs without deontic conflicts with the requirements of epistemic rationality, is that believing a logical truth never wrongs anyone. But none of our leading examples of doxastic wrongs are cases of believing logical truths, and it is in any case not plausible that you can wrong someone by believing a logical truth. Similar points go if the beliefs that are rationally required include non-logical truths as well, so long as they are still relatively limited.

If any of the views in the last paragraph are correct, then at most few beliefs are epistemically required. You are doing poorly, as a believer, if you do not believe these things. And many are epistemically forbidden—you are doing poorly, as a believer, if you believe these things. Finally, some are morally forbidden—you are doing poorly, as a moral agent, if you believe these things. But the goals of doing well as a believer and doing well as a moral agent are in no way in tension, because as Figure 11.1 illustrates, there are many ways of believing all of the things that you are rationally required to believe while believing none of the things that you are rationally forbidden from believing and believing none of the things that you are morally forbidden from believing.

Consequently, we don't believe that a lack of coordination between epistemic and moral standards governing belief can be problematic simply in virtue of leading to deontic conflicts between the demands of epistemic rationality and the demands of morality. But we *do* believe that there is something more general to be troubled by, in the neighborhood. There is a more forceful way of saying why a lack of coordination between moral and epistemic standards governing belief would be bad.

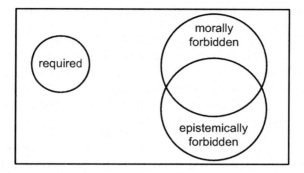

Figure 11.1 Moral and Epistemic Requirements Without Deontic Conflicts

3.2 The Problem of Coordination, Second Pass

The more forceful way of putting the problem of coordination does not depend on the assumption that there are any proper deontic conflicts between moral and rational epistemic requirements on belief. It targets the bare assumption that morality forbids things that epistemic rationality does not—the shaded area in Figure 11.2:

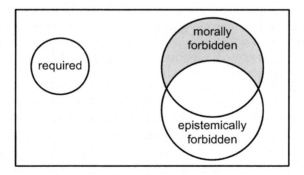

Figure 11.2 Morally Forbidden but Epistemically Permissible Beliefs

We believe that nothing can occupy this shaded area. Suppose for purposes of *reductio* that it does. If morality forbids beliefs that epistemic rationality does not, then there will be cases of belief that are rational in every way required for knowledge, but are nevertheless morally wrong. But we believe that there are no such cases. Indeed, it is puzzling how it *could* be wrong—and in particular, how it could wrong some individual—to believe something about them that satisfies every rational standard required for knowledge.

In order to draw out what is puzzling about this possibility, we will again focus on the characteristic role of apology, in relationship to directed wrongs. Apologies, it is important to acknowledge, are a currency that helps to grease the mechanics of interpersonal relationships under a wide variety of circumstances, allowing reconciliation in the face of conflict. As such, it is often wise to apologize in many cases in which an apology is not, strictly speaking, owed, and successful interpersonal relationships may involve many such apologies. But we take it that apologies are owed, and therefore most at home, in the case of directed wrongs. If you wrong someone, you owe them an apology, and if you owe someone an apology—as opposed to if it is merely wise to give them an apology—then you must have wronged them in some way.

The close relationship between apology and directed wronging is supported by consideration of the relationship between apology and excuse, as well as the relationship between apology and acting in a way that is all-things-considered wrong. Some actions wrong someone but not are not wrong all-things-considered; this can happen because we encounter tradeoffs. For example, even if it is morally permissible to turn the trolley onto the side track, that does not show that turning the trolley does not wrong the single person on the side track; it may wrong her but nevertheless be justified all things considered. And strikingly, apology does still seem owed in this case.

Similarly, an action can both wrong someone and be wrong all-things-considered, but be excused. And we owe apologies for excused wrongs, as well. If you slip and spill red wine on someone's brand new white carpet for which they have been saving for months, you owe them an apology even if you were bumped by someone else. The fact that apologies are still owed in cases in which an act is permissible all-things-considered and in which though wrong, it is excused, supports our contention that owing an apology closely tracks having committed a directed wrong.

The problem for doxastic duties that extend beyond what is required by epistemic rationality is that apology does not seem owed, by someone whose belief meets every epistemic standard short of truth required for knowledge. To appreciate this point, it helps to imagine, as we have done before, the case in which you come home smelling of alcohol though you have not fallen off of the wagon. We contended before, in section 1.1, that if your spouse apologizes only for what they did upstream from forming your belief or downstream after forming their belief, this does not feel like enough—there is something else left, unapologized-for, which is still a wrong.

Imagine, in this context, your spouse saying, "well, I'm sorry for believing that you fell off the wagon, even though my belief was epistemically impeccable, short of being true". This does not seem to us to be much of an apology. And the reason why it does not seem to be much of an apology, it seems to us, is that satisfying every epistemic standard appropriate to belief short of truth looks like the right kind of thing to defeat any presumption of being a wrong. It is therefore a bit like saying, "I'm sorry for taking back the book that you borrowed from me, even though I had every right to do it", which is again, we believe, not much of an apology.

Doxastic Wronging 199

If this is right, then there cannot be beliefs that are both rationally epistemically permissible and also constitute doxastic wrongs. That is, doxastic wrongs are all epistemically impermissible. As a result, our picture of the deontic space of beliefs must look more like Figure 11.3:

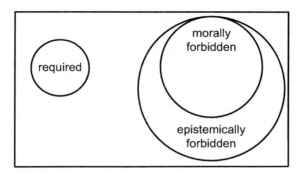

Figure 11.3 Coordinated Moral and Epistemic Requirements

This is a completely consistent picture. But unfortunately, given one more plausible background assumption that is commonly accepted in epistemology, this picture is not consistent with many of the best examples of apparent doxastic wrongs.

The problem is that if moral and epistemic considerations were completely independent of one another, then epistemic and moral impermissibility would not be expected to coordinate in the way required by Figure 11.3; instead, the space of possibilities would be as depicted in Figure 11.4:[20]

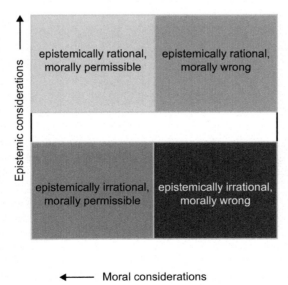

Figure 11.4 Independent Moral and Epistemic Considerations

If epistemic permissibility and moral permissibility are in fact coordinated, it follows that moral and epistemic considerations cannot be completely independent. So at least one of the following must be the case: either the moral requirements governing belief must be restricted in order to respect the epistemic requirements governing beliefs, or else the epistemic requirements governing belief must be expanded in order to respect the moral requirements governing beliefs.

Unfortunately, the first of these possibilities—restricting the moral requirements governing belief to respect the epistemic requirements governing belief—is not consistent with the full range of plausible and pre-theoretically compelling cases of doxastic wrongs. For example, Tamar Gendler (2011) offers the case of John Hope Franklin, an African-American member of an elite social club in Washington DC who is mistaken for staff by a fellow club member. In this case, the evidence that is possessed by the club member who forms the belief that John Hope Franklin is staff is quite good, in probabilistic, purely truth-directed terms, in comparison to many cases of ordinary beliefs that we form on an ordinary basis, because the club's members are nearly all white, and its staff is nearly all black. This problem is that this belief appears to be high on the evidence scale. So in order for this belief to constitute a doxastic wrong, the standard of sufficiency for evidence must be very high across the board. But then it would follow that very many ordinary beliefs about the weather, the day's news, and so on would all be epistemically irrational, because they would not meet the correspondingly high bar for evidence (Figure 11.5):

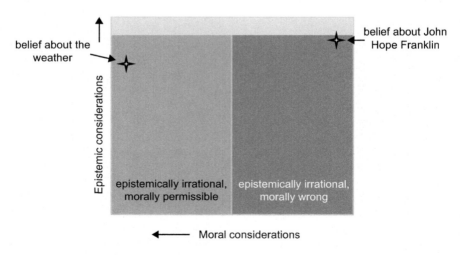

Figure 11.5 Moral Requirements Limited by Epistemic Requirements

To avoid this consequence, we need a story of how the standard of sufficiency can be raised without also being raised across the board. This is what we will do in section 4.1.

In this section we have argued for two conclusions: first, that if there are doxastic wrongs, then there must be some coordination between the moral and epistemic norms governing belief, in order to rule out the possibility of morally wrong beliefs that meet every standard required for knowledge. And second, that the coordination between moral and epistemic standards governing belief cannot come *only* by restricting morally wrong beliefs to cases of beliefs that are *independently* epistemically irrational. From these two conclusions we may infer that if there are doxastic wrongs, then the epistemic requirements governing belief must be sensitive to the moral requirements governing belief.

4.1 Moral Encroachment on Epistemic Rationality

In the last section we showed how the fact that epistemic rationality makes apology inappropriate generates a puzzle for the existence of doxastic wrongs—at least for the existence of doxastic wrongs in the kinds of plausible cases in which we believe that they are interesting and important, as opposed to cases in which they merely represent an additional layer of what is wrong with a belief that is independently recognized as epistemically irrational. If there are such doxastic wrongs, then in order to avoid the puzzle about inappropriate apology, the epistemic norms governing belief must be sensitive to the moral requirements governing belief.

This conclusion flies in the face of the epistemic orthodoxy of most of the last two and a half millennia. Distinctively epistemic rationality, it is commonly assumed—that is, the strongest kind of rationality that is required for knowledge—depends only on truth-related factors such as evidence, reliability, and subjunctive connections to the truth. In particular, according to core evidentialism, a view that we take very seriously indeed, what it takes for a belief to be epistemically rational is nothing other than that it is supported by sufficient evidence. So as long as the bar for sufficiency of evidence does not depend on moral factors, it follows that the epistemic requirements governing belief cannot be sensitive to moral considerations. So it is no wonder that evidentialists have not believed that we can wrong one another in virtue of what we believe about one another.

But we infer, in contrast, that the bar for sufficiency of evidence *does* depend on moral factors. As the moral considerations against belief increase, so does the evidence that is required in order to epistemically justify that belief. Our picture, in short, looks something like the following (Figure 11.6):

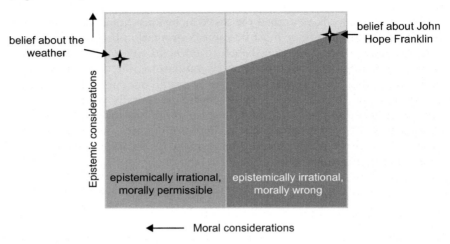

Figure 11.6 Epistemic Permissions Limited by Moral Permissions

This picture is not inconsistent with core evidentialism. On our view, any belief is epistemically rational just in case it is supported by sufficient evidence. But the bar for sufficiency on evidence is sensitive to moral considerations. This reconciles the sets of morally and epistemically forbidden beliefs, so that there are no beliefs that wrong someone despite being epistemically impeccable. On this view, we cannot fully understand knowledge or purely epistemic rationality unless we come to grips with when and why beliefs can constitute wrongs.

This completes our defense of the possibility of doxastic wrongs from the hardest challenge behind the Problem of Coordination, and our argument for the deep connection between the possibility of doxastic wrongs and the need to make room for moral encroachment on purely epistemic rationality. But we'll consider one important objection, in closing. On our view, epistemically rational beliefs never constitute moral wrongs. But one might try to construct counterexamples to this principle. For example, on a natural view, the right to privacy is the right that others not know certain things about you, at least without permission. If you have a moral right that we not know certain things about you at least without permission, and you have not given us permission, and we know those things, then maybe it is precisely the fact that our belief has a very *positive* epistemic status—in particular, that it is knowledge, and hence epistemically rational—that makes it wrong you.

We agree that it follows from our account that the right to privacy cannot consist in or entail a right that others not know things about you without your permission. But this, we think, is an acceptable result. As natural as it

Doxastic Wronging 203

might seem to describe the right to privacy in terms of a right against knowledge, in fact we believe the right to privacy is much more expansive. If it were simply a right against knowledge, it could be protected by Gettierizing anyone who believes something deeply personal about you. For example, if there are lots of fake nude celebrity photos on the internet, it would not interfere with someone's privacy to publish real stolen nude photos of them, because given the abundance of fake photos, no one could come to know anything about you on that basis. This seems deeply wrong to us. Even with invasions of privacy, the wrong is one of belief, not of rational belief, or of knowledge.

4.2 A Word in Defense of Moral Encroachment

If you take the answers we've provided to the problem of control and the problem of epistemic conflicts seriously, as we have argued that we ought, then the existence of doxastic wrongs gives us an argument for a kind of pragmatic encroachment on epistemic rationality, and correspondingly, we take it, although we will not pursue this further here, on knowledge.[21] Some, of course, will take this to be merely another way of sharpening the problem of epistemic conflicts for the existence of doxastic wrongs. Some may also take this to merely be another way of sharpening the problem of control. That is only to be expected; one philosopher's modus ponens is another's modus tollens. But we believe that cases like ours—cases involving doxastic wrongs—are both the best cases for pragmatic encroachment on the rationality of belief, and a return to pre-philosophical common sense. Sometimes philosophy may serve as a corrective to common sense, of course, but philosophy is hard, and can also lead us astray.

As we have been noting, the idea that there are doxastic wrongs is a natural one. But has been held by many theorists to be philosophically problematic. Jason Stanley has noted that the intuitions supporting traditional pragmatic encroachment reveal a powerful connection between belief and action that epistemologists had been ignoring. Similarly, though this is not a thought that we have had the opportunity to develop here, we suggest that cases of doxastic wronging are important because they dramatize the role that our beliefs about one another play in constituting our interpersonal relationships—a powerful connection between belief and human sociality. If this defense of ordinary thought stands at odds with theoretical commitments, all the worse for our theoretical commitments.

Notes

1. Book of Common Prayer.
2. For further discussion, see Schroeder (unpublished).
3. This interpretation is argued for explicitly and directly in Basu (MS).
4. Conee and Feldman (2004).
5. Stanley (2005, p.12).

6. We borrow this apt expression from Hatcher (2017), with whom we join in rejecting the assumption. As we understand this metaphor, the sense in which beliefs are supposed to be at the mercy of the evidence is that what you believe depends simply on what evidence you have been given, and is not the result of choice or agency.
7. Williams (1970, p.141).
8. Alston (1988, p. 270).
9. Flowerree (2016, p. 6).
10. McHugh (2012) similarly argues that voluntariness is not a central condition, but rejects Hieronymi's criterion—answerability—in favor of reasons-responsiveness and thus also rejects (1).
11. Hieronymi (2006, p. 54).
12. Nelson (2010, p. 87).
13. For further discussion see Basu (2018), especially chapter 1.
14. Sir Arthur Conan Doyle, *A Study in Scarlet*.
15. See Nagel (2008) for more on applying Kruglanski's work to issues in epistemology, e.g., our understanding of stakes and knowledge ascriptions.
16. Compare Schroeder (2012, 2013).
17. We have not exhausted the ways in which this could be established. For example, it is consistent with the idea that we are responsive to epistemic reasons, and the epistemic reasons are not exhausted by the evidence. See, for example, Schroeder (2012).
18. Compare Stroud (2006).
19. We don't mean to deny, here, that one can wrong someone by what you do not believe about them. The authors are divided over this question. We just mean to be arguing that there is a problem of conflicts even if we do deny this.
20. In the diagram, we use the vertical dimension to represent evidential support for beliefs, with higher support toward the top of the diagram, and the horizontal dimension to represent the moral dimension of beliefs, with more morally problematic beliefs toward the right of the diagram. There are many different ways to make each of these dimensions more precise, and we do not intend our diagram to decide between them; merely to make a very rough picture of what is going on a little bit more visually tractable. Intuitively, the horizontal line that distinguishes epistemically rational from epistemically irrational beliefs is the threshold for what makes evidence "sufficient" to justify belief.
21. Others who have come to the same conclusion that there is moral encroachment on epistemic rationality or knowledge include Pace (2011), Fritz (2017), and Moss (2018).

References

Alston, William (1988). 'The Deontological Conception of Epistemic Justification.' *Philosophical Perspectives* 2: 257–299.

Basu, Rima (2018). *Beliefs that Wrong*. PhD Thesis, University of Southern California.

——— (ms). *The Wrongs of Racist Beliefs*. Unpublished manuscript.

Benbaji, Hagit (2016). 'What Can We Not Do At Will and Why.' *Philosophical Studies* 173(7): 1941–1961.

Book of Common Prayer. www.bcponline.org/.

Conee, Earl, and Richard Feldman (2004). *Evidentialism*. Oxford: Oxford University Press.

Fantl, Jeremy, and Matthew McGrath (2002). 'Evidence, Pragmatics, and Justification.' *Philosophical Review* 111(1): 67–94.

Flowerree, Amy (2016). 'Agency of Belief and Intention.' *Synthese* 194(8): 2763–2784.

Fritz, James (2017). 'Pragmatic Encroachment and Moral Encroachment.' *Pacific Philosophical Quarterly* 98(s1): 643–661.

Gendler, Tamar (2011). 'On the Epistemic Costs of Implicit Bias.' *Philosophical Studies* 156(1): 33–63.

Hatcher, Michael (2017). *A Deontological Explanation of Accessibilism*. PhD Dissertation, USC. https://search.proquest.com/openview/17ecbcf034eb521b866ea2 43da550826/1.pdf?pq-origsite=gscholar&cbl=18750&diss=y.

Hieronymi, Pamela (2006). 'Controlling Attitudes.' *Pacific Philosophical Quarterly* 87(1): 45–74.

——— (2008). 'Responsibility for Believing.' *Synthese* 161(3): 357–373.

Keller, Simon (2004). 'Friendship and Belief.' *Philosophical Papers* 33(3): 329–351.

Kruglanski, Arie W. (2004). *The Psychology of Closed Mindedness*. New York: Psychology Press.

McHugh, Conor (2012). 'Epistemic Deontology and Voluntariness.' *Erkenntnis* 71(1): 65–94.

Moss, Sarah (2018). *Probabilistic Knowledge*. Oxford: Oxford University Press.

Nagel, Jennifer. (2008). 'Knowledge Ascriptions and the Psychological Consequences of Changing Stakes.' *Australasian Journal of Philosophy* 86(2): 279–294.

Nelson, Mark (2010). 'We Have No Positive Epistemic Duties.' *Mind* 119(1): 83–102.

Pace, Michael (2011). 'The Epistemic Value of Moral Considerations: Justification, Moral Encroachment, and James' "Will to Believe".' *Noûs* 45(2): 239–268.

Schroeder, Mark (2012). 'Stakes, Withholding, and Pragmatic Encroachment on Knowledge.' *Philosophical Studies* 160(2): 265–285.

——— (2013). 'State-Given Reasons: Prevalent, If Not Ubiquitous.' *Ethics* 124(1): 128–140.

——— (unpublished). 'Sins of Thought.' Unpublished paper, presented at *the Third Annual Theistic Ethics Workshop*, College of William and Mary, October 2017.

Shah, Nishi (2002). 'Clearing Space for Doxastic Voluntarism.' *The Monist* 85(3): 436–445.

Stanley, Jason (2005). *Knowledge and Practical Interests*. Oxford: Oxford University Press.

Steup, Matthias (2012). 'Belief Control and Intentionality.' *Synthese* 188(2): 145–163.

Stroud, Sarah (2006). 'Epistemic Partiality in Friendship.' *Ethics* 116(3): 498–524.

Weatherson, Brian (2008). 'Deontology and Descartes' Demon.' *Journal of Philosophy* 105(9): 540–569.

Williams, Bernard (1970). 'Deciding to Believe.' In *Language, Belief, and Metaphysics*, ed. Howard E. Kiefer and Milton K. Munitz, 95–111. Albany: SUNY Press.

12 A Note on Knowledge-First Decision Theory and Practical Adequacy

Juan Comesaña

1. Introduction

According to Williamson (2000), your evidence at a given time is given by all the propositions you know at that time. According to traditional decision theory, in figuring out what to do you should consider all the states that are compatible with your evidence. The combination of the two views, knowledge-first decision theory, has it then that in figuring out what to do you should consider all and only those states compatible with what you know. If knowledge by inductive inference is possible, however, knowledge-first decision theory would have you rule out for considerations states which you shouldn't rule out. In this note, I first present this problem for knowledge-first decision theory, and then suggest a fix for it based on the idea that a proposition cannot be known unless it is practically adequate.

2. Knowledge-First Decision Theory

Traditional decision theory has it that a decision problem is determined by a matrix such as Table 12.1:

Table 12.1 Decision Matrix

	S1	*S2*
A1	O1	O2
A1	O3	O4

The row headings on the table represent the acts available to the agent, the column headings the states of the world that the agent considers possible, and the cells the possible outcomes of the actions. O1, for instance, is the outcome that results if the agent performs action $A1$ and the world is in state $S1$. It is assumed that the agent's preferences between outcomes can be represented by a utility function which assigns a number to each outcome. It is also assumed that a probability function is defined over the set of possible states of the world. Different representation theorems show how such utilities and probabilities can be derived from

A Note on Knowledge-First Decision Theory   207

simple preferences of the agent, but I will not be concerned here with such reductions. Assuming that the relevant utility and probability functions exists, then, traditional decision theory is the claim that an action is rational just in case it maximizes expected utility. The expected utility of an action A is a weighted average of the utilities of all the possible outcomes of A, where the weights are provided by the probability function in question.

When a possible state of the world is assigned 0 by the probability function, then it doesn't have any effect on the expected utility calculation. A crucial question for a normative interpretation of decision theory (that is to say, an interpretation according to which it models how agents *ought* to decide) is: which states should be assigned probability 0? This question can be put in Bayesian lingo: are there any constraints on which *prior probabilities* subjects can assign to different propositions? Subjective Bayesians (such as Jeffrey 1965) are happy to leave the choice of priors completely unconstrained, save for the requirement that they be indeed probabilities. Some other decision theorists think that this is too subjectivist to have any real normative bite, and so provide some further constraints (for instance, Lewis (1980) argues for the "Principal Principle", regarding deference to chances). At the other extreme, Objective Bayesians hold that that there is a unique rational prior. Williamson himself is an Objective Bayesian of this extreme kind. This version of Objective Bayesianism is often dismissed as a non-starter (for instance, Kelly 2005), takes its falsity for granted), but it shouldn't. It is the equivalent, in the fine-grained framework, of the thesis of Uniqueness in the traditional binary epistemological framework, a thesis so embedded in epistemological theorizing that until recently it wasn't even explicitly discussed. Its denial amounts to a kind of epistemological relativism that is no more acceptable in the fine-grained than in the binary realm.

Be that as it may, what I am interested in this chapter is not Williamson's objectivism (with which I agree), but rather another aspect of his overall view which is also related to the issue of to which states can subjects assign probability 0. Traditional Bayesianism has a nominal answer to this question: precisely those states incompatible with the evidence the subject has at the time. The answer is merely nominal because Bayesians, as such, do not have a theory of evidence. Again, Subjective Bayesians will say that a subject's evidence at a time are whatever propositions the subject assigns credence 0 to at that time. Williamson, however, identifies a subject's evidence at a time with what the subject knows at that time, a view enshrined in the equation E = K. The overall Objective Bayesian picture from Williamson, then, is there is a unique rational prior assignment of probabilities to states, and that the probability assignment that is rational for a subject to hold at any given time is the result of conditionalizing that prior on whatever the subject knows at that time.[1] This means that, for Williamson, a subject should take into account only those states which are compatible with her knowledge at any given time.

208　*Juan Comesaña*

3. A Problem for Knowledge-First Decision Theory

The view that a subject need only consider those states which are compatible with what she knows in figuring out what to do has a number of untoward consequences. Here I concentrate on just one.[2]

Assume that it is possible to come to know a proposition p inferentially on the basis of another proposition q which doesn't entail p. Of course, given E = K, whenever a subject knows a proposition p, p itself is then part of her evidence, and so the subject's total evidence does entail p—because any proposition entails itself. But E = K is still compatible with the possibility of inductive inferential knowledge as I have just characterized it. It is not true in general (and perhaps it is never true) that when a subject has inferential knowledge of a proposition p the inferential basis is p itself. We can distinguish between the subject's total evidence and the subject's "basing evidence". If E = K is right, these two will often come apart: the propositions which we use as an inferential basis form a proper subset of all the propositions we know at a given time. So, E = K is compatible with the claim that it is possible for a subject to have inferential knowledge of a proposition p even if her basing evidence does not entail p. Indeed, many philosophers will see compatibility with this kind of inductive inferential knowledge as a constraint on any adequate epistemological theory.[3]

To be specific, let us suppose that you know that train A will leave on time today, based on hard to specify evidence which includes your background knowledge about the on-time statistics for train A and several other pieces of evidence. This evidence is indeed hard to specify, but we will also assume that it doesn't entail that train A will leave on time. It is compatible with all that evidence, for instance, that some accident up ahead on the tracks prevents train A from leaving on time today. For the sake of specificity, let us say that the conditional probability of the ur-prior on your basing evidence for the proposition that train A leaves on time today is .903.[4]

Let us now also specify your practical preferences. You are going where train A would take you, but it is crucial that you get to your destination on time. If train A leaves on time, then you will indeed make it, with some time to spare. The alternative is to get an Uber, which will get you there on time, but will also cost significantly more. Indeed, let us assume that your preference for being on time (whatever the cost) vs. not being on time is such that, given a probability of .903 that train A will be on time, taking an Uber has a higher expected utility for you.

Given this setup, the problem for knowledge-based decision theory is the following. Given that you know that train A will be on time, in figuring out what to do you should not take into account a state of the world where train A is not on time. Therefore, given the higher cost of taking an Uber, it obviously maximizes expected utility for you to take train A. So, according to knowledge-based decision theory, you should take train A. But this is the wrong result: given the specification of the case, you should take an

A Note on Knowledge-First Decision Theory   209

Uber. There are two relevant probabilities in question: one is the probability that train A will be on time, conditional on everything you know; the other is the probability that train A will be on time, conditional on the evidence on the basis of which you believe that train A will be on time. Assuming, as we are doing, that you know that train A will be on time on the basis of some inductive evidence, these two will come apart. Which of them, then, is the relevant one—that is to say, which of those two probabilities should we use to weigh the utilities in question? Obviously, we should use the basing evidence probability. Using your total probability artificially inflates the likelihood that train A will be on time. You should not exclude the possibility that train A will not be on time, as you would have to do if you were to use your total evidence (according to E = K) for that purpose. Therefore, knowledge-based decision theory has the wrong consequence here.

4. The Practical Adequacy Condition on Knowledge

The problem for knowledge-based decision theory arises from a combination of two factors: there is a proposition you know (that train A will leave on time), and yet your rational credence in that proposition is less than 1. Whenever this happens, it will be possible to come up with a preference structure such that it is rational for you to act as if the proposition in question is false.[5] Knowledge-based decision theory, however, has it that you should always act as if every proposition you know is true.

The claim that, if you know a proposition, then you should act as if it is true, is held not only by proponents of E = K and knowledge-based decision theory, but also by a number of other philosophers. Indeed, some philosophers have elevated this claim to the position of an independent necessary condition on knowledge.[6] Say that if your rational credence in a proposition is high enough for it to be rational for you to act as if it is true, then that proposition is practically adequate for you.[7] What some philosophers have claimed, then, is that a belief cannot amount to knowledge for a subject unless it is practically adequate for that subject. Thus, in the situation described previously, you would not know that train A will be on time, because that proposition is not practically adequate for you.

The idea of the practical adequacy condition on knowledge is that your preferences can prevent you from knowing a proposition no matter how likely that proposition is on your basing evidence (provided that it is less than certain). It is not that knowledge in itself requires an arbitrarily high probability of the proposition in question on your basing evidence, but rather that your preferences set a lower bound for that probability. A consequence of this is that the view that practical adequacy is a condition on knowledge is committed to the truth of some rather odd-sounding counterfactuals, such as the following: had it not been so important to you to be on time, you would have known that train A will be on time. Notice that the

210 *Juan Comesaña*

view that practical adequacy is a condition on knowledge is compatible with the possibility of knowledge on the basis of non-entailing evidence—it just is not compatible with the possibility of knowledge on the basis of evidence insufficient for practical adequacy.

5. Practical Adequacy to the Rescue?

If you cannot know a proposition unless it is practically adequate for you, then the problem for knowledge-based decision theory disappears. The problem, recall, arises from the fact that it is possible to know a proposition on the basis of non-entailing evidence. For if this kind of knowledge is possible, then we can tinker with your preferences while keeping fixed the rational credence in the proposition in question, with the result that the proposition is not practically adequate. But, of course, if practical adequacy is a condition on knowledge, then this last step fails. We cannot freely tinker with the subject's preferences while keeping fixed whether she knows the proposition or not, for tinkering with the subject's preferences can *make it the case* that she no longer knows the proposition in question. And, of course, the kind of tinkering needed to make the proposition no longer be practically adequate is precisely the kind of tinkering that, according to practical adequacy condition, destroys knowledge.

Thus, the practical adequacy condition can help with a serious problem for knowledge-first decision theory. Whether the help is welcome or not depends, of course, on whether the practical adequacy condition is itself plausible. In this note, I merely wanted to notice a point of contact between two influential views in contemporary epistemology.

Notes

1. The conditionalization of a probability function Pr on a proposition E is the conditional probability function $Pr'(-|E)$, which is in turn defined as a ratio of unconditional probabilities: $fracPr$ $(-\wedge E)$ $Pr(E)$. The conditional probability is undefined whenever $Pr(E) = 0$. Williamson's updating rule is a kind of ur-prior conditionalization rather than the traditional Bayesian conditionalization rule. For more on conditional probabilities see Hájek (2003), and for more on ur-prior conditionalization see Meacham (2016).
2. For more on the problems with knowledge-based decision theory, see Comesaña (forthcoming).
3. My own view on this is more complicated. See my dispute with Pryor in Comesaña (2013b), Pryor (2013), and Comesaña (2013a).
4. This ridiculous level of specificity serves in part to highlight the problem of false precision (see Kaplan 1996), but that problem is orthogonal to the issues in which I am interested here.
5. To act as if a proposition is true is to maximize utility in worlds where the proposition is true, and *mutatis mutandis* for acting as if a proposition is false.
6. See, for instance, Fantl and McGrath (2002).
7. The terminology of "practical adequacy" is from Anderson and Hawthorne (2019).

References

Anderson, Charity, and John Hawthorne. (2019). "Knowledge, Practical Adequacy, and Stakes." In *Oxford Studies in Epistemology*, Vol. 6.

Comesaña, Juan. (2013a). "Reply to Pryor." In *Contemporary Debates in Epistemology*, edited by Matthias Steup Ernest Sosa and John Turri, 239–243. UK: Blackwell.

———. (2013b). "There Is No Immediate Justification." In *Contemporary Debates in Epistemology*, edited by Matthias Steup Ernesto Sosa and John Turri. UK: Blackwell.

———. (forthcoming). "A Plea for Falsehoods." *Philosophy and Phenomenological Research*.

Fantl, Jeremy, and Matthew McGrath. (2002). "Evidence, Pragmatics, and Justification." *Philosophical Review* 112(1): 47–67.

Hájek, Alan. (2003). "What Conditional Probability Could Not Be." *Synthese* 137: 273–323.

Jeffrey, Richard. (1965). *The Logic of Decision*. 2nd ed. Chicago: The University of Chicago Press.

Kaplan, Mark. (1996). *Decision Theory as Philosophy*. Cambridge: Cambridge University Press.

Kelly, Thomas. (2005). "The Epistemic Significance of Disagreement." In *Oxford Studies in Epistemology*, edited by John Hawthorne and Tamar Gendler. Vol. 1. Oxford: Oxford University Press.

Lewis, David. (1980). "A Subjectivist's Guide to Objective Chance." In *Studies in Inductive Logic and Probability*, edited by Richard Jeffrey. Berkeley: University of California Press.

Meacham, Christopher. (2016). "Ur-Prios, Conditionalization, and Ur-Prior Conditionalization." *Ergo* 3(17).

Pryor, James. (2013). "Reply to Comesaña." In *Contemporary Debates in Epistemology*, edited by John Turri Matthias Steup and Ernest Sosa, 2nd ed. UK: Blackwell.

Williamson, Timothy. (2000). *Knowledge and Its Limits*. Oxford: Oxford University Press.

List of Contributors

1. Charity Anderson (Baylor University)
2. Brad Armendt (Arizona State University)
3. Anne Baril (Washington University in St. Louis)
4. Rima Basu (Claremont McKenna College)
5. Stewart Cohen (University of Arizona)
6. Juan Comesaña (University of Arizona)
7. Dorit Ganson (Oberlin College)
8. Mikkel Gerken (University of Southern Denmark)
9. John Hawthorne (University of Southern California)
10. Brian Kim (Oklahoma State University)
11. Matthew McGrath (Rutgers University)
12. Kate Nolfi (University of Vermont)
13. N. Ángel Pinillos (Arizona State University)
14. Mark Schroeder (University of Southern California)

Index

acceptance 17–18, 30, 119, 127, 130–134
adaptation 141–143, 149–151, 155
agnosticism 11, 15
aims 39, 76, 127, 129; *see also* goals
Anderson, Charity 3–4, 7
anti-realism 127–130, 135
Armendt, Brad 8

bank cases 4–5, 57–59, 61–64, 112–113
Baril, Anne 6–7
Basu, Rima 8
Bayesianism 17, 207
Bayesianism, radial 17
beebe, james 153
belief: categorical 12, 18, 23, 27, 75, 88–89, 172; degrees of 6, 8, 10–13, 15, 17, 22–23, 32, 83, 172; deliberative 74–75, 78, 80; dispositional account 22, 30; full 147; function of 38–40, 42, 45, 48–50, 75, 152; gettiered 71–72, 77, 83, 85–87; justified 10, 38, 42–44, 56, 58, 60, 64, 69, 73, 119, 142, 160–164, 198; outright 24–27, 29, 30, 32; pragmatically warranted 73, 75–77, 83, 86, 88; rational 103, 177–178, 202–203; reductive theory of 6, 11–12, 14, 15, 17, 19–20, 23–24, 27, 30–32; sensitive 147–149; stakes-sensitive 8, 170–172, 175–178; suspension of 10–15, 19
brain-in-a-vat (BIV) 83, 91, 142, 148–149, 151, 156, 163
Brown, Jessica 26, 143
Brunero, John 61

categorical attitude 73; *see also* belief, categorical
certainty 102–103, 11, 26, 31
chance 20, 24, 31, 33, 145

choice 8, 17–18, 25–26, 28–30, 75–77, 89, 109, 170–171, 175, 177, 187, 193; rational 70, 73–75, 89, 175; theory 130–134
closure, epistemic 7, 88, 107–109, 111–114
closure, single-premise 7, 88, 107, 109
cognitive function 39–40
Cohen, Stewart 7, 144
coherent, practically 75–77, 83, 88, 95
Comesana, Juan 8, 106, 210
commitment 6, 62, 128, 178
conditionalization 4, 97–98, 108–109, 111–112, 176, 179, 207, 210
confidence 1, 5, 10–14, 18–23, 25–32, 141; *see also* credence
constructive empiricism 129–135
context-sensitivity 6, 84, 80, 171
contextualism 67, 101, 117
credence 5–7, 12, 14–18, 20–24, 28–30; justified 29; rational 5, 209–210; *see also* confidence

Death in Damascus case 173
decision instability 173
decision problem 17, 73–81, 85, 88–89, 95, 96, 97, 173–174, 179, 206; framing a 73, 77–78, 83, 88–89, 96
decision theory 70, 72–75, 77–83, 177; causal 173; constructive 78–83; knowledge-first 206–210
deliberation: practical 75; theoretical 158
deliberation dynamics 170, 174–175
deliberative desires 74–75, 78
DeRose, Keith 4–5, 57, 117, 136
Descartes, Rene 141
doubt 40, 90, 144, 146, 149–151, 154–156, 158, 161, 164, 182
doxastic wrongs 181–185, 187–188, 198, 203

214 *Index*

epistemology, action-oriented 38, 39, 42–45, 48, 50–51, 53
equilibrium 174, 175, 177–178, 179
evidence: knowledge 207; strength of 77, 81–83, 92, 94, 97; total 73, 76, 102–103, 208–209
evidentialism 45, 201–202
evolution 152–153, 155–156, 158–161, 164, 165, 166
externalism 6, 7, 56, 62, 65–66, 67, 119

factors: objective 73, 81, 83, 137; practical 6, 8, 11, 32, 56, 58, 66, 67, 71, 73, 94, 116–118, 122, 125–127, 129, 130–135, 137; subjective 81, 83; truth-relevant 43–44, 69–70, 85, 117
faith 6, 41, 43, 52
fallibilism 5, 21, 26, 137
Fantl, Jeremy 1, 3, 4, 26, 27, 28, 56, 57, 58, 63, 70, 71, 101, 102, 111, 117, 122, 132, 136, 142, 185
Fodor, Jerry 129, 155, 156, 165, 166
Friedman, Jane 15, 33, 146, 165

Ganson, Dorit 6, 27, 29, 94
Gendler, Tamar 195, 200, 205
Gerken, Mikkel 7, 117, 119, 120, 125, 126, 132, 133
Gettier cases 7, 70–73, 77, 81, 83–87, 89–90, 94, 95, 97, 159
Gibbard, Allan 173, 178
goals 62, 73, 79, 87, 96, 134, 137, 193, 196; *see also* aims

Hajek, Alan 11, 210
Harper, William 173, 178, 179
Hawthorne, John 1, 3, 4, 5, 7, 56, 70, 71, 117, 122, 142, 146
Heuristic 1, 12, 30, 33
Hieronymi, Pamela 60, 188, 189–191, 204
hope 13, 114

ice case (also frozen pond case) 101–102
ideal, rational 75
ignorance 24, 151–154, 159
impurism 117–118, 123, 136, 137
induction 51
infallibilism 5, 90
intellectual factors 10
intellectualism 93
intention 28, 162, 188
interest-relative invariantism 93, 117
internalism 6, 56, 62, 65–66, 67
intuitions 58–59, 66, 69, 71, 162, 185, 203

James, William 20
Jeffrey, Richard 95, 96, 115, 176, 178, 179, 207
judgments: constructive 80; deliberative 74–75, 78, 80, 88; skeptical 8, 141–142, 143, 144, 146–147, 149, 150, 159, 161, 164
justification 1, 50, 52, 60, 66, 73, 95, 119–121, 137, 144, 161, 163–164, 183–184; discursive 119–120, 124, 136

Kim, Brian 7, 56, 178
knowledge: ascriptions 117–118, 122, 125, 127, 204; attributions 153; scientific 7, 116, 118–121, 124–127
knowledge-action principle 8, 28, 137, 141–143, 151, 165; *see also* norm, knowledge-action
knowledge-first 8, 94, 206–210
Kolodny, Niko 61

Lewis, David 85, 136
Lichenstein, Sarah 78
lotteries 14, 19–21, 24, 31, 92, 98, 106, 145–148, 151, 156, 164
luck 70–72, 87, 94
luck, epistemic 70, 71, 72, 77, 94

McGrath, Matthew 1, 2, 3, 4, 26, 27, 28, 29, 56, 57, 58, 63, 70, 101, 102, 111, 117, 122, 132, 136, 142, 185
Memory 115, 186
mental module 155
mental state 38, 142, 156, 165
moral encroachment 8, 181, 201–203, 204

Nelson, Mark 190–196, 204
Nolfi, Kate 6, 51, 52
non-evidential 22, 32, 35–36, 38, 42–43, 45, 194
norm: epistemic 8, 19, 32, 39–40, 42–46, 53, 181, 185, 195, 20; knowledge-action 6, 8, 28, 141–143, 151, 165; *see also* knowledge-action principle
Nozick, Robert 17, 147, 165

objectivity 118, 120, 122–123, 127–128, 135
obligations 20, 46; deontological 185, 187, 191; epistemic 20, 185, 189, 191

Peirce, Charles Sanders 51, 97
perception 119, 124, 141, 156–157, 161, 183

permissible, epistemically 197, 199
permissible, morally 198, 199, 200, 202
permissible, rationally 15, 75, 80, 95
phenomenon 101, 113, 137, 147
Pinillos, Angel 8, 14, 32, 136, 146, 165
possibility, skeptical 83–84, 91–92, 98
practical adequacy 3–4, 7, 8, 88–89, 95, 106, 108–111, 209–210
practical interests i, 106, 118, 146, 157, 158, 170
pragmatic encroachment i, 1, 3–7, 10–12, 25–27, 30–32, 35–45, 45–50, 56–66, 69–70, 101–106, 107–114, 115, 116–136, 137, 140, 165, 172, 185, 203
pragmatics 2
pragmatism 5, 27, 45–48, 52, 118, 134
pragmatism, hybrid doxastic 6, 12, 22, 23–27, 31
preference: conditional 95, 108; deliberative 74–75, 77, 78; reversals 78
probability: conditional 82, 91, 110, 111, 208, 210; epistemic 107, 113–114, 115; evidential 82–83, 91, 103; objective 82; subjective 11, 17, 91, 98
purists 117–118

rational expected utility 207
rationality 17, 73, 76, 80, 94, 96, 143, 176, 201, 203
rationality: epistemic 7, 15, 19–20, 103, 184, 194–201, 201–203, 204; practical 7, 17
realism 127–130
reason: objective desire theory of 61; practical 4, 10, 56–59, 60–62, 66, 67, 188; subjective desire theory of 63, 74, 193; theoretical 15, 22, 24, 30, 31; treating as 56, 59
reasoning: ampliative 103–104; practical 1–4, 26, 30, 56–66, 102, 125, 135, 143, 188
reasons: epistemic 3, 119, 125, 127, 188, 190; external 62–63, 64, 189; favoring 124, 134; internal 62–63; motivating 32; normative 60; possession of 104, 106
reason-theoretic 7, 72, 85
relative alternatives 85
relativism 117, 207
reliabilism 37, 43, 56, 69–70, 146, 151–153, 162–164, 173

Ross, Jacob 27–30, 95, 165
Roush, Sherlyn 127, 130–135
Ryle, Gilbert 12, 22, 29, 32, 34

salience 86, 146–147
Savage, L.J. 88–89, 95, 96
Scanlon, Tim 60
Schroeder, Mark 8, 27–30, 94, 95, 164, 165, 181–203, 204
Schwitzgebel, Eric 22, 27, 32
semantics 101, 117–118, 136–137, 164, 165
Shah, Nishi 188
Situation: choice 17–18, 28; epistemic 45, 190, 209; practical 38, 69–72, 77, 83, 87, 185
skeptical mechanism 142–144, 147, 149, 156, 160–164
skepticism 67, 70–93, 94, 141–164, 165, 166
Slovic, Paul 78, 96
small worlds 88
stakes: high 4, 59, 69–70, 112–114, 123, 133, 172; ignorant high 61, 62; low 36, 59, 69, 112–113, 124, 172
Stanley, Jason 1, 3, 5, 56–57, 61–62, 70–71, 117, 118, 122, 132, 136, 142, 185, 203
strength of epistemic position 107, 110–111, 113

taking for granted 69–82, 88, 92–93, 94
Tang, Weng Hong 31, 33
theoretical reasoning 15, 22, 24, 30–31
train cases 36–38, 57–58, 108–109

utility, expected 7, 75, 102, 108, 111–112, 114, 175, 207–209

value i, 18, 43, 127, 132, 151, 172, 176
value, epistemic i
van Fraassen, Bas 21, 33, 129–130, 134

warrant 26, 42, 46, 56, 58, 66, 73, 119–123, 136; pragmatic 73, 95; scientific 119
Weatherson, Brian 32, 70–71, 93, 94, 133, 188
Williams, Bernard 62, 67, 204
Williamson, Timothy 106, 136, 165, 206–207, 210